EDUCATIONAL PSYCHOLOGY

EDUCATIONAL PSYCHOLOGY

Dr P K Johri

2007

SBS Publishers & Distributors Pvt. Ltd.
New Delhi

All rights reserved. No part of this publication may be reproduced, stored in a retrieval system, or transmitted in any form or by any means, electronic, mechanical, photocopying, recording or otherwise, without the prior written permission of the publisher and the copyright holder.

ISBN : 81-89741-39-X

Price - Rs 125

First Published in India in 2007

© Reserved

Published by:
SBS PUBLISHERS & DISTRIBUTORS PVT. LTD.
2/9, Ground Floor, Ansari Road, Darya Ganj,
New Delhi - 110002, INDIA
Tel: 23289119, 41563911
Email: mail@sbspublishers.com

Contents

1. **FUNDAMENTAL ELEMENTS**   1
   Fundamental Process • Study Method • Function of Sense Organs • State of the Brain • To Further • Concept of Form • Concept of Attention • Traits of Attention • Factors of Attention • Importance of Sets • Importance of Consistency • Studying Cultures • Social Values

2. **BASIC CONCEPTS**   18
   Psychology and Soul • Psychology and Mind • Psychology and Consciousness • Psychology and Behaviour • Definition of Behaviour • Definition of Education • Definition of Educational Psychology • Psychology vs. Education • Facets of Educational Psychology • Knowing Psychology • Psychology as Education • Educational Psychology: Opportunities • Educational Psychology: Vastness • Teacher and Psychology • Educational Psychology: Various Levels • Growth of a Learner • Views of Learning • Importance of Educational Psychologists

3. **EVOLUTION AND GROWTH**   38
   Societal Progress • Factors of Growth • Societal Growth • Importance of Culture and Society • School's Significance • Meaning of Societal Growth • Growth of an Infant • Growth of a Child • Childhood: Impact of Group • Child and Teacher • Social Development: Factors • Helping and Vying • Bodily Development • Definition of Bodily Growth • Stages of Growth • Properties of Infancy • Progress of Motor • Increasing Weight • Growth of Body in Childhood • Developing Body • Blood and Breath • Growth of Motor • Different Functions • Bodily Growth and Sexuality • Growth: Various Kinds • Stratification of Scammon

• Typology of Kretschmer • Physical Growth: Importance in Education • Infant's Growth and Education • Child's Growth and Education • Teacher's Knowledge of Growth • Development of Feelings • The Meaning • Properties of Emotions • Emotion of Major Importance • Emotion during Childhood • Elimination • Child's Feelings • Emotional Growth: Importance in Education • Child's Stability: Guidelines • Role of Teacher in Emotional Matters • Emotional Issues: Factors • Importance of a Teacher • Winding-up • Role of Intellect • Growth of Intellect • Mental Development: Dimensions • Memory Growth • Progress of Mind: Factors • Infancy: Progress of Intellect • Role of Wisdom • Different Growths • Area of Concern • Memory Growth • Creativity in Progress • Faculty of Logic • Growth of Language • Childhood and Intellect • Different Languages • Difficulties in Speaking • Childhood and Reasoning • Power of Imagination • Child's Mental Nourishment • Growth of Intellect in Education

4. **DEVELOPMENT AND CHARACTERISTICS OF ADOLESCENT** 92

What is Adolescence? • Is Adolescence a Problem? • Adolescence Period: General Characteristics • Physical Needs of the Adolescents • Emotional Developmental Needs and their Satisfaction • Educational Provisions for Adolescents

5. **CULTIVATION AS A DISCIPLINE** 103

Understanding Progress • Definition of Growth • Definition of Progress • Development vs. Growth • Study of Growth and Development • Concepts of Progress • Importance of Progress • Development: Phases • Factors Affecting Progress • Starting of Life • Role of Heredity • Nourishment by Nature • Genetics and Atmosphere • Growth and Development: Different Factors • Role of Learning • Impact of Education on Growth

6. **SIGNIFICANCE OF INDIVIDUAL** 127

Concept of Learning • Humanistic Concept • Evolution of Personality • Methods of Evaluation • Situational Contact • Importance of Identity

7. **PERCEPTION OF LEARNING** 140
   Traditional Conditioning • Learning of Instruments • Learning of Motor • The Style • The Difference • Cognitive Concepts • Oval Knowledge • Goading of Knowledge • Role of Neurophysiology • Role of Nervous System • Importance of Spinal Cord • Brain Formation • Functions of Brain • Role of Endocrine System • What Brain Does? • Role of the Cerebellum

8. **MENTAL FITNESS** 158
   Scope of the Problem • Classroom and Hygiene • Mental Health: Guidelines • Teacher's Mental Health • Teacher's Health: Reasons • Teacher's Health: Encouragement

9. **INSTINCTS AND HABITS** 186
   Study of Instincts • Variability of Instincts • Instincts under Change • Animal's Instincts • Instincts Everywhere • Instincts of Man • Features of Human Instincts • Psycho-Genesis and Law • Past vs. Present • Initial Periods • Great Interests and Instincts • Development Chocked • Winding-up

10. **THE INTELLECT** 223
    Hereditary Factors • Role of Intelligence • Assessment of Abilities • Role of Wisdom

11. **PERCEPTION OF THOUGHT** 235
    The Classification • Some Concepts • Research Consequences • Freudian Concept • Piaget's Theory • Gestalt Perception • Study of Behaviour • Cognitive Method

12. **GRADES OF LEARNING** 241
    Grades of Learning Ability • Role of Age in Learning Ability • Age and Various Abilities • Types of Children • Defining I.Q.'s and M.A.'s • Role of Intelligence Tests • Peculiar Traits • Different Abilities • Role of Psychology • Scope of Personal Differences • Personal Differences • Motivational Factors • Guiding Processes • Increase in intellectual differences with age • Special Child • Disabled Child • How to Deal Personal Differences? • The Inference

13. MAKING DISCIPLES READ 282
Meaning of Reading • Method of Reading • Aims of Reading • Reading Performance: Factors • Personal Dissimilarities • Step-by-step Progress • Types of Reading • How to Develop Work-type Reading? • Kinds of Reading • Problems of Reading • Problems and their Impact • Solutions to Problems • Role of Language

BIBLIOGRAPHY 308

INDEX 312

CHAPTER ONE

Fundamental Elements

It may be stated with emphasis that 'Perception' is the process, in which we look at the world to discriminate among the various stimuli, and interpret them with regard to their meaning and appreciate their significance. Whatever is 'experienced perceived is given meaning' is another way of explaining it. Our feelings, tastes, smells, images, all must fall under perceptual process. If we hear a sound we can identify it as being the sound of a motorcycle or aeroplane or some other machine. We can similarly discriminate the things we see for example cow or a goat or a dog. Perception is thus a mid-way process. Our experience of the world—*i.e.* perception arises from the sensory inputs plus the ways we understand and look at the things. Therefore, it occurs between the sensory process and behaviour. However perception itself is some thing abstract and cannot be observed directly. It can be studied by at the various conditions and responses.

FUNDAMENTAL PROCESS

Process of Perceiving

Various physical energies in the environment act on the sense organs. The receptors in them are stimulated from which nerve impulses are transmitted to the brain. Perception of objects and events are produced when these nerve impulses are processed.

The following sequence of events leads to perception.

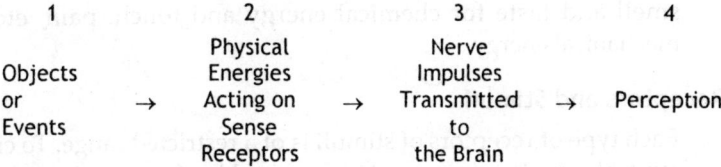

1	2	3	4
Objects or Events →	Physical Energies Acting on Sense Receptors →	Nerve Impulses Transmitted to the Brain →	Perception

Fundamental Elements ■ 1

Detection

Perception serves an important function for us. It is not the mere copy of objects as experienced by the sense organs. In other words, it transforms raw sensory input into meaningful and useful information. It helps us know (Perception—Giving meaning to sensation). What happens in the environment and what goes on within our own bodies. Such knowledge enables us to deal with our environment more efficiently in relation to what we want or desire.

Discrimination

Discrimination of stimuli in the environment is essential for perceiving something. This means that one should necessarily sense a thing before he can perceive it. In other words, perception is based on sensation. For perception to take place, not only the presence of the object is to be sensed, but also the various features of the objects such as shape, colour, size etc.

Sense Organs

Sense organs are the channels of sensation. Popularly we know of five senses namely, seeing, hearing, smell, taste and touch. Besides these, the sense organs in the muscles joints and tendons account for a feeling or pressure within the body.

This is called kinaesthetic sense. In addition to these, the vestibular receptors in the head are responsible for the sense of balance. The receptors in the skin, besides affording a sense of touch are also responsible for the three other senses of pain, warmth and cold.

Sensitivity Elements

In each of these sense organs, there are a number of sensitivity elements known as receptors. A receptor is a specialised nerve ending that is sensitive to a particular kind of stimulus generating an appropriate type of energy of sufficient intensity or strength.

These energies can be chemical, thermal, mechanical or electromagnetic in nature. For instance, vision responds to electromagnetic energy while warmth and cold for thermal energy, smell and taste for chemical energy and touch, pain, etc. for mechanical energy.

Receptors and Stimuli

Each type of receptors of stimuli is of a restricted range. To cite an example, our hearing receptors are capable of responding to sound vibrations between 20 and 20,000 cycles per second. This means that no sense organ is infinitely sensitive.

STUDY METHOD

Patterns and Groupings

When several objects are present in the visual field, we tend to perceive them as organised into patterns or groupings. The Gestalt psychologists studied such organisation intensively in the early part of 20th century. They emphasized that organised Perceptual experience has properties, which cannot be predicted from a simple analysis of the components. In other words, Gestalt psychologists said that 'the whole is more than the sum of its parts.'

Organisation partially explains our perception of complex patterns as unitary forms, or objects. We see objects as objects only because grouping processes operate in perception.

Law of Proximity

The organising principle of proximity, or "nearness". We see three pairs of vertical lines instead of six single lines. The law of proximity says that which are close together in space or time tend to be perceived as belonging together or forming an organized group.

Figure

Similarity

This is the other important organizing principle of perception. Most people see one triangle, formed by the dots with its apex at the top and another formed by the rings with its apex at the bottom. They perceive a triangle because similar items—the dots and rings—tend to be organized together. Otherwise they would see the following figure. In figure A has a hexagon or as a six-pointed star like while figure B where all the dots are the same.

Grouping according to similarity, however, does not always occur. The following figure C is more easily seen as a six-pointed star than as one figure composed of dots and another figure made up of rings. In this case, similarity is competing with the organizing principle of symmetry, or "good figure". Neither the circles nor the dots by themselves form a symmetrical pattern. The "law of good figure" says that there is a tendency to organise things to make a balanced figure, which can be achieved only by using all dots and rings to perceive a six-pointed star. The law of good figure wins out over the law of similarity because the rings by themselves or the dots by themselves do not form symmetrical good figures.

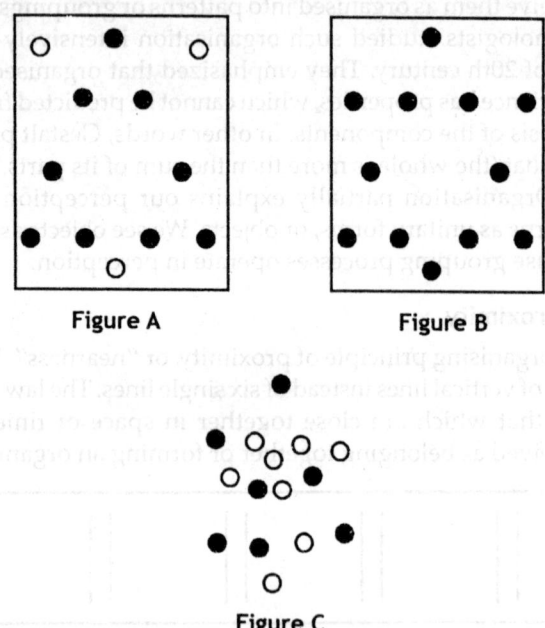

Figure A   Figure B

Figure C

Continuation

Continuation is the tendency to perceive a line that starts in one way as continuing in the same way. For example, a line that starts out as a curve is seen as continuing on a smoothly curved course. A straight line is seen as continuing on a straight course or, if it does change direction, as forming an angle rather than a curve.

FUNCTION OF SENSE ORGANS

The minimum stimulus to which a sense organ can respond is called absolute threshold. This absolute threshold differs, depending upon the individual, the senses involved and a number of varieties of conditions of observation. Similarly, the smallest difference in stimuli that can be differentiated is known as the differential threshold. Different kinds of experimental methods are used to measure both the absolute threshold and differential threshold.

STATE OF THE BRAIN

Two principal parts of the nervous system are the spinal cord and the brain. Since the brain plays a key role in such psychological activities as learning, thinking and perception we will try and see how the brain functions in perception.

The cerebrum is the crowning structure of the brain and its organization is tremendously complex. The three general functional types that can be differentiated out of this complexity are: (*i*) specialised sensory areas, (*ii*) motor control areas and (*iii*) association areas.

(*i*) *Specialised Sensory Areas:* These are located in the parietal occipital, and temporal lobes. A portion of the parietal lobe, lying just at the back of the fissure of Rolando is the principal area of sensitivity for pressure touch and temperature. This area does not seem to be responsible for pain sensitivity. Pain sensitivity seems to be located in the thalamus. Thalamus also mediates the sensitivities mentioned above. For some reason or other, if the tissues of the parietal lobe are destroyed thalamus seems to take over these sensitivities. The area for sensitivities for vision is located in the tip of the occipital lobe. Damage to this area in one of the hemispheres results in impairment of visions; total destruction of this area in both the hemispheres of the brain brings about total blindness.

The area of sensitivity for hearing is located in the temporal lobe. Each ear is connected with both the hemispheres and hence if injury occurs in only one hemisphere, particular or minor hearing disturbances occur. Destruction to this are in both the hemispheres will result in serious impairment. The remaining hearing sensitivity is situated in the sub-cortical centres.

(*ii*) *Motor Areas:* The centres which control voluntary motor activity lie in a portion of the frontal lobe which is situated just in front of the fissure of Rolando. Experimental evidences are available to suggest that this is either damaged or destroyed retraining is still possible.

3. *Associative Areas:* Associative neurons in man are concentrated in functions, through inherited connections, and connections modified by training. For example, the neurons responsible for understanding the meaning for auditory sounds are found in the same general areas. The associative areas are categorised as sensory, motor and frontal.

TO FURTHER

(a) *Neurons:* The sensory associative areas comprise of associative neurons for specialised stimuli such as sound, smell, light, and so on. The sensory associative areas are not particularly concerned with sensory sensitivity alone.
(b) In *motor associative areas,* associative neurons meant for the control of motor processes, are found. When these areas are damaged, it leads to the impairment of the ability to understand the meaning of motor activities.
(c) *Frontal associative areas* play a vital role in mental activities such as reasoning, memory and motivation. Ability to recall and to solve problems gets impaired when this area is damaged or destroyed immobility and passivity also may result because of injury to this area.
(d) Besides the cerebrum, the cerebellum is a centre that plays a vital role in motor coordination, which helps us in making our movement precise, accurate and smooth. It makes use of kinaesthetic and vestibular impulses and aids in the maintenance of balance and postures.

CONCEPT OF FORM

Depth perception was a puzzle to scientists and philosophers for hundreds of years. They could not understand how we could see a three-dimensional world with only a two dimensional, or flat, retina in each eye. Today we realize that the ability to perceive depth is no more amazing than is any other perceptual accomplishment. We are able to make use of information, or cues, in the sensory input to "generate" the three dimensional world that we see. Thus, the question is: What are the cues we use to see depth and distance? Parts of the answer lay in the cues received by each eye separately the monocular (one-eyed) cues for depth perception. Another part of the answer is found in the cues received from both eyes working together—the binocular (two-eyed) cues.

CONCEPT OF ATTENTION

A writer had observed as:

(a) At any one particular point of time, our sense organs are exposed to an innumerable number of stimuli. Out of these, only a few of the stimuli are clearly perceived. From among the rest, some are perceived less clearly and the rest are very hazy and do not make adequate impact on the sense organs, for them to be perceived. This means that out of the multitude of our experiences only a few are attended to and hence attention, is a fundamental process on which perception rests.

(b) The division in attention as being central and peripheral brings in our field of experience two aspects namely the focus and margin. The events and stimuli that are perceived clearly are in the focus of our experience. They stand out prominently in our experience since we attend to them. The events and stimuli in the margin are perceived hazily. Though their presence is felt, they are perceived very vaguely. There are still other events, which are outside the field of experience and hence are not consciously perceived.

TRAITS OF ATTENTION

The nature of attention may best be illustrated by an example. When we are absorbed in watching a movie, our attention is focused on the screen and we see the main characters and events. The details in the scene such as the arrangement of furniture, actors in the background, etc., are hazily seen and these are not registered properly and strongly. Besides, we may be dimly being aware of other events in the theatre. For instance, we may feel the hardness of the seat, presence of the audience; the kind of conversation might takes place between some of them etc. However, we are not aware of any of these, while our attention is on the movie. We realize many of these things only after the picture is over.

Fundamental Elements ■ 7

FACTORS OF ATTENTION

Even in instances where we are engrossed in a task or activity, our attention does not stay continuously in such a task. On the other hand, we find attention 'wandering, oscillating or shifting. In the example given above, the individual's attention may shift from the movie to the audience, the conversation etc. In other words, what was once in the focus may shift to the margin and vice versa. This kind of shifting of attention is governed by certain principles. These principles are with regard to two kinds of factors. One refers to the external factors in the environment and the other refers to the factors from within the individual such as motives, set and expectancy.

External Factors

There are several external factors that govern things to be brought to the focus of attention. The following of them are important: (*i*) Intensity and size, (*ii*) Contrast, (*iii*) Repetition, (*iv*) Movement (*v*) Novelty.

Internal Factors

The factors we mentioned so far are external stimulus factors. Equally important are certain other factors, which are personal in nature. Some of them are movies, interests and other states within the person.

Illusions

Illusions are familiar examples of perceptual processes at work. An "Illusion" is "not" a trick or a misperception; it is perception. We call it an illusion simply because it does not agree with our other perceptions. Our perception of the line lengths in Muller-Lyer illusion does agree with the perception we would have if there were no arrows.

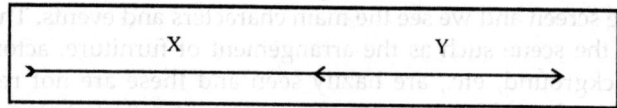

Muller-Lyer Illusion:
Is X longer than Y?

The presence of the arrows in the figure causes us to process the sensory input in such a way that we perceive the lines as unequal in length.

An example is given of a similar version of this horizontal-vertical illusion as shown in following Fig.

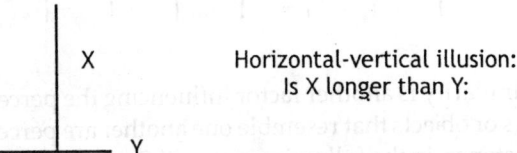

Horizontal-vertical illusion:
Is X longer than Y:

Illusion demonstrates that what we perceive often depends on processes that go far beyond the raw material of the sensory input.

IMPORTANCE OF SETS

Set of Expectancy

This is another factor determining the objects or events that would be chosen and perceived by people. It is a matter of common observation that we 'see' what we are 'set' to see. For instance, if you are awaiting the arrival of the postal worker, the creaking noise of the door makes you run out of the room to receive the mail.

Organization

Though much of our perceiving is through the sense organs and not learned, certain aspects of perceiving are organised and learnt. These organising tendencies take different forms such as: (*i*) grouping, (*ii*) figure-ground perception, (*iii*) contour, (*iv*) closure and (*v*) apparent movement.

Grouping

An important kind of organising tendency is known as grouping. The presence of various stimuli makes us perceive them in some kind of pattern groups. There are several ways in which grouping occurs. The various factors which play a significant role in grouping are: (*i*) proximity or nearness, (*ii*) similarity (*iii*) symmetry or good figure and (*iv*) continuation.

Proximity is important for the formation of pattern in perception of figures. For instance, the lines in the following figure are perceived in pairs because of the nearness of one line to the other. They are perceived as four pair of lines rather than as eight lines.

Fundamental Elements ■ 9

Similarity is another factor influencing the perception pattern. Things or objects that resemble one another are perceived together. For instance, in the following you will find that all the triangles are perceived as group and all the circles another group, even though they are scattered in a manner where the factor of proximity does not operate in a predominant way.

Even though the factor of similarity influences the perception pattern, still it may not hold when the principle of good form of symmetry operates. For example, in spite of the fact that there are two distinct groups of figures in the following diagram we perceive all these figures together being perceived as a hexagon. The tendency to form a symmetrical or balanced figure influences the tendency to group things or objects.

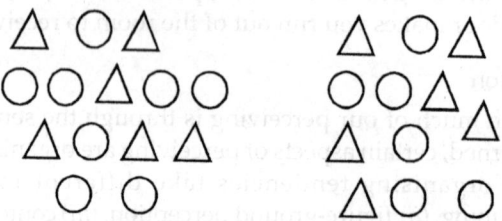

Another important principle in grouping is that of continuation. This refers to a tendency to see a figure as continuing, even though there may be gap or a break in the line. The principle illustrated above in the process of grouping explains as to how complex patterns of stimuli are perceived as a unit. In short, grouping helps us to perceive things as a whole and in a meaningful manner. Otherwise perception would apparently be fragmentary (Gestalt).

Figure Ground

The tendency to perceive the figure and ground is also a fundamental tendency. It is closely related to the tendency of grouping and is also a basic one. When an object is perceived, usually it is perceived against a background of experience. For instance, when we see the utensils are the figures. Similarly when we 'see' words written on the blackboard, the blackboard forms the background and the words are the figures. For object perception to take place, the capacity to differentiate the object from its background is essential, since the object of our daily perception occur in the background of our experience. In figure-ground perception, we are to be conscious of the fact that figure as well as ground has certain characteristics of their own. The figure has a form or shape; it has other object or quality, it appears to come out of the ground and is prominent.

Contour

Differentiation of objects from general ground with regard to visual perception is made possible because of our ability to perceive contours. Distinct and clear-cut differences in the colour or degrees of brightness contribute to the formation of contours.

IMPORTANCE OF CONSISTENCY

Stability of Perception

There is stability of our perception of the world around us. Objects and events perceived by us are stable. For instance, the size of a person does not appear to change or alter with the distance from which we see him. Similarly, the shape of a room does not change because of the change in the angle of our vision. Likewise, irrespective of the movement of our head, the direction from where a sound is originated does not change. Now, we will see the reasons for constancy of the perception of objects in the world around us.

Constancy in perception occurs with "regard to the shape, size, colour and brightness of objects." These occur in spite of the difference in stimuli coming even from the same objects.

Shape Constancy

When we stand directly in front of a window the retinal images are of a rectangle. However, when we move to a side and see the same window, the retinal image is not that of a rectangle but of a trapezoid. In spite of this, the window is perceived to be a rectangle. This is what is being referred to as shape constancy.

Size Constancy

The size of a retinal image is dependent upon the distance from which an object is seen. The farther away an object the smaller would be the image on the retina. In the same manner the nearer the object the bigger would be the retinal image.

The constancy of the size of objects in perception is dependent upon our ability to perceive distance. In the cues of distance (depth) are available, it results in good size constancy. If the cues of distance are completely removed our perception of unfamiliar or strange objects are directly dependent upon the retinal images. Partial loss of distance cues requires our ability to have size constancy to some extent. However, elimination of depth or distance cues does not much effect the size constancy for familiar objects. This is due to our previous experience and knowledge of the object.

Constancy of Brightness

The constancy of visual objects, in their appearance with regard to the degree of whiteness, greyness or blackness is being referred to as brightness constancy. Irrespective of the illumination under which an object or a surface is viewed, the brightness appears not to vary. A crow looks black even in bright light and cotton as white even in dull light. Likewise a sheet of white paper placed under different shades of light appears to be white and not as different shades of grey paper. The above phenomenon occurs because of a pure white object reflecting all the light falling upon it and pure black object absorbing almost all the incident light, and different shades of grey reflecting appropriate percentage of incidental and absorbing the remaining light. The more the percentage of light reflected the lighter the grey. The percentage of the total light reflected by a surface is known as albedo.

Plasticity

Visual deprivation—restriction of the visual input in some fashion—is especially potent during what is known as the sensitive period for visual development. A sensitive period is time in the early development of a person or animal during which environment has its greatest effect on behaviour or on the brain underlying behaviour.

Perceptual Learning

Based on past experiences or any special training we have had, each of us has learned to emphasise some sensory input and to ignore others. E. Gibson has defined perceptual learning as "an increase in the ability to extract information from environment as a result of experience or practice with the stimulation coming from it". Perceptual learning can be considered a variety of cognitive learning.

Cognitive Styles

People are said to differ in the ways they typically and characteristically process information. The general processing strategies that characterize different people are known as perceptual cognitive styles.

Among the many dimensions along which people vary in perceptual cognitive style are:

(a) The degree to which their perceptions (and other aspects of their behaviour and personality) are flexible or constricted (Klein, 1970), and

(b) Their field dependence or field independence (Witkin & Goodenough, 1981).

People perceptions are at the flexible end of the flexible-constricted dimension are said to have a wider focus of attention, to be less affected by interfering influences and to be less dominated by internal needs and motive than are people at the constricted end.

The dimension of field dependence—field independence has to do with the perception of wholes or parts. A field-dependence person is said to unify and organize sensory inputs so that it is difficult to break down what is perceived into its parts or elements; the perception of field-dependent person is thus said to emphasize the whole over its component parts. Such a person, because of his or her difficulty in breaking the whole down into its parts, may have difficulty with tests requiring that a simple figure be found within a complex whole. Field-independent people, who emphasize the parts in perception, do well on such embedded-figure tests and on other perceptual tests requiring the emphasis of parts over the whole.

This viewpoint was called the "new look" in perception. Although many of the "new look" experiments were flawed and some of the specific theoretical ideas of the "new look" have been sharply criticised, the general idea that individual differences in motives and needs affect perception persist. In other words, we may attend to the organized sensory inputs in the ways that match our needs. For example, people who are hungry, thirsty or sexually aroused are likely to pay attention to events in the environment, which will satisfy these needs.

Projective tests, such as the well-known Rorschach inkblot test, capitalize on the influences of motivation on perception. The ink blots or pictures used in projective tests are ambiguous; they can be perceived in any number of ways. The idea is that people's motives will, to some extent, affect the ways in which they organize and perceive the test stimuli. A psychologist may be able to infer from the perceptions what motives are dominant in a particular person.

STUDYING CULTURES

Perception

Social psychology covers such a wide array of behaviours; it may be helpful to discuss few distinctions that will serve to map the area. In even the simplest social interaction, the interplay between participants is rapid, and a great deal of information is exchanged. The essence of interaction is that all participants modify what they do and say according to what others are doing and saying. While such mutual interdependence provides much of the joy and vitality in our interactions and others, it also makes it difficult to arrive at a clear analysis of the determinants of social behaviour.

From social perception, we will move to a discussion of social-influence situations. Social influence is a change that occurs because of contact with one or more persons.

Social Perception

How do we come to know other people? Our social perceptions of others are initially based on the information we obtain about them and, in some instances, the attributions (inferences) we make about the cause for their behaviour. It is, of course, important to have accurate knowledge of others before deciding what kind of interactions to have with them. Our perceptions of other's personalities and feelings—as well as the causes for their behaviour—guide us in deciding how we will respond to them and what sort of relationship we will have with them.

Impression Formation

Forming impressions of other people are probably so natural to everyone that like breathing, one only thinks about the process if some thing goes wrong. "Impression formation" is a process by which information about others is converted into more or less enduring cognitions or thoughts about them. When we first meet someone, we have access to considerable information—how the person looks and what he or she does and says. According to one point of view, we are not overwhelmed by the abundance of this information because we are able to group it into categories that predict things of importance to us. These categories are their perceived interrelationships from the basic "cognitive framework" by which we understand others. The characteristics defending cognitive categories can be as broad as "women" or "men" or as narrow as "myself".

Implicit Personality Theory

For understanding other people, the category most frequently used is the trait. Traits are classification schemes for describing the behaviour of individuals. Our language provides us with many options for describing behaviour, such as assertive, friendly, punctual or talkative. For example, in 1936, Alport and Odbert identified about 1800 trait names in a Standard English dictionary. Traits are a compelling set of categories used to describe, remember and communicate our own and other people's behaviour.

Our own implicit personality theory, similar to our general cognitive framework, includes both assumed relationships shared by most other members of our culture and assumed relationships that are unique to us. The shared assumptions are a result of similarities of experiences within a particular culture, where people share a common language, common exposure to mass media, and common socialization or child rearing experiences. The unique assumptions are a result of our own individual experiences, especially with people of importance to us in our family, school, neighbourhood or church. Implicit personality theories help us to simplify the information we receive in social interaction, colour the way we interpret events, and guide our responses to other people.

Combining Information

Most people believe there is some value in making a good first impression, and research shows that such efforts are not wasted; a "primary effect" does often occur in impression formation. Furthermore, we generally give more importance to information concerning negative traits than to information concerning positive traits that others might possess. (Hamilton & Zanna, 1972; Ambile & Glazebrook, 1982). Each of these factors affects the weightage people give to various pieces of information when forming an impression of another person.

Some information patterns contain apparently contradictory information. (Try, for example, to imagine someone who is both hostile and dependent). Asch and Zukier (1984) asked subjects to imagine people who were described by such contradictory traits in order to study how perceivers resolve discrepancies. The others assumed that perceivers would try to preserve the unity of the other person. The contradictions were resolved by inferring a greater degree of complexity about the other person.

Kelley's Attribution Theory

Kelley's attribution theory emphasized our use of consensus information, consistency of behaviour, and distinctiveness of behaviour in making inferences about the internal or external causes of another's behaviour.

Final Word on Social Perception

The processes by which we form our social perceptions of others are efficient means for guiding our reactions to others. Our social perceptions are grounded in our observations of others—their physical characteristics and their behaviour in particular settings. Our observations provide the information that is converted into meaningful inferences by our cognitive framework. At a minimum, this process involves placing the information into cognitive theories, which are related to other categories. We can thus, make simple inferences from minimum data or combine rich sets of information into overall impressions. Under some circumstances, we can also make inferences about the causes of other people's behaviour as well as our own behaviour. Despite the smoothness by which the process works, however, it does not guarantee accuracy or comparability with other's observations. We each make a personal contribution to the process because we may have different ways of categorizing the information, individual aspects to our cognitive framework, or some unique way of combining information. Nevertheless, the end result of social perception process determines how we react to others and how we see ourselves.

SOCIAL VALUES

"Conformity" is a term used to refer to the situation in which individuals change their beliefs or behaviour so that they become more similar to those of other group members. Conformity pressures can arise in any situation involving other people. Although some instances of conformity are very similar to examples of imitation, they typically involve more than one person modelling the behaviour and require the focal person (FP) to respond in the presence of the agents. In conformity situations, the agents have at least some interest in changing the FP's behaviour. Indeed in these situations, if the FP's behaviour does not change, it is termed "deviant", while no special term exists for describing the FP's lack of change in imitation situations. Although conformity pressures can exist in situations that are structurally close to imitation situations, they also occur in circumstances that are starkly different. In particular, conformity pressures arise when the FP and the agents are members of an intact group and the agents not only make persuasive interventions but also have the power to apply sanctions.

Interpersonal Attraction

Interpersonal attraction is an important part of social relationships. Involved in interpersonal attraction are the factors of proximity, attitude-similarity and physical attractiveness.

Major Sides

The growth of interpersonal relationship follows a path through various levels of involvement. Interpersonal relationships start with the stage of unilateral awareness. They then move through the stage of surface contact, in which interactions are governed by general cultural norms and rules of etiquette, to the stage of mutuality, characterized by increasing concern for the partner's outcomes in the relationship.

Justice in Social Relationship

The "Justice rules" are employed most often as standard of fairness in social relationships. These include a contribution rule, based upon the investment each person makes in the relationship; a needs rule, which requires that outcomes be distributed equally among the participants. Each of these rules represents a standard against which people's outcomes may be compared with what they are thought to "deserve".

CHAPTER TWO

Basic Concepts

In modern times, during this age of science and technology, psychology has been considered as one of the youngest; yet one of the most influential sciences. It has influenced education in different ways and practically given a new turn, a psychological turn to the human mind. For a skilful teacher of the present-day society, knowledge of the child has been considered to be more important than the knowledge of the subject matter. Therefore, teachers in the modern society should be equipped with those psychological skills and competence, which are badly needed for the successful guidance of learning, adjustment and the growth of the child.

The subject 'Psychology' has two aspects-pure and applied. Pure psychology formulates broad principles brings out theories and suggests techniques for the study of human behaviour, which finds in its applied aspect, *i.e.* Branches of Applied Psychology, Clinical Psychology, Crime Psychology, Industrial Psychology, Occupational Psychology and Educational Psychology. Therefore, Educational Psychology is nothing but one of the branches of Applied Psychology in the practical shape It is an attempt to apply the knowledge of Pure Psychology to the field of education. It consists of application principles and techniques to human behaviour in educational situations. In other words, Educational Psychology is a study of the experiences and behaviour of the learner in relation to educational environment. In order to develop a clear understanding of the term 'Educational Psychology', it is necessary to understand the meaning of psychology and education separately.

PSYCHOLOGY AND SOUL

About 2000 years ago, Psychology appeared as a separate branch of study. It was the genius of Aristotle that gave birth to this science.

Yet, in its modern form, it is one of the latest of all disciplines. It has been changing its meaning from time to time. According to Rudolf Goeckel the term psychology has been derived from two words, "Psycho" and "Logos", Psycho means soul and Logos means "Science of" or "Talk about". Thus psychology means "The science of soul". Goeckel named it as Psychologia. Soul is a being, which dwells in the body and at the end of life it leaves the body. Since soul is a metaphysical entity, scientific investigation is not possible. Therefore the modern psychologists have discarded psychology as the science of soul. Therefore, the definition of psychology as the science of soul was discarded.

PSYCHOLOGY AND MIND

The philosophers again developed another definition of psychology as the "Science of Mind". After sometime controversy arose on the nature of mind. People began to feel that like soul, it is equally impossible to define mind scientifically. Ultimately this definition was discarded.

PSYCHOLOGY AND CONSCIOUSNESS

Psychology was again defined as the science of consciousness or immediate experiences. Ultimately, it was observed that consciousness forms only a very negligible part of the personality of an individual and the scope of psychology goes much beyond the study of consciousness. It also studies the sub-conscious and unconscious states of human mind. On this ground, the psychologists rejected this definition.

PSYCHOLOGY AND BEHAVIOUR

The above definitions given by philosopher-psychologists before the beginning of experimental psychology were considered to be very much inadequate and were rejected. Now it is defined as "the science of behaviour". To understand this definition, let us now discuss in brief the meaning of the science and behaviour.

DEFINITION OF BEHAVIOUR

Science has been defined as "systematic study of knowledge" concerning the relationship between the cause and effect of a particular phenomenon. In order to collect the scientific data and systematised material, science employs various kinds of methods of enquiry such as observation, classification, formulation of hypothesis, analysis of evidence, etc.

It also organises and develops our knowledge of the world where we live in. Psychology too aims at the same thing. It uses scientific methods to study human behaviour. It also helps us to understand, control and predict human behaviour.

Behaviour is a specific response, which can be seen and observed in an active way. Psychology as the science of behaviour also aims at studying the behaviour of the individual and groups. We can study the behaviour of an individual in social milieu. As a social science it studies scientifically the socio-cultural problems of particular society. Hence it is the science of behaviour.

DEFINITION OF EDUCATION

"Education is an activity, which goes on in the society." It attempts to develop the personality of an individual and then prepares him for membership in a society. "Man without education would still be living just like an animal. It is education, which transforms man from a mere two-legged animal into a human. It helps him to behave like a man and prevents him from behaving like an animal. Any modification brought about in the behaviour of an individual as result of his interaction with the environment constitutes learning." Thus modification of behaviour of an individual for healthy social adjustment in the society is education.

DEFINITION OF EDUCATIONAL PSYCHOLOGY

The term Educational Psychology is the combination of two words Education and Psychology. So far, we have discussed the meaning of Psychology and Education separately. Let us now focus our attention to the meaning of Educational Psychology.

Psychology is the science of behaviour. It aims at studying the behaviour of individual and the group. Besides, this it also helps us to control the behaviour of the organism as a whole. Education on the other hand, implies the modification of the behaviour of an individual. In order to modify the behaviour of an individual, the teacher must study the behaviour of the individual first. To study the behaviour of the child the teacher must take the help of true

Psychology and to modify the behaviour of the child he must take the help of Education. Thus, Education and Psychology are interrelated. Pure Psychology helps to study behaviour and Educational Psychology as an applied branch of psychology applies psychological principles of Education to modify human behaviour.

Educational Psychology as outlined above is a branch of psychology concerned with human learning and development in educational settings. It involves scientific study of techniques that can be used to enhance learning. Studies conducted by the Educational Psychologists generally deal with the following three important areas.

System of Teaching: It includes teaching methods, styles, management techniques etc.

System of Learning: It includes application of principles of cognitive and developmental Psychology, taking into account individual differences and learning styles.

The Atmosphere: It includes social context of the classroom or home environment.

PSYCHOLOGY VS. EDUCATION

Sl. No.	Education	Psychology
1.	Modern education is a group phenomenon. Hence some of the group psychological laws can be applied to the process of education viz. group dynamics.	1. Psychology also deals with groups.
2.	Modern education is defined as for behaviour, of behaviour and by behaviour. Hence psychological laws, processes and findings can be applied to education.	2. Psychology is surely a behavioural science.
3.	Educational goal today is all round development of the individual. Hence psychology aids teachers in affording better educational development of children.	3. Developmental psychology gives required insight into human development in all its aspects.

(Contd.)

Sl. No.	Education	Psychology
4.	Modern education caters to the needs, interests and abilities of children. Hence knowledge of psychology of needs and interests enables teachers to plan their educational programmes in a desirable manner.	4. Psychology enables understanding of needs, interests and abilities of children.
5.	Education involves proper organisation of teaching learning situation. Hence it is a common meeting group of both the subjects.	5. Psychology of learning gives insight into these areas.
6.	Education aims at the development of personality and character. Hence there are psychological aspects in this area also.	6. Psychology analyses these aspects of development minutely.

According to Arthur Coladarci of Stanford University, Educational Psychology is the empirical foundation of education. It consists of those aspects of education, which can be observed, tested and experimentally verified, and as such Educational Psychology is the scientific foundation of Education. However, effectiveness of Educational Psychology is proved only when its methods and findings become a part of educational practices, when the teachers apply psychological methods and when they develop and experiment attitudes towards their efforts.

Judd describes Educational Psychology "as a scientific study of the life stages in the development of an individual from the time he is born until he becomes an adult".

Charles E. Skinner states, "Educational Psychology is the branch of psychology which deals with teaching and learning."

According to Walter B. Kolesnik "Educational Psychology is knowledge of the study of those facts and principles of psychology which helps to explain and improve the process of education. Educational Psychology thus is the body of scientific knowledge about two activities—Education and Psychology".

FACETS OF EDUCATIONAL PSYCHOLOGY

We often put a question—What is the Nature of Educational Psychology? The answer to this question becomes almost clear when we try to examine the meaning and definitions discussed earlier. Its nature is scientific, as it has been accepted that it is a science of education. Its relation with education and educational psychology is also to throw light on its nature. We can summarise the nature of educational psychology in the following way.

KNOWING PSYCHOLOGY

(i) *Educational Psychology is a Positive and not a Normative Science:* Usually normative sciences like Ethics and Philosophy decide the aims of education. It is not the function of Educational Psychology to decide the same. However, once it is decided Educational Psychology will help us in telling whether aims are attainable or intangible. As a positive science, Educational Psychology will be concerned with the discovery of techniques, by which the educational goals can be attained out of scientific study. When psychology declares that a particular aim is unattainable, philosophers will then rethink and modify the goals of education.

(ii) *Educational Psychology is a Behavioural Science:* As noted earlier, the scientific study of how learning and other human behaviour have relevance to education is the principal concern of Educational Psychology. Thus, Educational Psychology may be thought of as a behavioural science with two main referents—human behaviour and education. In the educative process human beings are the objects of investigation about whom generalisations are developed and knowledge is sought. The second important referent of education, Educational Psychology is concerned with behavioural questions that are related to the objectives and practices of education.

(iii) *Educational Psychology is an Applied Science:* The action of Educational Psychology is to be found not only in the nature of the subject itself but rather in its application in the classroom. Teachers primarily deal with groups of children not with psychological theory or experimental results, but their learning is constantly being applied to a unique set of circumstances. That is why teaching is a profession and not a trade.

Educational psychology is just an application of psychological principles in the field of education and also changing the behaviour of the individual. It is to predict behaviour, control and influence it. Thus it becomes an applied branch of Psychology.

(iv) *Educational Psychology is a Social Science:* Social psychologists study humans who interact frequently, if not continually, with each other and live in groups ranging from the family to the society. Social psychologists are not only concerned with the effect of the groups (whether family, peer, professional, cultural or social) upon the individual and vice versa, but are also interested in a wide variety of other personal interactions.

(v) *Educational Psychology is a Counselling Psychology:* We use the word counselling to refer to the functions of psychologists whose principal job is to deal with people who are in need of help or advice but not primarily who have emotional difficulties. A branch of psychology closely related to counselling is to be found in the work of the school psychologists—planning, teacher training, problem of parents and the like. Educational Psychology thus encompasses counselling psychology.

(vi) *Educational Psychology is an Educational Science:* General psychology may be considered as the primary behavioural science. The domain of psychology is very broad, including the study of collective behavioural problems of individuals in educational situations. Educational Psychology collects necessary knowledge from general psychology to apply the same in educational setting. For example, to discover what makes teaching effective and what makes learning effective. We need the help of several special areas of general psychology. In Developmental Psychology the teacher learns about human growth from infancy (and even before) to maturity-how physical, intellectual, emotional, and social potentials mature and change as a child grows; what conditions foster healthy growth, and what conditions block it. Many changes in teaching methods and curriculum have come about as more has been learned about the ways in which children typically develop and how their needs change. Another focal point of attention has been the special problems of the child who is "different" in some way.

The Psychology of learning is concerned with acquisition and change of our patterns of behaviour, how those processes take place most efficiently, how learning of different kinds can be measured, what conditions help us retain what we learn and use it appropriately in new situations, and how learning varies with different levels of ability. Many kinds of learning "content" are involved in schoolwork from simple muscular responses to highly complex intellectual process. A teacher's need for studying the psychology of learning is obvious.

It becomes evident that modern psychology offers a great deal of help to educational psychology to apply scientific principles to educational settings and thus educational psychology becomes an educational science.

(vii) *Educational Psychology is concerned with Human Factor in Learning:* The Encyclopaedia of Educational Research (1960) defined the nature of Educational Psychology as follows: Educational psychology is concerned with human factor in the learning. It is a field in which concepts derived from experimental work in psychological laboratories are applied to education, but is also a field in which experimentation is carried out to test the applicability of such concepts to education and to round out the study of topics of crucial interest to teachers. It is the study of the learning teaching process in its various ramifications.

(viii) *Educational Psychology is a Growing Science:* Historically, Educational Psychology began with William James and Edward Thorndike in the USA in 1808. Since then the field of educational psychology has been influenced by works in related fields such as developmental psychology, educational measurement, cognitive psychology, personality theory, counselling, individual differences, and most recently computer science researchers, who are involved in scientific study of techniques that can be used to enhance the teaching learning process are contributing many new ideas to be applied in the field of education.

PSYCHOLOGY AS AN EDUCATION

(i) *Not the Nature of Subject but its Application in the Classroom is its Real Nature:* The nature of Educational Psychology is in no way concerned with the nature of the subject matter itself but with its application in the classroom situation. Knowledge of psychological theory alone cannot help the classroom teachers to deal with the students. Their knowledge in theory should be connected with classroom practice.

(ii) *Psychological Foundations of Education cannot be Educational Psychology:* Psychological foundation of education cannot be considered as deeper a science as Educational Psychology. It is to be considered as intermediary discipline that attempts to orient the students into the realms that are common between education and psychology. It is more concerned with the implicational aspect and not so much with the theoretical aspect of Educational Psychology. It aims at the application of the psychological knowledge to the field of education. It mainly emphasises on understanding the psychological aspects that serve as the educational foundation.

(iii) *Educational Psychology is not Mysterious:* Many people imagine that Educational Psychology is something magical or mysterious and that somehow educational psychologists have a superior or almost super human way of looking into the thoughts and feelings of the students. The notion is in other words, that there is a psychological method or approach, and that any one who knows how to use this and uses it successfully has an advantage over anyone who lacks it but in a true sense Educational Psychology is no more mysterious today. It is an ordinary applied science. It has no magic, no mysterious ways and no dark or hidden routes by which it gets its knowledge. Whatever educational psychologists have learned, they have learned through observation, and through careful observation in the classroom. Hence, Educational Psychology is neither magical nor mysterious.

(iv) *Educational Psychology is not Common Sense:* Some people go to the opposite extreme and assume that Educational Psychology is essentially nothing more than common sense. To them, Educational Psychology is nothing but what wise people have discovered from their experience, whether they have ever had formal training in the subject or not.

It would of course, be overstating the case to say that educational psychology has a monopoly of knowledge of human behaviour and its modification. The fact remains that application of scientific psychological principles in educational settings and the psychology of common sense in educational setting are different.

For one thing there are statements that are accepted by common sense but not accepted by psychology. One example of this is the common notion that those who are insane or seriously mentally ill have "lost their minds". In the other words, insane people are considered to be unable to reason adequately or accurately. This common-sense idea of insanity is far from the truth. Although intellectual abilities are sometimes disturbed in mental illness, a great, many individuals who are insane are not suffering for lack of ability to reason. If given an intelligence test, they do as well as others. In such cases, the difficulty is not in the intellectual realm at all but rather in the field of emotion. Thus, psychology must insist that insanity cannot be regarded as the "loss of mind".

On the other hand, a good many things that are accepted by psychology are not accepted by common sense. An example relates to the phenomenon of colour. The common sense view of colour is that the colour is in the object, which we see. Thus, if we see yellow flowers and blue flowers in a vase on our desk, common sense says the yellowness and the blueness are actually in the flowers themselves. From the standpoint of modern science this view is entirely unacceptable. We have every reason at present to believe that the colour is not in the object but rather in the perceiver.

EDUCATIONAL PSYCHOLOGY: OPPORTUNITIES

Scope means, the limits of a particular subject in the field of its operation. What is to be included in its study or what subject matter does it contain comes under its scope. Educational Psychology, as discussed so far, deals with the behaviour of the learner in educational settings and should limit itself within the four walls of the teaching-learning process and educational environment. It must try to solve the problem evolving in actual teaching-learning situations and help the individuals involved in this process.

The psychologists who deal with the problems of education are concerned with what to teach, when to teach and how to teach. A famous psychologist, Lindgren points out that Educational Psychology is concerned with understanding the learner, the learning process and the learning situation. The scope of Educational Psychology may be discussed under the following heads.

(i) The learner (student),
(ii) The learning process,
(iii) The learning situation,
(iv) The learning experience, and
(v) The teacher.

The Learner

The term 'learner' applies to students who individually or collectively participate in the educational programmes. These students taken collectively constitute the class. In fact, the behaviour of the class is none other than the behaviour of the students. There can be no teaching without they're being a learner. Therefore, Sir John Adams once remarked, "Teacher teaches John Latin. Teacher must have the knowledge of John's psychology; therefore, the teacher must study psychology."

The teaching of Latin without the knowledge of John will not be effective. John (the learner) thus becomes the center of the teaching-learning process. From psychological point of view, John is a child and he should consider, not his needs, ambitions, fears and other emotions are not the same as those of an adult. Treat him, therefore, as a developing organism, which is unique, and not as a small model adult.

Two learners of the same age differ from one another in a number of ways. When one has a liking for music and dislike for mathematics and science another may have, dislike for music and for mathematics and science. Hence, while preparing the curriculum for the learners we must take into consideration the dual differences that exist among the learners.

However, intelligent a learner may be, he cannot become successful in life if he lacks motivation. Hence motivating the learner is very important. In the classroom, situation from the psychological view, not only motivation but also the developmental characteristics of personality, mental health, individual differences intelligence, etc, of the learner come under the scope of educational psychology.

The Learning Process

Learning is the process by which we acquire and retain attitudes, knowledge, understanding, skills and capabilities and these cannot be attributed to the inherited behaviour patterns or his physical growth. Capacity for learning is related to innate physiological factors. Rate of learning depends on both inherited environmental factors.

Various Names of Learning

(a) Affective learning has to do with feelings and values and therefore influences our attitudes and personalities.

(b) Mental processes which produces cognitive learning, is achieved by such as reasoning, remembering and recall. It helps in the problem of remembering and recall. It helps in problem solving, developing new ideas and evaluation.

(c) Psychomotor learning has to do with the development of skills that require efficient coordination between our brains and muscles, as when we read or write or carry out physical skills such as balancing, skipping or jogging.

A number of other processes have been put forward to explain how we learn. All of them have conceived of learning as a process that progresses in stages.

The Learning Situation

It is difficult to imagine any period of our life situations, when we are not learning something, even though we are not always aware that we are learning. While walking down a street on any ordinary day, we continually modify our behaviour. Learning is commonly through experiences in response to environment. Thus learning situation covers all life experiences that modify our behaviour.

From academic point of view a learning situation refers to the classroom setting, which is composed of students, a teacher and a room. All have unique characteristics. In addition to these features we also have the behaviour of teacher and students. Behaviour includes not only overt physical activity such as talking, and doing, but also cognitive process like cognising, thinking and evaluating. In the classroom and the school, the teacher is to help bring about desirable changes in student behaviour. Through the teacher's interaction with students and the students' interaction with one another, many desired interests, motives, social skills and several outcomes in the cognitive and psychomotor domains are acquired more efficiently than if there was no practical interaction.

The Learning Experience

Although Educational Psychology does not connect itself directly with the problem of what to teach or what learning experiences are to be provided for the learner, yet it has the full responsibility of suggesting techniques of acquiring the learning experiences. Once the task of deciding the aims and objectives of a piece of instruction at a particular stage is finished the need of Educational Psychology is felt. At this stage, Educational Psychology helps in deciding what learning experiences are desirable, at stage of growth and development of the learner so that these experiences can be acquired with a greater ease and satisfaction. In this area, Educational psychology has the subject matter, which deals with the knowledge and principles of psychology that facilitates the selection of the desirable learning experiences for the learner.

The Teacher

It is not enough for a carpenter to be good at sawing and polishing wood because every kind of wood has different characteristics and behaves in different ways under his tools. The skilled carpenter need to know about trees, their variety, their characteristics and how to make the best use of them, so it is with teaching. Teaching skills alone are not sufficient. He must understand the children as learners. He must try to recognize those characteristics that are significant in helping each child to learn more effectively.

Any teacher who knows anything about the learners is aware that growing up is more than growing bigger. Children are not little adults nor are adults big babies. It is essential, therefore, that teachers who are closely concerned with children during that period of life some of the most important developments take place should know as much as possible about the process of growing and developing.

One of the first things we notice when we try to understand the learners is how differently they are, how each develops at his pace and along his own path of progress. No child is typical. He is in his own way unique. Yet like the doctor who must recognise which symptoms are serious and which are trivial, the teacher must distinguish between those variations that are normal and those that may indicate a child's need for special attention.

Understanding the learner from psychological point of view is an attempt to find out as much as possible about a particular learner by spending some time with him and learning about his physical, mental and personality characteristics and relevant facts about the environment in which he is growing up. Recording of such child studies is important so that the information can be used in wider studies or, where necessary for helping a child with problems.

EDUCATIONAL PSYCHOLOGY: VASTNESS

In an important sense, it is not desirable to limit the scope of Educational Psychology to the above five areas only. Educational Psychology is a developing and a fast growing science. Like any other developing branch of science it multiplies itself every year.

New ideas are coming into picture because of the results of new researches and experiments in the field. Society is dynamic in nature. So also is education. The new problems in the process of education and their solution are coming with a faster rate. Educational Psychology is trying harder and harder with the result of the development of new concepts, principles and techniques. For example, traditionally developmental psychologists were concerned with the study of the child development, but in recent years adolescence, adulthood and old age have drawn increasing interest. A major concern of developmental psychologists has been the process of socialization-how the immature, and relatively helpless infant is transformed into a functioning member of society.

An important part of socialization is the process whereby language is acquired and this is an area of vigorous research activity. Although developmental psychology has been with us since the very beginning of psychological study, its current popularity is increasing. This example proves that it is unwise to fix the boundary of Educational Psychology by defining its scope. It will not only harm the progress of Educational Psychology but also prove as a great obstacle in the progresses of education.

The boundaries of Educational Psychology, therefore, must be left free for its future expansion so as to facilitate the inclusion of all that is created in this field. As a result of which we can solve most of the problems of education and help the teaching-learning process to meet the demands of exigencies.

TEACHER AND PSYCHOLOGY

The contemporary age has witnessed an ever-growing interest in the welfare and education of children. Because of the recognition of the significance of the period of childhood, the present age has been called "the children's century". Modern education is also described as child-centered. Besides this paedocentric knowledge and understanding of children, the teacher should have knowledge of Educational Psychology. It will give him larger awareness of the nature, abilities and needs of the students he teaches, of the processes involved in his work and his own capacities and limitations.

EDUCATIONAL PSYCHOLOGY: VARIOUS LEVELS

Teachers in modern schools, whether primary or secondary, are often amazed at children's eagerness to learn, their creative problem solving, persistent efforts in self-development and their academic, athletic and artistic accomplishments. Trained teachers who are curious and scientifically oriented often wonder why and how children learn as much and even more effectively. The answers to these questions are relevant to the knowledge of psychological principles. The teachers can obtain positive results, if they can apply psychological principles in the classroom, laboratory, on the playground and in any learning situation.

Teachers and prospective teachers at the secondary stage of education therefore should try to enhance their understanding of their students by studying Educational Psychology. Thus they can provide proper guidance for effective learning.

Education Psychologists have much to offer the secondary school teachers in understanding the learners, because they have extensive resources at their disposal. In their research, they have access to children of all ages and ability groups in ongoing complete learning situations. They also help the teachers in their understanding of the principles of teaching, especially in the field of learning, in understanding developmental tasks of adolescents, individual differences and mental health. In all these fields, the teachers and prospective teachers become successful in understanding the learner.

GROWTH OF A LEARNER

Modern education is concerned with the development of both the individual and society. It is the duty of the Teacher to develop the constructive potentialities of every learner as fully as possible. At the same time he should aim to preserve and enhance the conditions of constructive living in society. In addition to these, he should turn to the accumulated and continually expanding knowledge, which makes up our cultural heritage and he should see that it is rich in curriculum resources. For the teacher should believe in a subject-child—community-centered education. When the teacher seeks the development of the learner, he should look to the following aspects.

(i) The teacher should enable the learners to achieve an inquiring mind, skills for effective communication, knowledge for maintaining, protecting and improving his health and for satisfying interests and skills and ethical character.

(ii) The teacher should enable the learners to achieve comfortable, useful and happy social relationships in their families, with friends and with other people at work and play. The learner should develop respect for humanity in general.

(iii) The teacher should enable the learners to attain economic efficiency by becoming an intelligent consumer and by preparing material suited to his talents and interests and to the needs of his society.

(iv) The teacher should enable the learners to develop civic responsibility, which involves a sense of social justice, an understanding of his society, participation as a citizen, tolerance, interest in conservation and devotion to the ideas of democracy.

In summarizing the role of the teacher in the development of knowledge of the learners, we can say that the teacher should look to the development of a community of individuals enjoying an increasingly satisfying constructive way of life. They involve the attainment of intellectual proficiency, occupational competence, effective group participation and leadership.

Besides the above areas, the teacher also gets help from Educational Psychology for the development of the learners in the following areas as well.

(i) Physical development, health and body care, including individual health, and elementary aspects of public health, grooming and understanding of growth.

(ii) Individual, social and emotional development, including mental health, emotional stability, growth of personality, and self-understanding and evaluation.

(iii) Ethical behaviour standards, and values, including observance of moral and civil laws, observance of the customs and mores of the culture, and the development of such characteristics as sportsmanship, kindness and helpfulness.
(iv) Social relations, a category which grows out of the preceding two and is devoted to the individual as a person in his personal, and social relations with others with whom he associates in home, community, and place of work.
(v) The social world, which considers the behaviour of the child in relation to the broader social setting of community, state and nation and includes geography, civics, economics, government, and the traditional Indian way of life.
(vi) The natural environment, as revealed by the physical and biological sciences, which emphasize learning to think scientifically and the use of scientific methods both as scientists and for solving problems in everyday living.
(vii) Aesthetic development, including both appreciation of the arts and personal participation in art, music, crafts and other creative activities.
(viii) Communication, including an understanding of the language, effective use of language skills in reading, handwriting, composition, usage, spelling, punctuation, speaking and listening.
(ix) Quantitative relationships, consisting arithmetic, including number system; knowledge of how it is widely used in solving quantitative problems in society, and the development of problem-solving skills.

VIEWS OF LEARNING

Within each of these nine broad and interrelation areas, objectives are further classified as indicative of four "types of behavioural change".

(i) Knowledge and understanding, which would include the objective of learning "how to use table of contents of a book".
(ii) Skills and Competence, under which we would place such objectives as "skill in untangling unfamiliar words".
(iii) Attitudes and Interests, under which we would include "enjoyment of a wide variety of reading materials", and

(*iv*) Action Patterns, which "refer to broad generalized ways of behaving" such as ways of responding to problem situations through the union of intelligence with good working habits and scientific methods of thinking. According to Campbell-Stewart, Educational Psychology helps the teachers in the following ways:

(a) *To Outline Aspects of the Learning Process:* Teaching methods rest fundamentally upon the psychology of learning. A teacher aims at modifying the experience and responses of his students in many ways. He should, therefore, know the conditions of the learning process thoroughly. Psychology helps him by rendering a most systematic and exhaustive analysis of the learning process.

(b) *To Outline the Main Phases in Psychological Growth from Infancy to Maturity:* The infant, the boy, the adolescent and the young man have different outlooks and attitudes. A systematic study of the characteristics of each one of these developmental phases will not only be interesting but also rewarding for a teacher who desires to be successful and effective in the classroom. Detailed information regarding these stages of growth is furnished by psychology.

(c) *To Match Subject Matter and Processes to be Learned to Labels of Development and Psychological Principles:* A practical outcome of the study of development stages is the equipping of the teacher with the skill to match the class instruction with the mental levels of the learners. Educational Psychology also helps in the formation of the guiding principles, which are the bases of this correlation of the curriculum and teaching to the psychological growth level of the learner.

(d) *To give Some Training in Assessing and Making Allowance for the Social Matrix beyond the School in which the Child and the Teacher Live:* As the child leaves the school he is exposed to many social influences, a large number of which are only too often adverse, nullifying the healthy socio-cultural effect of the education received at the school. Streets, cinemas, cafes, etc, are few instances of the sources of these undesirable influences in the beyond the school social matrix. Educational Psychology aims at training the teacher in adopting suitable remedial measures. Some of these measures are: organization of sports and games, conducting of psychological test, guidance of the students and their parents, etc.

(e) *To give the Teacher insight into his own Psychological Process and his own Role as Teacher:* A teacher should learn to control his own conflicts before he starts teaching. If he does not do so the students merely serve as more or less suitable materials on which "to react his unconscious and unsolved difficulties". Knowledge of Educational Psychology helps the teacher to know himself.

Some of our teachers develop an undesirable attitude towards their students due to poverty, ill-health, insecurity of service, incompetence to do the allotted work, emotional tensions, inability to get on amicably with colleagues, etc. These and host of other unfortunate factors affect the teaching-learning situation adversely.

Our society, on the other hand is unfavourable towards the teaching profession. Teaching has been accepted as a 'failure belt'. It is the refuge of the "unproductive men and unmarriageable women". Because of such an attitude of the society towards teaching profession, our teachers do not feel for their profession. If this is re-enforced by an already existing painful tension in the mind, of the teacher, his plight becomes all the more miserable because of this additional inner enemy.

Educational Psychology helps the teacher to know his own inner nature. He also understands the mechanism of the factor leading to his failure as a teacher. The knowledge of his own self and his profession helps him to improve both as a person as well as a teacher.

Educational Psychology also helps the teacher in proper management of the classroom to promote learning and minimize disruption. It teaches him how to present his lessons to both large and small groups-and when to do which. It also teaches him how to predict certain learning patterns of students of different ages and from different backgrounds to comprehend the importance and limitations of the theories employed in teaching strategies, and to utilize the many tools and techniques that are available to him. Besides, studying. Educational Psychology will remind a teacher how challenging teaching can be, and how gratifying it is when a teacher devotees his time and energy to this work.

IMPORTANCE OF EDUCATIONAL PSYCHOLOGISTS

Educational psychologists incorporate knowledge of the teaching process, the learning of the teaching process, and the learning environment in strategies that are designed to enhance learning. They study topics such as cognitive and developmental psychology, principles of measurement and classroom management. Educational psychologists also conduct experiments, some in the classroom and some in laboratories to find their own answers to unresolved questions and so on.

Basic Concepts ■ 37

CHAPTER THREE

Evolution and Growth

SOCIETAL PROGRESS

Human being is the best creation of God, but he does not receive the best education by the study of science or religion, philosophy or political science, education or Psychology, Art or literature or by earning a Ph.D. or a D. Litt. degree from a recognized university, but by the study of truth about how to live and how to be socialized. Sociability not only establishes his superiority over other animals but also provides him with capability of making sound adjustment and maintaining effective and influential social relations.

Traits, habits and instincts come into being during childhood. Then they provide the criterion for the characteristic reaction of man to his environment. The child's respect for his elders, love for the youngsters, co-operation with peers and hospitality towards strangers, etc, depend on the process of the development of his personality in the environment of school and family. The more he learns sociability in this stage, the more he becomes sociable in his later life and the less he faces problems. So both the school and the home play an important role in the social development of the child.

Man is a social being. He comes in contact with the society and starts his interaction with it from the moment of his birth. The span of social relations gradually increases and continues till death. So it is a process from womb to tomb. Considering from social point of view, the childhood is the most valuable phase in human life. Real socialisation starts from childhood. The social habits along with the social instincts that he gains and his interaction with different persons and environment shapes his personality for the whole of his life. Hence it is a prime necessity on the part of a teacher to have the knowledge of how the social personality of a child develops and what are its main constituents.

FACTORS OF GROWTH

At the time of birth, the child is neither social, anti-social nor unsocial. It depends upon the environment and experience of his life. His personality is shaped accordingly. At the time of entering the school, the child does not have egocentrism. Rather he expresses interests in the persons, objects and events of his surroundings. He takes part in group-activities. Qualities like distributing things among friends, co-operation, friendship, social interaction and leadership are the main characteristics of his behaviour at that time. With the increase of his experience with other elements of the world, these qualities become the traits of his personality.

SOCIETAL GROWTH

Social development is a multi-faceted process in which children acquire talents and behaviour that allow them to function, within a social environment, in a manner that is mutually beneficial to their well-being and that of others. Through social development, children and youth establish inter-personal relationships, acquire a sense of sex-role identity, and develop social standards and a sense of conscience.

Social development is influenced by many different socialisation forces. These affect children's acquisition of the habits, values, and knowledge that facilitate their attainment of goals and enable them to function satisfactorily as members of society. In other words, children learn a complex network of clues that indicates the appropriateness of their actions for specific situations. For example, students' behaviour in one teacher's classroom may be very different from their behaviour in another classroom or on the playground.

A variety of social agents, or determinants, influence the socialization process needed for effective social interaction. These social determinants may include biological factors, social structure and cultural-group membership, the unique social interactions that children and adolescents have with parents and other, cognitive and situational determinants.

Children are not just passive recipients in their acquisition of social behaviour; rather they are active participants in their environments through their social interactions. Students actively incorporate the standards of external social agents and they process those mental structures that enable them to construct schemes or programmes that facilitate appropriate behaviour in other social situations.

IMPORTANCE OF CULTURE AND SOCIETY

Social development varies with children's social and cultural system. Children are encultured differently based on their cultural backgrounds and on parental beliefs related to the nature of children and how they should behave as adults. For example, American-Indian, Oriental, and Anglo-American children are encultured to have different values and behaviour. However, it appears that children's acquisition of social traits and skills is independent of culture and that the process of social development is similar across cultures and social systems.

SCHOOL'S SIGNIFICANCE

School or any educational institution occupies a special position among the various factors that influence the social development of a child. School is basically a social institution. It can be called a society in miniature. So it can serve as a model of society with all the social characteristics. The amount of influence that school can have on the child depends on the caliber and will of the teacher.

Along with the discussion of child's physical, perceptual and cognitive development, psychologists are highly interested in infant's social and moral attachments. The reasons are many.

Firstly, the human beings are highly social and a child's birth is a social event in itself. Then as he grows he is influenced and shaped by the social and moral behaviour of people surrounding him. He also influences others. So it is a two way relationship and needs a good understanding among those involved.

Secondly, during early years an infant's behaviour is not clear but confusing as it does not have any uniqueness. Without a proper examination, we can't find out the possible psychological roots as causes of such behaviour.

Thirdly, there is the question of nature and nurture of the child. Different aspects of child's personality should be known to us. We must know about the inherent aspects and the factors that change due to influences of circumstances. Here social experiences take an important place in the child's life.

Finally, the effect of early deprivation trauma should be studied. The factors that produce a well-adjusted and balanced child and the cause that produce a permanent scar in an individual's psychology, must be properly studied.

Different methods and ways are open for the experimenter to study early sociability of human beings. Simple cases can be studied by mere observation. Then there longitudinal studies continuing for many years and experimental studies. We may conduct cross-cultural studies to know the difference in sociability of human beings caused by different social backgrounds. Then there are the studies of child's social behaviour in different socio-economic set-ups. Sociability of upper class, middle class and lower class children tend to be different and its cause and effect is to be properly studied.

MEANING OF SOCIETAL GROWTH

Various thinkers have defined social development in the following way:

1. *Garrett:* "Socialisation or social development is a process whereby the biological individual is converted into a human person". This definition is based upon the distinction between the term individual and person. We cannot name each and everybody as person. The person always possesses some personality. The personality is the product of social interaction between him and his social environment. Socialisation and social development—the process of social interaction-helps the individuals to attain personality characteristics.

2. *Sorenson:* "By social growth and development we mean increasing ability to get along well with oneself and others". In this way Sorenson explains that during the process of social development there is a progress in the social abilities or skills of an individual. With these increasing abilities he tries to bring improvement in the maintenance of social relationships. He tries to mould his behaviour and seek adjustment and harmony with others.

3. *Freeman and Showel:* "Social development is the process of learning to conform to group standard mores and traditions and becoming imbued with a sense of oneness, intercommunication and co-operation."

This definition lays stress on the following:

(i) Social development refers to the process by which a person acquires the necessary knowledge, skills and dispositions that make him an acceptable member of his own group.
(ii) It develops group loyalty and encourages mutual dependence, co-operation and cohesiveness.
(iii) It is the process which helps an individual to behave in accordance with social traditions and mores and thus makes him able to adjust to his social environment.

In the light of all these views we can come to the conclusion that social development or socialisation is a process

(i) which begins with the infant's first contact with other people and continues throughout life.
(ii) it is the net result of his constant interaction with his social environment.
(iii) it helps in learning and acquiring various social qualities and characteristics, and
(iv) with the result of such learning the individual becomes adjusted to his social environment and can maintain proper social relationships.

GROWTH OF AN INFANT

The child's attitude, social relationships and pattern of behaviour are to a great extent determined by his early social experience. In the beginning all these are "home-grown" and the foundation of sociability is laid in the homes.

Sociability is not innate and it must be learnt. Every social behaviour is an acquired trait. The period between six weeks to six months, is said to be a 'critical time' in the development of attitudes. For a sound and organised social development both "the types of opportunity" and "number of contacts" are important. Mothers, in upper and middle socio-economic families can give favourable opportunities to their children for contact with the members of their families while those who belong to the lower groups lack such opportunities. So their social immaturity is shown in a quiet, retiring and disinterested attitude towards people and social activities.

At birth the infant's perception is non-distinctive. He wants his physiological needs fulfilled. It does not matter who fulfils them.

She may be his mother or a caretaker, it may be a soft pillow or a hot water bottle. When the child is six weeks old, the first social smile appears and between second and third months of life, the baby's ability to distinguish people from inanimate objects develops. He then becomes more attached to people and shows different types of emotional behaviour when detached from them. But still he is unable to distinguish people. Some psychologists call this stage as "discriminating responsiveness to people". It is the beginning of true social behaviour.

The baby, between the second and third months becomes interested in people. He tries to attract his attention towards him or watch his facial expression. He shows special relationship with his mother.

When the baby is four or five months old, he wants to be picked up and to be given a soothing and warm touch. He smiles, in response to the person who speaks to him. After one month he can distinguish between scolding and smiling, friendly and unfriendly voices. At the age of six or seven months he differentiates between familiar and strange persons. He smiles at friends and shows anxiety towards unfamiliar persons.

During this period "attachment behaviour" shown towards the mother is intensified. He smiles at her and tries to vocalise a word to her.

The age of eight or nine month is a period of imitation for the child. He imitates the speech, simple motor activities and gestures of others. When he is one year old, elders can refrain him from doing a thing by uttering the word 'No'.

When the child is one and a half years old he shows "Negativism". It means stubborn resistance to requests and demands of adults. The resistance may be physical or the child may remain silent or even tense.

At the end of second year a state of equilibrium is seen in a child. He co-operates with adults in many simple daily activities and follows their directions. Now he becomes more social in his behaviour. He plays with others and especially with the children of his own age. He even shares his playing materials with them.

Most babies become interested in viewing coloured pictures, television and listening to radio. Though they cannot understand the meaning of the subject matter, still they observe and become fascinated by the constant change in light, colour and pictures on the screen of the television or on the pages of the comic books.

GROWTH OF A CHILD

Childhood consists of two phases known as early childhood and late childhood. Pattern of socialisation changes from one phase to another. Early childhood has been characterised as the "first stage" of socialization. At this stage he gathers training and experience to be a member of gang in late childhood. Area of relationship of the child increases every year and his talking, playing, etc, increases accordingly. The importance of social development during early childhood lies in its qualitative aspect rather than quantitative aspect. That means, it is not important to count the number of social relationships the child has, rather it is important how he develops intimacy with his environment. His future socialization depends upon the pleasurable social contact at this stage.

Early childhood is a crucial time, so far as social development is concerned, because the child during this time, learns the basic social attitudes and the pattern of social behaviour. From two to three years of age, the child's level of social relation is generally low. After three years of age his socialization shows the prominent symptoms of conversational interactions, dominance, leadership, dependent submissiveness, conformity or compliance with the wishes of others, etc. He also shows some unsocial or antisocial behaviour, but they are also important to the socialization of the child. Some prominent social traits develop during early childhood, which are discussed below.

Firstly the child shows negativism or resistance to adult authority which reaches its peak between the age of three and four years. After that it declines. According to Macfarlane, "Negativism is an interesting combination of self-assertion, self-protection and of resistance to excessive pressures. Children learn that resistance is their best defence in the face of erratic training or when quick tempered persons push slow tempered persons too fast. The child's negativism takes the form of verbal responses and silence. They sometimes do not hear or understand an order or request or they try to neglect them".

Another trait of socialisation of the child is imitation, which implies that the child becomes interested in other children in and around him and tries to imitate their speech, action and emotions. By doing this he tries to prove himself a member of the group. The child does not imitate at all. He chooses the person or persons from whom he gets warmth and affection and imitates their behaviour.

At times the child develops a desire to excel or outdo others. This results in rivalry and he tries to brag about his possessions. This is common in case of siblings in a home. When the child is frustrated he expresses aggression. By showing aggressive behaviour he tries to establish his dominance over others. From rivalry and aggression quarrelling starts and the child takes away the toys of another child, distracts his work, screams, cries, kicks, hits and bites. These outbursts are short in duration and easily forgotten. At the age of three years such quarrelling is frequent and after that improved social adjustments bring about a decrease in the frequency and intensity of quarrels. Children of the lower socio-economic levels quarrel more than those of the higher. Boys are more quarrelsome than girls.

Upto the age of four years, the boys and girls play together, without any specific preference for a particular sex. After four the discriminating attitude begins and it becomes prominent after five years. Then they play different games. In the opinion of Marshal it is a kind of aggressiveness shown by the boys towards the girls. The girls are also antagonised by this.

Between the age of two and three years the child plays alone without any interest in other children. Then comes "Associative play" and "Co-operative play" in which he is a part of a group. At the age of four years he starts team play. He becomes conscious of other's acceptance or rejection of his play activities. He starts playing 'neighbourhood-games' such as tag, hide-and-seek, cat and mouse, cops-and-robbers, etc. Games at this age are simple, involving few rules and lack any type of competition.

Late childhood has been named as "gang age" in view of an increasingly strong desire of the child to be a member of the gang. During this stage, social-development is rapid and the child is no longer a selfish, self-centered individual. He is a well-adjusted, cooperative member of his peer-group. Child's behaviour shows more maturity than before. When the child reaches the age of six, his negativism decreases, though again at the age of ten and eleven they show a type of rebelling attitude against adult authority by which they try to establish their self appropriateness.

The circle of friends of the child widens as he does not want to be confined to his home and family members. When the child enters the middle school, his puberty begins and boys as well as girls spend more time outside the home. Generally a gang consists of children of same sex. They form teams not only to play but also for other activities like stealing fruits, smoking and some other socially unacceptable behaviour.

By forming gangs they raise money for charity, make things or act out plays depending upon the nature of the community they belong to.

The child learns to compete with others, to co-operate and work as a member of a team, to accept responsibilities and to see them through, to take the part of others when mistreated or neglected and to be a good sport in adversity as well as in success. During the childhood, boys and girls prefer the companionship of the individuals of their own sex. The girls think themselves more matured than the boys of their age but at the same time they see them enjoying more social independence. So they develop antagonistic and unfavourable attitude towards the boys. Boys and girls of this age develop an attitude of hero worship towards someone who possesses qualities they admire. The children select a member of their gang as leader, who must be superior in most respects to the rest of the group especially in intelligence, dependability, diplomacy, self-confidence, emotional stability, athletic ability and awareness of the wishes of the others. Again the leader must be an extrovert.

CHILDHOOD: IMPACT OF GROUP

Late childhood is also called 'play age' because during this period overlapping of play activities is the characteristic of the younger years and those of adolescence of different social class backgrounds differ, qualitatively and quantitatively. Bright children are generally more solitary and take part in fewer activities. Within the play activities of boys construction of tools, drawing, painting and clay modelling are marked, while girls prefer sewing, drawing, painting and singing. The child who fails to establish good social relations spends more time in day dreaming than the socially well-adjusted child.

During late childhood the child develops interest in understanding people and things which formerly hold little or no meaning for him. After the child enters the school he becomes aware of his racial group and religious-group membership and tries to follow the attitude of elders. He develops a self-concept and understands his social class. He defines his social class status in terms of the occupation of his parents. The self-concept of boys and girls is different. The boys think that they should be able to run fast, play rough games, need to be smart, climb, swim carry things and above all they must have more ability than girls. On the other hand, the girls think that they must stay close to the houses play quietly and gentler than boys; sitting and talking about dresses; they need to know how to cook, sew and take care of children.

CHILD AND TEACHER

For the development of social traits in the child and to build him as a good citizen, the school, family and society are to play a very crucial role. In all these environments social development of the child is well-directed and well-shaped by teaching learning process. Education in very valuable for the child. Parents and elders should teach their children how to co-operate and keep good relation with all family members. Direction, advice and above all encouragement are basic for the development of the child. They should not be neglected but be given love and affection. Otherwise his social growth is retarded. He becomes autocratic and selfish. Selflessness, tolerance and co-operativeness are the qualities which should be inculcated in the child. Hard and rigid behaviour, sometimes causes mental instability. Many parents out of fear of danger, do not give their children independence to do any work and they themselves do that work for the child. By this, the quality of self-independence is hampered.

In case of schools or other educational institutions proper environment should be created to facilitate social growth of the children. School can arouse in the children qualities like friendship leadership, co-operation, responsibility, pity, unity, etc. This cannot be achieved only by advice. For this co-curricular activities should be encouraged. Sports and games, staging of drama, discussion, excursion, scouting, Red Cross, etc., are helpful for the child in the development of social traits. Human relationship is the foundation of sociability. So it is the first and foremost duty of the teacher and school to see how best students can keep direct relation among themselves and engage in constructive work.

SOCIAL DEVELOPMENT: FACTORS

Sympathy

It is a social quality. One should not only express explicitly sympathy in the sorrow of others, rather he should cooperate in order to do away with the misery of others. This is true sympathy. Sympathy should be active but not passive. It starts from home. Its learning cannot be rendered simply by means of advice. If the child receives sympathy from his family members and gets required help in the time of need, he develops exactly the same quality for others. These qualities may not be explicit in the child, for the child's power of observation, imagination, thinking and gathering experience may not be enriched. So he fails to express sympathy for others.

For this reason the elders, by means of concrete examples should eradicate qualities like hate and jealousy from the child's mind. The child first applies these qualities to his own people. This is extended to others at a later stage.

Friendliness

Sympathy and sentiment for one and all creates friendship. A child of two or three years can make contact with other children of his own age if they are left together at a particular place. This contact develops into friendship. Generally similarity in interest, age, height, social and economic status serves as foundation of friendship, selflessness, co-operation, etc. It has been observed by examining the students of a class that many students are interested to create new friends and some others lead isolated life. This happens due to individual differences in the personality. The child with whom others become interested to mix and make friendship with are called 'stars' and friendless students are called 'isolates'. Apart from this, there are some students who become intimate with only one friend and there are others who have many intimate friends. The former is called 'paid' and the later is called 'friendship gang'. This difference should be marked by the teacher and he should steer them in the right way. He should take steps to facilitate the isolate child to enlarge his circle of friends and become sociable.

The followings are some reasons for the isolation of the student.

(a) *Anti-Social:* Some children show rough behaviour. They show anti-social behaviour like disturbing others at the time of study, quarrelling frequently, beating others, stealing books and money, tearing up of the books and notes, etc. For such reasons other children are not interested to keep relation with him and finally he is isolated.

(b) *Socially Indifferent:* Some children are always thoughtful, inattentive and shy. They are introverts. Thought, imagination and attention of such students are always self-directed. They are not hopeful in creating friendship and lead a busy life. Their mental health needs to be restored. For, the teacher should apply principles of love, sympathy and consolation and engage them in responsible work by which they can be brought back to social mainstream. Sometimes the suggestion of psychologists proves useful in such cases.

(c) *Underdeveloped:* The students whose social and moral maturity does not keep tune with their growth in chronological age lie behind other general students and feel isolated.

The students who are friendly with all and with whom others want to make friendship show some distinct qualities. The qualities that make a student popular and friendly to all are his patience, good health, efficiency, responsibility, dependability, co-operation, service and help to others, and love for all, etc. Again good adaptability and emotional balance make him popular among friends.

HELPING AND VYING

Co-operation is one of the finest social traits. When the child, for the first time leaves his family and enters into the other environment his span of social relations widens. He develops group behaviour. After becoming the member of a group, he tries to be co-operative. Group co-operation gives birth to group competition. One group of children compete with another group for which all members of a group are to be united. It is difficult to say which of the two qualities — co-operation and competition starts first in human life, because during infancy and early childhood brothers and sisters in a family compete among themselves to be nearer and dearer to their elders. This type of competition is also possible in a classroom.

It should not be misunderstood that family only serves as a ground for competition. It also facilitates co-operation. Experience and moral educations makes competition change into co-operation. Competition cannot be blamed, since without competitive attitude, the child cannot continue his endeavour for development and perfection. But both co-operation and competition have their own limits. They should respond to the needs of the society. Though competition is helpful for the child, it has some drawbacks, because at times such a competitive mentality makes the child jealous and he undergoes tension. So proper balance should be maintained between these two qualities and that is the duty of the teacher. Apart from these if the competition is fair and constructive, social health is restored.

For the all-round development of the child, good social moral upliftment should be given proper attention in the school curriculum. The behaviour of the child should be closely and intensely observed by the teacher which will guarantee the healthy development of the child social and moral.

BODILY DEVELOPMENT

The whole series of anatomic and physiological changes taking place between the beginning of prenatal life and the close of senility may be considered as the physical growth. The study of physical growth of both children and the adolescents is very interesting and helpful also. Ordinarily, people make an estimate of the age of the children from their size and treat them accordingly. They also expect them to behave in a manner appropriate to the level of their physical growth. But the basic growth of the child is determined by two factors: heredity and environment. The hereditary factor refers to the characteristics of their family and race and environmental factors refer to healthy or unhealthy surroundings in which the children live, their nutritional and climatic factors, etc.

The behaviour of the child gets influenced by physical development in two ways: direct and indirect. Directly, it determines what children can do. For example, a child, who is developed according to his chronological age, can compete with his peers in games and sports on equal terms. If not, he fails to compete with them and gets himself isolated from the peer group.

Indirectly, physical development influences the attitude of the child towards self and others. In other words, it is his adjustment to the human environment. For example, children who are overweight cannot adjust with their thinner-mates. As a result of which they develop a feeling of personal inadequacy. If, on the other hand, their friends refuse to play with them because they are too slow, they develop a feeling of "martyrdom" in addition to the feeling of inadequacy. Such a feeling creates a havoc in the personality development of the children and the adolescents.

DEFINITION OF BODILY GROWTH

Physical growth brings bodily and physiological changes (internal as well as external) in an organism from the conception till death. These changes take place in the following dimensions.

(i) *Changes in Physical Structure:* Changes in terms of height, weight, body proportions and general physical appearance are considered as changes in the gross physical structure of an individual.

(ii) *Change in Internal Organs:* Changes in the functioning of glands, nervous system and other body systems like circulatory, respiratory, digestive, muscular, lymphatic and reproductive are known as changes in internal organs.

Physical growth does not occur at a regular rate. It occurs in periods, phases or waves. Sometimes it appears slowly and sometimes rapidly.

Researchers are recognizing more and more that a child's physical development has a strong influence on his personality. Researcher Tanner, put it this way:

"All the skills, aptitudes, and emotions of the growing child are rooted in or conditioned by his bodily structure. Behind each stage of learning lies the development of essential cell assemblies in the brain; behind each social interaction lies a body image conditioned by the facts of size and other features.... How fast a child grows and what type of body structure he has can exert a crucial influence on the development of his personality. The child's sense of identity is strongly linked to his physical appearance and ability."

STAGES OF GROWTH

The period of infancy covers knowledge of the entire pre-school age, from birth to about 5 to 6 years. In the first few weeks the human embryo and foetus grow at an extremely rapid pace both in size and structure through the multiplication of cells. Within a period of nine months, from the time of conception, the human organism grows from an almost weightless cell to about seven to eight pounds. By the time the human infant is born the rate of growth shows an enormous decrease as compared with that of the foetus. Even then the most rapid physical changes and the most striking growth of the whole postnatal life takes place during the first year. This early period of rapid growth is uniquely significant for education.

PROPERTIES OF INFANCY

(i) *Rapid Growth and Development:* Infancy is the period of growth and development. Inner as well as outer organs, develop rapidly at this stage. There is rapid growth in terms of height, weight and size. There is rapid development of emotions and almost all the emotions are developed in the child during this stage. This stage is marked by intensive motor activity and restlessness.

(ii) *Dependence:* An infant depends upon his mother, father and other family members for the satisfaction of his basic needs. He is a helpless creature and can move and function only with the help of others. Even for the emotional satisfaction, he depends upon others. He expects that everybody around him should love him and give him his entire affection and attention. He wants to love and to be loved and in this exchange he totally depends on the mercy of others. In this way the child at this stage is dependent but as he moves into the later years of his infantile behaviour he slowly proceeds towards independence.

(iii) *Self-assertion:* Although the child is a helpless one and depends upon others for the satisfaction of his needs, he is quite self-assertive. He tries to dominate his superiors and elders. His wishes must be fulfilled. He thinks he is always right and those all around him should obey him. He is the prince without a crown.

(iv) *Period of Make-believe and Fantasy:* Infants live in the world of their own creation. This is a period of rich but baseless imagination. As at this stage the infant has limited potentialities and aspires more than what he can actually get in actual life. He compensates himself in fantasy and make-believe.

(v) *Selfish and Unsocial:* In infancy the child is almost completely ego-centric and selfish. He does not want to share his toys or give any of his possessions to anyone else. He wants to have all the things, even love, admiration and affection reserved for him. He does not care for the social and moral codes and principles and places his self-interest at the premium.

(vi) *Emotionally Unstable:* Infancy is the period of violent emotional experiences. The emotions at this stage are marked by intensity, frequency and instability. They are spontaneous and the infant is hardly able to exercise control over them. He is not able to hide his feelings and in this way, the emotional expression of the infant is generally in the overt form.

(vii) *Sexual Development:* Although the sex organs at this stage are not developed, yet the sex tendency is in a continuous stage of development. The findings of psychoanalysts like Freud and others have clearly shown that the sexual life of the infant is as rich as that of an adolescent. The infant passes through the three stages, sexual development stages of self-love, homosexual and heterosexual. At the initial stage, the child-derives pleasure from his own body by sucking his thumb or touching the sex organs. Later on he seeks the satisfaction of his sex impulse outside and develops sentiments of love for the mother or father depending upon his sex. Finally the child develops heterosexual tendency and in this respect the male child gets attached to the mother and the female child to the father.

(viii) *Respiration and Circulation:* During infancy, the lungs develop rapidly and breathing capacity is increased. The heart also grows in size and its action becomes stronger but slower than at the embryo stage. The pulse rate which was one hundred and thirty for boys and one hundred forty for girls at birth drops gradually so that it is ninety-five for boys and ninety for girls. Parents and teachers must realise that the developmental rate of the heart varies with children. Recognition of this fact can help us to prevent tragedies resulting from too great a strain laid on this organ.

(ix) *Muscular Development:* The very slow development during infancy shows a slight acceleration at age three. Development proceeds from the bigger to the smaller muscles. Thus, an infant thrusts out his arms in play, but immaturity of the smaller muscles of his wrists and fingers prevent their manipulation.

PROGRESS OF MOTOR

This is determined by maturation of necessary muscles. A child will sit up, stand or walk only when the necessary muscles have matured. But this process of muscle maturation is very slow during infancy and these motor skills are acquired very slowly. Prior to this maturation, actions are awkward and they involve many unnecessary movements. In trying to grasp an object, an infant will exhibit several unnecessary movements of the shoulders, upper arms and elbows. The use of the thumb occurs only after the ninth month. As the infant advances in age, greater maturity of the muscles results in the unnecessary movements being dropped and action being refined. There is also greater strength and speed in the movements.

INCREASING WEIGHT

When the human infant is born, he weighs about 7 to 8 pounds. In length, he is about 20 inches. In the very first year the weight triples and the length increases by about 40 per cent. The rate of growth slows down considerably during the next three years and after that it becomes steady.

Growth in weight is influenced to a great extent by nutrition. Infants from poorer families are weightless and are shorter in stature as compared with infants from rich families. There is also variation in growth rate due to sex-difference. The male infants are larger than female infants of the equal age.

GROWTH OF BODY IN CHILDHOOD

Childhood begins with the school going age round of about 5 or 6 years and ends with the beginning of adolescence, *i.e.* about 12 years in case of the girls and 14 years in case of the boys. During childhood period, height and weight progress at a fairly uniform rate. But, motor development including posture, motor skills, co-ordination, locomotion, etc., which begin from infancy, go on unchecked.

DEVELOPING BODY

The rate of physical growth continues to be slow. Between the ages of six and nine years, children grow about three to four pounds annually. This slow trend continues during the next phase also. Between the ages of nine and twelve years, increase in height is only an inch per year. Weight increases by about two or three pounds per year but this increment varies from month to month. This slow period of growth is called the pre-puberty lag. The growth is slowest for girls between the ages of nine and ten years, while boys grow slowest between ten and eleven years.

An average six year old is about three feet tall and thirty-five to forty pounds in weight. As the growth rate is slow at age nine, the child is about three and half feet tall and nearly fifty-five to sixty pounds in weight. Girls are generally shorter and lighter than boys.

The most significant physical change occurring during this period is the lengthening of the limbs. The legs especially grow vary fast and children appear long-legged. Though children are generally healthy, postural defects are likely to appear now. In our efforts to correct this, we must try to find out the causes which may be infection, malnutrition, fatigue or even emotional disturbance.

BLOOD AND BREATH

The lungs continue to grow and the breathing capacity increases. The heart has not yet attained its full growth. Between the ages of nine and twelve these organs are almost, but not fully developed. Hence we must prevent children from exerting themselves too much.

The slight acceleration in muscular development that had set in after age three, still continues. Muscle tissue increases and coordination improves. By age six, a child has reasonable mastery over the basic skills. Hence the child is very active, and enjoys games that involve much physical activity. But his imperfect muscle-co-ordination makes him prone to falls. Since the muscles of the orbit are not developed fully, long reading sessions are prohibited for the six years old. Between the ages of nine and twelve, muscle growth increases and co-ordination also improves. The child's actions are more refined and skillful. Reading sessions can also become longer now.

GROWTH OF MOTOR

Children between the ages of six and nine have a reasonably good mastery over the basic motor skills of sitting, standing, walking and simple finger manipulation. Improving muscle co-ordination helps the child to acquire new skills and improves the already acquired ones. Thus, the six and seven years old may be seen trying to climb a stairway by taking two steps at a time. They also try climbing and jumping down from high places. By age twelve, muscle co-ordination is almost perfect. At this stage improved co-ordination of hand and finger muscles helps the child to produce good handwriting.

DIFFERENT FUNCTIONS

A child at this stage is full of energy and action. The school authorities, therefore, should take care that the early education of the child takes cognizance of this significant physical factor. Consequently, primary education should be predominantly informal. It should have ample provision for interesting and diversified activities.

Most of children grow according to the average pattern of development characteristic of their age level. Some children however, differ markedly from the average in many respects. Some of them go through the whole developmental process more rapidly. Others more slowly, than the average growth rate typical of their age. Some children show striking individual peculiarities in the trend and speed of growth at various levels of development. They may thus be advanced at one stage of their development and retarded at another. Throughout these developmental variations however, every child keeps on undergoing almost ceaseless growth in various parts of its body.

BODILY GROWTH AND SEXUALITY

During the first ten years, the boys are slightly superior to girls in most of physical growth. The tempo of physical development, however, is faster on the whole in girls than in boys. On the average, the period of rapid growth, following the onset of puberty, starts two years earlier in girls than boys. The significant year in which most rapid growth usually occurs is the 12th in the case of girls (about one year before the first menstruation) and the 14th or 15th for boys. Between the age of 11 and 15 years the girls usually excel the boys in weight and height. Growth in girls, however, stops abruptly after the menarche. The average girl reaches her mature stature by 16½ (sixteen and half) years. The average boy, on the contrary, continues to grow until he is almost 19.

The body proportions of young boys and girls are very similar in general. Boy's skeletal frames become broad at the shoulders. Their general growth is characterized by heavy muscles and greater strength. In girls the pelvis widens and the hips broaden. Pads of thicker fat in certain areas of the body result in the typical softness of the female figure. These developmental proportions are typical for the two sexes. Nevertheless, there are a great many children whose course of growth does not fit in with the average pattern of physical development described above.

GROWTH: VARIOUS KINDS

Many attempts have so far been made to classify individual children into physical types. The most commonly recognized racial and familiar traits usually forming the basis of such classification are variations in skin colour, form and colour of hair, shape of head, ear and nose, colour and shape of eyes, general structure, span and weight. It may be pointed out that these variations are more or less permanent. They persist in the individuals from family to family and from generation to generation. In changed environments, these physical traits may undergo some modifications but their general nature remains fundamentally unchanged on the whole.

STRATIFICATION OF SCAMMON

One classification of physical types is presented by Scammon. His four types of children based on their physical growth are as follows:

1. *The Lympoid:* This is a physical type in which the rate of growth of the child increases rapidly until 11 to 12 years and then decreases almost as rapidly to the adult level.
2. *The Neural:* It is the type of rapid early growth at 3 or 4 years gradually slowing down and reaching almost adult level by 12 to 14 years.
3. *The General Type:* It is characterized by a rapid rise in growth in early infancy followed by another rise around puberty.
4. *The Genital Type:* It is marked by a slow growth in the early years which becomes very rapid at puberty.

TYPOLOGY OF KRETSCHMER

Another interesting classification based on physical peculiarities, is presented by Kretschmer. His physical types are also four in number. Their salient features are:
1. *Pyknic Type:* This is characterized by round trunk and short extremities.
2. *Asthenic Type:* Small trunk and long extremities are the distinctive features of this type.
3. *Athletic Type:* This type shows a moderately proportional development of the body.
4. *Dyspalastic:* This is a mixed type of physical growth.

A thorough knowledge of physical typologies might not be very helpful for a teacher in his actual school work though it proves very insightful for the school medical officer. Some general information regarding the salient characteristics of physical growth among children, however, is almost indispensable for any successful teacher because obviously proper guidance in the field of physical health is as essential for a child as any other help and guidance.

PHYSICAL GROWTH: IMPORTANCE IN EDUCATION

It is not possible to have watertight compartments between physical, cognitive, emotional, social and moral development. They are closely interlinked. The growth and development of any one of these aspects affects the growth and development of the other. Therefore, physical growth is not an exception to it. It influences the other aspects of growth and development in other directions also. For example, growth and development of the nervous system influences the growth and development of intellectual powers. Emotional and social adjustment is also linked with physical growth and development. While the children having normal physical growth and development are accepted by their age group, the physical deviates, who are very small, very large, too fat, etc., remain isolated.

They are often nicknamed, ridiculed and denied participation in the play and recreational activities enjoyed by children of the same age. It brings serious maladjustment and personality problem. The young child, if intelligent enough, becomes aware of the fact that he differs in appearance and physical abilities from other children. His attitude towards self is injured and self-confidence is shaken. In this case either he becomes shy and timid or becomes aggressive in order to compensate for his inferiority feeling. Besides this, the balanced growth and development of the internal as well as external organs depends on the balanced functioning of the body systems. The functioning of the body systems decides the interest, attitude and the total behaviour of an individual. For example, glands and their functioning affect his emotional behaviour to a great extent. Similarly his anatomical development, the development of circulatory, respiratory system, etc., give the persons the required abilities for participating in various motor activities.

Thus physical development has a great impact on the total make-up of an individual. Therefore, it needs a very careful attention. It can help the teachers to achieve one of the most important aims of the educational process to bring an all round balanced development.

INFANT'S GROWTH AND EDUCATION

Children between the ages of three and five years are too young to cope with the work of the primary school. But they are mature enough to start preparing for it. Kindergarten training is therefore, very important. It is here that the child gets the first experiences of school life. He memorises short nursery rhymes, sings with others, learns to obey simple commands and follows directions. He gets accustomed to being separated from his mother and learns to adjust to a fixed schedule. He is also taught to work and play with other children of his age. Hence, the song-dance-and-play atmosphere of the nursery school is just a happy place where learning is a joy.

Activity must form an integral part of nursery training. As the children acquire new motor skills, they have an innate urge to practice them. Action songs, games that involve varied activities like running, skipping and jumping are enjoyed by them. As repetition and drill are also enjoyed, the same action or drill can be repeated profitably.

CHILD'S GROWTH AND EDUCATION

Children between ages six and nine years have a keen desire to read and write. But their muscle coordination is still imperfect. Hence the teacher must not over-emphasise reading and writing.

Handwriting also cannot be expected to be very good at this stage. Between age nine and twelve, reading can be encouraged. The teacher can also help the child to improve his handwriting.

TEACHER'S KNOWLEDGE OF GROWTH

(i) Knowledge of the pattern of physical growth and development can help a teacher in knowing what can be expected normally from the children at a particular age level. In turn it can help us to arrange school programmes like curricular and co-curricular experiences, methods and techniques of teaching, timetable, textbook and material, seating arrangement and learning environment, etc.

(ii) The contemporary age has witnessed an evergrowing interest in the welfare and education of children. It is on account of the period of childhood that the present age has sometimes been called "the children's century". Therefore knowledge of the health and proper physical development is very much essential for a teacher in a modern classroom. Modern schools have to play a decisive role in the task of growth and development process and can render valuable help in this direction.

(iii) Knowledge of physical development will help a teacher to be aware of the physical deviates, their psychology and problems of adjustment. Consequently he can help them in their social and emotional adjustment as well as in school learning.

(iv) Psychologists are of the opinion that the needs, interests, desires, attitudes and in a way the overall behaviour of an individual is controlled to a great extent by physical growth and development. Hence at a particular age level what would be the expected behaviour of the child growth and development pattern? For example with the study of the trend of the physical development in adolescence one can be aware of their growing physical, emotional and social needs. Accordingly, adolescents can be helped by the teacher in the adjustment to their rapid development and changes.

Since physical development plays an important role in the life of children, the parents and the teachers should pay attention to certain significant educational implications.

A child can become efficient in all fields of life, if he possesses a good physical health. Therefore physical development during infancy and childhood days deserves attention. In every school, there should be a regular programme of health education. Children should get enough of opportunities to participate in games, sports and physical exercise. Necessary information about physical culture, personal hygiene, food values, cleanliness, etc., should be provided in an interesting way. Interesting talks and film strips introducing the children to the various developmental stages should be arranged in schools. As a result of which they can develop a correct picture in their mind about their own changing selves and role in life. Besides this, it will work as a safeguard against the development of irrational worries regarding abrupt development, which take place in the children's bodies.

DEVELOPMENT OF FEELINGS

Emotion is the magic word that makes human life dynamic and makes him a multicoloured shell on the shore of the sea of society. It is like a battery charged by the nature in the organism that provides him with great primeval forces of great power to adjust and cope with the environment. Emotions add colour, spice, lyric and adventure to our lives. Along with this, it connects the mental and physical activities of man together. Between the hide and seek game of happiness and sorrow, human life becomes a daring adventure. Emotions control most of our activities. The best achievements as well as the worst deeds of human beings are the product of different emotions at different times. History is sufficient proof to project that starting from Mahabharata war till the wars of today, the root cause of all the destructions, is nothing but human emotions. While some emotions make our life horrible, others make it happy. Hence, for human beings it has become a necessary evil and so it occupies an important place in curriculum of psychology and education as well.

Emotion is a very complex phenomenon. So its study raises a number of difficulties. Almost all psychological phenomena notably perception, memory, learning, etc, except thinking and reasoning are involved in its study. Many types of emotions like pleasure, frustration, love, affection, fear, anger, sorrow, jealousy, hate, etc, make life happy and at times sorrowful being controlled by different types of emotions. At different times man may become a God or a monster in different situations of life. Emotions, not only influence our behaviour but also control our style of living, social adjustment and development of personality. One fault of our educational system is that we do not take into account seriously the emotional condition of the child while imparting education to him. If we can steer the emotions of the child in the right way, it will act as a constructive element in human personality.

If studied comparatively, emotions play a more important role in the life of a child than in the life of an adult. Child's power to think on a particular problem is limited. So he takes the help of a few emotions like fear, astonishment, anger and disgust to express his mental conditions. If the emotional state of children moves in a negative direction they do not become interested to learn; rather they fail to adjust themselves properly in the society. For example, if the child suffers from emotions like fear and anxiety all the time, his mental health is hampered and bitter introvertism and inferiority complex develops in him.

THE MEANING

Emotion may be defined as a stirred up state of the organism. In all emotions there is a strong disturbance of the whole organism which involves visceral disturbances and other internal changes producing definite external signs. Bodily manifestations like clenched fists, biting of teeth, shivering of the whole body and loud laughter, etc, often take place in emotions. As the term emotion is derived from the Latin term "emovere" which means to stir up, to agitate or to excite, to move outward, the feeling of an emotional state seeks an outlet in the form of an overt action. The intensity of such a feeling changes in proportion to change in the strength of an emotion.

Mainly three types of outer stimuli arouse emotion within us. They are person, object and situation. There are some other inner stimuli such as mentality, interest, ideal, health, self-respect, self-awareness, self-control, etc, which cause emotion. An emotional state continues till the stimuli function within or without us. In order to down or control the emotion we have to get rid of the particular stimulus responsible for it. A particular stimulus may create, a strong emotion at one time and a weak emotion at another. Secondly a particular stimulus may arouse emotions of different intensities in different persons. Both the outer and internal stimuli work in a particular emotional stage. For example, when a person of our age or a friend of ours ridicules or passes comments on us, we are not angry but when the same activity is shown by a younger one we become angry.

Emotions have a strong link with our urges, needs and interests. If they are satisfied, an individual is said to be enjoying a happy life and he is emotionally stable, balanced and healthy. But if they remain unfulfilled, frustration grows and the individual suffers from failure in adjusting himself with his environment.

Instinct is the source of emotion. Different instincts give rise to different emotions. Again, the same instinct may give rise to so many types of emotions in different individuals and in different situations.

Psychologists give divergent opinions regarding the number of original instincts. According to Descartes, the human child, at his birth carries six instincts. They are amazement, hate, sorrow, love, happiness and wishes. But according to McDougal, fourteen instincts cause twenty eight emotions. Some others opine that anger, fear and love are three basic and primary instincts.

On the other hand, American behaviouristic psychologists do not agree on the point that instincts that cause emotions are inborn. By experimentation they have proved that the child takes birth with only one instinct that expresses itself through different types of behaviours in different circumstances. This changing style of behaviour is considered by us as different emotions. They also proved that by conditioning, the emotional state can be expanded or controlled.

PROPERTIES OF EMOTIONS

1. It is a stirred up state, that shows both internal and external disturbances.
2. The emotions vary in intensity, from person to person and situation to situation.
3. Instincts work as stimulus to emotional responses and if they can be controlled, emotions can also be manipulated in a desired direction.

EMOTION OF MAJOR IMPORTANCE

The emotional response of the new born infant cannot be defined well or identified specially. But two distinct patterns are clearly noticeable in the reactions of the infant. They are pleasant and unpleasant responses. If the position of a new born is changed suddenly, if a sudden loud noise is produced or if the movement of the infant is obstructed, unpleasant response is elicited. The new born in unable to feel the degree or intensity of a stimulus. So his emotions of same intensity to all in the mother's womb lie dormant and does not show any emotional responses. As Backwin has stressed, "The ability to" respond emotionally is present in the new born as part of the developmental process and does not have to be learned.

After two weeks of birth, the infant enters into babyhood. During this stage, emotions can be well differentiated and they are aroused by different stimuli. Some observable emotions such as fear, anger, distress, delight, elation and affection, etc, are remarkably developed in the baby. During this stage the emotional state is short-lived and one emotion gives way to other emotions. Emotions can be conditioned easily at this time as the level of intelligence is very low. "A baby who has been frightened by the pain of an inoculation, for example, is likely to be conditioned to fear the doctor. Because he wears a white coat the baby's fear may spread to anyone wearing a white coat, such as a barber and in turn, he will fear having his cut."

EMOTION DURING CHILDHOOD

Anger

Anger is the most common emotion of a baby. When the movement of the baby if interfered with or wish thwarted he cries in order to show his anger. For example, if the child wants to have a particular toy and advances towards it but some one obstructs his advancement or sometimes the baby wants to be picked up but nobody gives attention towards him, anger is aroused within him. If the child becomes physically unable to reach a particular object he wants, he becomes angry. The baby often tries to express himself through speech. But he is unable to do so. In such a case also he feels angry. The anger response of the child is shown by an outburst of energy in screaming, kicking the legs and waving the arms in a random fashion. Sometimes they hold their breath, jump up and down, throw themselves on the floor, or hit or kick anything within their reach.

How to Handle Anger?

Anger aggravates matters very frequently and causes distress. Therefore the teachers and the parents should take the following steps to handle anger.

(i) When a child is angry, the adults should try to distract the attention of the child from frustrating experiences and direct it towards some other situation.

(ii) When an older child is angry, the adult persons should discuss about the situation and help him to have a correct view of the situation.

(iii) The parents, teachers and other adult members should try to avoid needless restraints, tedious repetitions and inconsistent demands.

(iv) There must be a provision to develop the required skill in the children which will help them to overcome an angry situation.

Fear

Generally babies are protected by the parents from any type of fear provoking stimuli. Even then, they learn to fear through imitation of those who are afraid or by remembering some unpleasant experiences. The most fear provoking stimuli in babyhood are loud noises, animals, darkroom, high places, sudden displacement, being alone, pain and strange persons, places and objects. Fear of stranger persons is one of the outstanding features of the emotional growth of the baby. It happens because the baby is not ready to see an unknown person approaching in place of the familiar person. So every situation of novelty or strangeness arouses fear in him. If a familiar person dressed in an unfamiliar fashion approaches the baby, he is frightened but when the unfamiliar dress is removed the fear is also removed off the baby's mind.

The responses shown by the baby in fearful situations are those he tries to avoid or withdraw himself from, namely the fear provoking stimuli. Whimpering, crying, temporary holding of breath are the other responses made by the child in such situations. Generally a fearful child turns his head and hides his face and if capable runs and hide himself in a place he thinks safer. Towards the end of babyhood his curiosity is aroused to see what is happening when he hides himself, and so he peeps out of his place to look at the person or object that aroused his fear.

ELIMINATION

When fear safeguards against harm, it is valuable. The child should avoid dangerous situations by the help of fear. But fear becomes dangerous, when a person cannot do anything because of the fearful situation. Such type of irrational fears are called phobias. Phobias cause much sufferings to an individual. Complete prevention of fear is not possible. But by the help of the following methods one can prevent fear.

(*i*) By the method of verbal appeal, an individual can get rid of fear. Such verbal appeals suggest the children how to develop the power of reasoning and how to build confidence.

(*ii*) The second method of prevention is negative adaptation. It helps to give an opposite response to the fear response. For example, when a child is afraid of a dog, he can overcome the situation if he is allowed to play with it.

(*iii*) Social imitation is another method where the child observes his friends and relatives acting in a fearless manner in a fearful situation.

(*iv*) Distraction is also a helpful method by which the attention of the child can be diverted towards an interesting feature of the feared object.

Affection

Affection of infant and baby is directed towards a person, an animal or a thing. "The baby fixes his gaze on a person's face, kicks, holds out and waves his arms, smiles and tries to raise his body, because these movements are so uncoordinated at first, he cannot reach the loved one. He can, however, usually reach the loved one by the age of six months. Affection of a baby manifests in his warm regard, friendliness, sympathy and helpfulness, mainly in action and less in words towards a person who takes care of his bodily needs, plays with him or gives him pleasure.

During the second year, the arena of affection of the baby includes objects, especially his toys. Along with human beings his affection is directed towards the "love object." Animal pets are also included within the love objects. With a family pet the baby can play without fear and feel warmth with a family pet.

The babies generally love those who give close physical contacts. The love reactions shown by the baby are hugging, patting or kissing the love object or person.

The baby's love for a person or a thing is influenced by his learning. His learning, mostly the conditioned learning makes him determine whom to love and how much to love. Only for this reason the baby's love for the different family members varies. In general, they love their mother more than any other member of their family due to constant companionship with her.

CHILD'S FEELINGS

In comparison to infancy and babyhood, the emotions during childhood are more common, more intense and more distinguished in character. During this stage, the child does not like to be under someone's guidance and control; rather he wants to enjoy himself in his own style. So irritability rises frequently at this time. Sometimes emotionality occurs from fatigue caused by strenuous and prolonged play. The main causes of emotion during childhood are psychological rather than physical as they were during babyhood. The level of aspiration of the children is very high. They think that they can do what their parents think impossible on their part. But the parents do not allow them to do that. At last when they fail to do what they thought, emotional state is aroused in them. Emotions and tensions grow in number and degree, when children enter schools, where they have to adjust themselves with dynamic and different social conditions. In such a situation the children make problems for their parents and peers and hence they try to avoid children for their unreasonable and constant emotional outbursts.

Different factors influencing emotionality during childhood are: health condition, differences in environment, patterns of emotional behaviour established during the babyhood days, undivided attention of the mother, sex and ordinal position of the child within the family, age difference with the sibling and the standard set by the parents for the child, etc.

During babyhood maximum of pleasant experiences and minimum of unpleasant experiences occur. But during earlier childhood, the situation is just reversed. As the child tries to come out of the closest guidance of parents and tries to lead an independent life, his emotions are intense. Sometimes he is frustrated. If he learns to tolerate frustrations, a balanced emotionality is developed and it helps the child in later age in not becoming aggressive.

Intelligence checks emotion. In late childhood he knows that if he expresses emotions, especially unpleasant emotions violently it will be socially unacceptable. "Hence a child acquires a strong motivation to learn to control the outward expressions of his emotions." He becomes careful about his expression of emotions outside the house. But inside the house he lacks that carefulness. So his parents often punish him for "not acting his age".

On the whole in late childhood, the emotional expressions are somehow pleasant. The child, through various activities shows that he is happy in his adjustments with his environment. Though most of the emotions are pleasant, unpleasant emotions often occur. The child sometimes suffers from anxiety and feelings of frustration.

A survey of some common emotions shows that they are also experienced by adults. But the stimuli and the manner of reaction are different. We will emphasize the difference on child.

Anger

The child in his early childhood comes across many anger provoking situations in his life. Secondly he thinks it is a better way to get the wish fulfilled by becoming angry. The anger provoking situations are quarrel over playing, dissatisfaction over toilet and dressing, obstruction caused to other interesting activities, unpleasant attack from other children and taking away the plaything, etc.

In the later childhood the child faces more anger-provoking situations than in early childhood. This is caused by his desire for more independence than he had when he was undergoing the period of early childhood. The various situations that arouse anger are interruption in course of an activity, constant criticisms, unfavourable comparisons with older children, blame or punishment based on misunderstanding, accusing him of lying and failure to achieve the goals set by him.

The younger child expresses his anger through 'temper tantrums'—that is, by crying, screaming, stamping, kicking, jumping up and down, striking, throwing himself on the floor, holding the breath, stiffening of the baby or making it limp, etc. The older child expresses his anger through sulkiness, negativism, refusal to speak, quarrelsome, fussiness and being generally disagreeable to everyone about everything. But older children have more controlling capacity over their emotions than that of younger children. Temper tantrum behaviour is eliminated when the child reaches the school going-age. The degree of frustration is more in case of older children. So some become aggressive in nature and some others become withdrawing in nature.

Fear

Fearfulness increases in early childhood. The child recognizes some situations which he fails to take into notice before hand. His intelligence is increased so he tries to understand a novel situation. If he fails to understand it he is frightened. When the novelty wears off the fear decreases. Fear is a painful experience for the young child. It becomes more specific in late childhood. Fear responses of young children are running away, hiding, avoiding physically and verbally, crying and whimpering, etc.

There are various reasons why fear develops in young children. Conditioning, imitation and memories of unpleasant experiences are the main factors contributing to arousal of fear. If the child hears some fearful sounds on radio or sees a fearful scenery in cinema he fears any sight and sound that bears similarity with that. Imitation plays a prominent role in the development of fear in young children. They see how their mothers are fearing a particular stimulus; so also they develop fear for the particular stimulus.

When the child is a little older, he tries to understand a situation Secondly he does not want to be ridiculed by others as he thinks to fear is a cowardly behaviour. Thirdly he develops a negative attitude towards the thing he feared or he develops a liking for it. So during late childhood fear decreases considerably. The child tries to understand 'what is the fact' and why it is happening, etc. Definition of fear for the child changes at this time. The most common fears in late childhood are fear for fire, darkness, illness, disease, doctors, operations, being bitten by a dog, etc. Girls show fears more frequently than do boys.

Concrete stimuli decrease and abstract stimuli join strength during late childhood. The fears are imaginary, fanciful, supernatural, etc. Children fear their losing self-prestige and try to hide their personal limitations. If a child is afraid, he does not show his fear. It is expressed in different forms such as shyness, worries, anxieties, etc.

Affection

The child expresses affection towards those persons and objects which give him pleasure and satisfaction. For the first time the child establishes a love-relationship with any particular person in his environment. Love is stimulated by the activities of other persons towards the child. During this stage the child should get love from his family and outsiders. If he does not get it he becomes 'self-bound' and feels stress in his emotional activities.

As Garrison has explained:

"Love seems to be a two way affair and grows best when it is both given and received. A constant rejection in the home may leave the child's capacity for giving forth affection undeveloped, or may cause him to seek affection from individuals outside the home. Over affection and indulgence may have an undesirable effect as lack of affection or rejection.......... There is therefore the danger that over affection for one or both parents will tend to exclude affection for children of the child's own age level".

So it is clear from the opinion of Garrison that too much of affection is as dangerous as lack of affection for the child. If parents love is not there, the child thinks himself secure, On the other hand, in case of over-affection, self-confidence is eliminated. He may be too introvert and may fail to establish friendly relationship with other children.

Children express their emotion of love both physically and verbally. They hug, kiss and pat the loved person or object. They opt for the companionship of the loved one for a longer time. They express their dissatisfaction when he leaves them. They imitate what he is doing and follow his styles and activities. This is also the same in case of pets and toys whom the child loves. During this stage girls are more affectionate than boys, and both choose children and adults of their own sex for the expression of their affection.

During late childhood the expression of affection is indirect rather than direct as it is during early childhood. The child does not like to be kissed or embraced especially in public. They feel grown up which forces them to be undemonstrative in their relations with others. But indirectly they keep the company of those whom they love. They try to help him in all possible manners. The love in its direct way bursts at unexpected times

EMOTIONAL GROWTH: IMPORTANCE IN EDUCATION

Educational institutions play an important role in the emotional development of children. Child's emotions can be steered either in positive direction or in negative direction by family and school. Some factors in educational curricula may make the child unhappy instead of making him happy. In traditional system of education the child gathers more unpleasant experiences than pleasant experiences. Some common emotions, that are negative in nature, and experienced in the traditional schools are anger, fear and jealousy. They do not help the child to maintain a healthy emotional growth. On the other hand, the pleasurable emotions help the children to develop love, affection and fellow-feeling towards others in the surrounding and ultimately an adjusted personality in future life.

There is no surety that the child, in his future life, will always face pleasurable situations. Rather he is sure to face both pleasure and sorrow in the long run. He must know how to adjust when situations of emotional tension arise. Only by that he can maintain his mental balance. He must tackle the dangers and problems that he confronts during his life. He must have tolerance, which he should put into use in adverse situations that arouse anger, worry, anxiety, frustrations etc. On the whole, if the pleasurable experiences in his life are more than the sorrowful sequences, balance in mental and emotional level can be maintained effectively. In case the sorrowful events come thick and fast, even a bold person can break down and lose his balance of mind.

CHILD'S STABILITY: GUIDELINES

Avoidance of cause or source of a particular emotion is the best way out in maintaining emotional stability. One must take into consideration what causes emotion in the child and then take preventive measures not to allow those things to happen to the child. Hurlock has pointed out five causes of arousal of emotion in children. They are:

(a) *Tiredness:* Physical tiredness makes a child to show anger, disgust and other severe emotional reactions. So when the child is tired he should not be given any task to work out.

(b) *Ill-health:* Ill health is one of the most important causes of frequent emotional outbursts.

(c) *Relationships with People of Severe Emotions:* There are people who are thick-skinned, furious and angry. If children are allowed to mix with them, they try to imitate their behaviour and develop such nature.

(d) *Submerged Wishes:* If the child is regulated under a strict and controlled atmosphere and rigid authority is imposed on him, wishes are not expressed freely which make his emotions arouse violently. So the wishes of the child should not be repressed in any way.

(e) *Embarrassment:*
1. If the child faces a particular situation, for which he was not ready, emotions arise and the child feels embarrassed.
2. The children should be taught about the proper way of expressing their emotions. Young children express their emotions in natural ways but adolescents are expected to express their emotions in a socially acceptable manner.
3. Some societies impose such rigid restrictions that the child does not get any chance to express his emotions. The society does not allow him to do certain things. But this is not good for the mental health of the child. He should be facilitated to express his emotions, at least verbally.
4. The educational institutions should help the child to find out the cause and understand the nature of unpleasant emotions. While undergoing an emotional stage it is not possible to change the behaviour of a child by injecting judicious thoughts into his mind. The only way out is to have a knowledge of the problems and wishes of a child and then provide him with measures to overcome them.
5. The child should not only be helped to express his emotions in an acceptable way but also he should be taught how to control them. Especially the emotions which are likely to cause embarrassment to others or destructive in nature, should either be avoided or controlled. This can be achieved by paying respect to the sentiments of the child.
6. The child should be directed and taught how to develop his capacity of internal control more than the external control of his emotions. This can be achieved by continuous endeavours.
7. The teacher plays an important role in educational system and hence apart from teaching lessons in the classrooms, he should be careful about the emotional

growth of children. The teacher's care, sympathy, affection, help and pity, etc, help the child to maintain a balanced emotional set-up. The teacher should have proper knowledge of emotional growth of the child. By this he can build a healthy atmosphere in the institution and the child will be able to gain a lot from it.
8. Judicious and rational thinking is the most effective in preventing emotional outbursts. So educational institutions should steer their curricula in such a direction that it will strengthen rationality and morality in children. Once the child is able to judge every problem in a disciplined way, unpleasant emotional outbursts will decrease as he knows what should be done and what should not be done. So his emotional growth moves in the right direction.

It is clear from the above discussion that a lot can be done by parents and educational institutions for the sound emotional growth of children. So in every sphere of family and school, proper attention should be paid and adequate steps should be taken to maintain emotional balance of children.

ROLE OF TEACHER IN EMOTIONAL MATTERS

Children showing emotional disturbances create problems for teachers in the school. They are generally naughty, destructive, aggressive and indisciplined. Sometimes, such behaviour crosses the limits and they go beyond control. Their temperament is wayward. After studying and analysing the behaviour of such children, a famous psychologist of London University opined that at first all emotion, which is opposed to the social customs and traditions, emerges in the mind of the child in the beginning. Opposed one after another, many anti-social and contradictory emotions emerge in different situations and make the child temperamental. As a result, the child expresses such aggressive behaviour. If this process continues, the future life of the child becomes an inflammable packet of Chinese crackers. Such a child creates innumerable problems for the teacher as well as for the school. If there is such a child, his temperament and mental problems should be understood correctly and measures should be taken to eradicate them for the benefit of the institution and the child himself. Hence it is a must for every teacher to have knowledge about the sources and causes of emotional disturbance of children.

EMOTIONAL ISSUES: FACTORS

There are some internal and environmental causes of such types of disturbances. They are discussed below:

1. *Organic Factors:* Some organic disturbances cause various emotional difficulties in the organism. Irregular secretion of endocrine glands is one of these. In some cases the physical structure and health condition of child hamper his emotional balance. If the child suffers from prolonged illness, if he feels much physical pressure on his body or if there is insufficiency in proper diet, emotional disturbances often occur. As a result of which angry, aggressive, and quarrelsome behaviour arises.

2. *Mental Factors:* At times some mental pressures force the child to show emotional disturbances. If long cherished hope is hampered he becomes frustrated.

3. *Social Factors:* For the healthy and sound emotional growth of the child the financial and temperamental environment of the family plays a significant role. The family, in which the parents lead an emotionally disturbed life and always quarrel with each other, can never create an ideal emotional background for the child. This affects the emotional growth of the child. Any child, (if unluckily,) is brought up in such a family, will show symptoms of emotional ill-health.

Likewise there are divided families where the father and the mother live separately. They produce children of emotional difficulties. On the other hand, a child always gets proper care, affection and protection from an emotionally balanced family.

Besides family and parents, social environment may also affect the emotional growth of the child. The locality, where the child resides, the schools where he reads and the friends with whom he is in constant touch make an element of social surrounding. If at any place the child comes in contact with the traits like suspicion, worries, anxiety, rivalry, anger, jealousy, etc,-they are reflected in the child's own emotional and physical behaviour.

4. *Sociological Factors:* The emotional growth of the child bears the mark of the geographical surroundings and the climatic environment within which the child has been brought up. A convenient, healthy and beautiful atmosphere always accelerates emotional growth of the child in a positive direction. But on the other hand, an unhealthy place with drains producing stink, dirty lanes, houses like cattle shed, crowded locality, etc, create abnormal emotional symptoms.
5. *Economic Factors:* Poverty is one of the most important causes of emotional disturbances. A hungry person is always aggressive. Children living in acute poverty cannot maintain their emotional balance.

So it is proved that the causes of emotional disturbances of a child are many in number. Sometimes more than one factor pressurises the child's mind at a time and he is abnormally tempted and forced to show emotional disturbances.

IMPORTANCE OF A TEACHER

It is a well established fact that in a whole class, an emotionally disturbed child is like a fly in the ointment. He soon affects other students and the peaceful atmosphere of the whole class. So it is the first and foremost duty of the teacher to point out the emotionally disturbed children when they are a handful in number and take possible preventive measures to eradicate the problem from its beginning. He should render special interest towards them and help them to solve their personal problems. If all children are emotionally balanced then he should maintain a pleasant, adequate, cooperative and mutual atmosphere in the classroom by which there will be no room for emotional disturbances. If the teaching process is heart-touching, classroom work is sensitive and facilities for extra-curricular activities are available easily, the student will be less prone to emotional disturbances. And in case any student shows such problematic behaviour, the teacher should be cautious enough to take up the measures discussed below.

1. *Re-education:* While the teacher applies a particular method of teaching and finds that some students show the symptoms of disturbances, he should at once change the method and again start teaching the same topic from the beginning. It is necessary to make the students understand why a particular

person, place or topic is boring. He should know the cause of boredom. He should be given chances to solve complex problems for himself. The student should be taught and directed as well as reinforced as to adjust himself with the difficult, problematic situations and persons. Re-education immensely helps the child in regaining his mental strength to overcome the emotional difficulties.

2. *Insight:* The root cause of emotional ill-health of the child is his disturbed thinking process. If at any rate the student is enabled to analyse his own problem with greater insight, most of the anger, aggression, mental pressure and temptations can be brought down. Things and events that pressurise a child's mind and give birth to high emotions should be arranged according to their intensity and importance, in order to help the child in restoring his mental health. It should be a unique feature of the child that he should always be attracted towards positive aspects of life. Only when the teacher has a clear understanding of his students character, behaviour, thinking process; language and temperament, can he arouse insight in them.

3. *Removal from Disturbing Environment:* It has been said that when an emotionally disturbed child is transferred from one school to another or when he is separated from one section of friends and included in another section of students some development occurs in his emotional level. This brings a change in the social environment of the child. The students get chances to adjust with new people and new events.

4. *Developing Emotional Immunity:* A particular condition that produces fear and annoyance, if repeated again and again, arouses excitement at a diminishing rate. For example, if a person wearing the mask of an animal appears before a child, he is annoyed. Then, if the same action is repeated, the child will not be afraid of it. This is because the child develops familiarity and becomes accustomed with that condition. Likewise if the child is inattentive and fails to perceive a certain stimulus, there is no reason that he should be emotional.

5. *Catharsis:* Catharsis means removal of an emotion or release from a tension. It is a common fact that emotional disturbances originate from mental tension. If there is any outlet for emotional tension, disturbances disappear. For

example, if a violently angry child is given a chance to express his anger verbally, or in any socially acceptable way, he does not show disturbances. Wrestling, boxing, debating are the various means through which the child expresses his anger, annoyance, disgust, etc, and his tension is eliminated. There are examples of many children giving up their disturbing behaviour and becoming great men in their future life.

6. *Emotional Education through Sports:* The child never applies all of his strength in performing a task. He retains some extra energy. When he does get any facility to apply this extra energy, he lays stress upon his mind and generates excitement. Hence to use this energy fairly and constructively, sports should be introduced in schools. When the emotional disturbance of the child is manifested in games and sports, it leaves a favourable and positive impact on his personality. So it is the foremost duty of the teacher to note that the students showing emotional disturbances take active part in sports and games in the school. Secondly the teacher should keep a watchful eye on the health of students. In case any decrease in the health of certain student comes to his notice, he should lose no time in advising him to build up his health. He may take the help of parents in this regard from time to time and inform them about their children's physical weakness, irregularity, inattentiveness, illness, etc.

7. *Maintaining Democratic Setup in the Classroom:* Children, in common, need love and affection of the teacher. So the teacher should have respect for the individual personality of every student, and should take into consideration their individual differences while teaching in the classroom. He should make arrangements for fulfilment of minimum requirements of students.

Along with psychological aspects, the teacher should impart moral and ethical education. The behaviour of the students should be ideal in every respect. He should know about the great men in history and follow them. The social development of the child should be balanced and positive and should be well acquainted with his circle of friends and take active part in every group activity. Feeling of loneliness is not good for the emotional health of a child.

8. *Influence of Teacher's own Emotional Health:* A teacher suffering from emotional disturbances spoils the child's emotional balance instead of doing him good. A violently angry, aggressive and extremely strict teacher causes similar emotions in the minds of students. So every teacher should, at the first hand, be cautious of his own emotional balance. He should have patience and be democratic in his approach.
9. *Taking Preventive Measures:* It is said that prevention is better than cure. It means that we should not wait for a problem to arise and then try to solve it. We should give no chance to the problem to arise. At the first sight of any kind of emotional disturbance in a child we should put our efforts into action and eliminate it. Otherwise it will get multiplied and trouble us a lot. The child, may be anti-social and cause problems to the society. Hence both the teacher and the parents should take preventive steps from the beginning. In no circumstances the emotional disturbances should be given any chance to grow.
10. *Treatment:* In case the emotional disturbances go beyond control, the teacher should suggest the child to be sent to mental clinic. Timely treatment may help the child to restore his emotional balance and help him in future.

WINDING-UP

The students showing emotional disturbances need personal care and sympathetic treatment with a good understanding of their problems. By showing them the right path, rendering correct guidance and timely treatment, their living in the society can be clean and disciplined. Carelessness makes them face more and more complex emotional problems and their abnormality goes on increasing. Hence they become the victims of various physical and mental frustrations. They are defeated at every step of their life and every defeat adds a bitter experience and intensifies their abnormality. So the teacher should try his best to save the children from such a condition and immunise them from any mild emotional disturbance by acknowledging their capacity and limitation. The individuality and personality of the children should be encouraged, the genius in them be aroused and cultivated and self-confidence be strengthened. By this the teacher fulfils his professional commitments and serves as society's strongest pillar.

ROLE OF INTELLECT

Each one of us is changing from conception till death continuously due to the impact of biological processes as well as owing to the influence of our environment As time passes the physical growth occurs and a human child becomes a full grown adult.

This can well be visualised. But side by side the other developments go on continuously. Those developments are rather felt than seen. For example, during the first year of age, the child who is unable to speak, uses sophisticated language when he grows up. This happens due to his rudimentary ability to solve problems of communication with others. So the sophisticated language of intellectual skills differentiates our species from all other forms of animal life. Changes occur in physical, mental, social, emotional and such other levels. A child reared up in a good social environment, can develop a sound personality and can overcome the bitter outcome of feelings of fear, anger, anxiety, etc, with an ability of better adjustment to the complexities of life.

By the 1920s, concept of the development of child was dominated by the thought of John Watson, the father of behaviourism. His impact, along with that of Freud, Binet, Hall and many others lead to the establishment of clinics to assess children and advice parents. Till then much was not known about children's thought, language and intellectual functioning. Watson discarded those internal events as in appropriate topics for research. But after using the concept of mediation it was learnt that the external behaviour of human beings and the reaction shown to the environment to know the ability of the child to build internal models of the world and to inculcate those models in order to learn from the past experience are necessary to draw conclusions about the future. The development of such ability in the child is known as intellectual development.

Intelligence is a concept rather than a thing which can be observed directly. It is the ability to think in terms of abstract ideas. It refers to mind in its cognitive aspect, particularly to the higher thought process. These higher thought processes are conception, comparison, generalisation, reasoning, etc. The topic "Intellectual Development" therefore, includes an account of the growth of these mental functions at different stages of development along with other allied mental functions.

GROWTH OF INTELLECT

Some people opine that the scholastic achievement of a child is his intellectual development. Though intellectual achievement includes scholastic learning, it is not limited to it. It is a well-known fact that the mental growth of the child is not solely dependent upon his pursuit of school subject. Intellectually, he learns a lot of things. But we cannot make a survey of the various aspects of intellectual development of the child in a single chapter. Therefore, here is an attempt to highlight in brief the salient features of some significant aspects of intellectual development during infancy and childhood.

MENTAL DEVELOPMENT: DIMENSIONS

As discussed above, mental or intellectual development takes into consideration the development of various mental abilities and capacities. How these abilities grow and develop from birth onwards is an interesting as well as useful thing to know. Though the development in the areas of various abilities proceeds simultaneously and is continuous, yet the studies have revealed possibility of the differences in the rate of overall mental development at various ages. Similarly it has been also noted that there is a possibility of greater growth and development in one aspect or area of mental activity than in another at one or the other stage of life.

General characteristics of trend or mental growth and development of various stages is concerned we have already discussed it in chapter two of this book. Now in the following pages we will try to discuss the changes and development in some of the important mental abilities or aspects of mental power of a small child as he grows older and older.

Sensation and Perception

Both sensation and perception are considered important aspects of mental development. Sensations are the elementary impressions gathered by sense organs. When these impressions are interpreted and some definite meanings are attached to them, they take the form of perception.

In the beginning, the child lacks in sensation as well as in perception. His sense organs are not developed. As a result, he cannot discriminate between things and understand their meaning.

Focussing of the eye towards the lamp, bright coloured objects, etc, can be said to be the beginning of an infant's perceptual growth. Later on, he distinguishes people from objects and then familiar people from strangers and in this way his environment gradually becomes differentiated into perceived objects. Those perceived objects become later on, associated with a verbal sound that he can recognize when heard.

When he is able to use his sense organs, he becomes increasingly conscious of the things around him and begins to ask a series of question such as why, what and who. At this time he has a poor perception of space, time, form, movement and distance. For example, due to lack of perception of the size of distant objects, the train when viewed from a distance, may appear to him as a toy train.

But gradually, his ability of perception gets developed. As the individual passes through the year of his adolescence, the sensory acuity reaches almost its peak and perceptual patterns become most organized and refined. His perceptions now become more definite, rich and detailed. They are now beginning to be influenced by his beliefs, opinions, ideals, etc, besides his needs, interests and mindset. They now need not be associated necessarily with concrete objects.

Concept Formation

Acquisition of concept is the generalised meaning that is attached to an object or idea. It is the result of one's perceptual experiences and involves both discrimination and generalization.

Discrimination begins early in life, sometimes after the child tries to generalize his perpetual experiences and thus begins to acquire concepts. Experience is a great factor in concept formation. In early childhood, the concrete experience in the form of actual objects helps the child in the formation of concepts. He tries to develop various contents from direct experiences.

In the later period, various experiences offered by reading, movies, lectures, etc, also provide the base for concept formation in the later years. It is not that only new concepts are formed; the old concepts may also get a new shape. They may be broadened, developed or the wrong concepts can be altogether abandoned. Normally, in development, concepts go from concrete to abstract, from vague to clear and from inexact to definite on the type of experiences one receives as he grows older.

In this way the concepts of the child in the beginning are characterized by vagueness, indefiniteness and inadequacy. For example, the child has very poor time concepts. As Crow and Crow put it "Time as such means little to the young child. He cannot distinguish among 'today' 'tomorrow' and 'next week' except as they represent words rather than actual duration of time."

Similarly his concepts of social relations and distance and depth are very vague and inadequate in the beginning. Gradually, as a result of learning and maturation, they became clear, specific and definite.

Development of Language

Development of language adds to the mental growth and development of an individual. The growth and development in speech, vocabulary and length of responses are some of the important aspects of language development.

At birth the child can utter some crying sounds. By the age of one and little later he may learn to speak a few words. After this, his vocabulary increases rapidly. Much of the speech pattern that the child learns is the result of imitation of others in the environment. During the course of learning to speak, it is possible that certain speech disorders like omissions, stuttering, stammering, etc, may develop. Therefore the parents as well as the teachers of small children must remain very cautious about this.

The vocabulary of children in the beginning is too limited. There is a continuous increase in the size of one's vocabulary during childhood. Later on, as the result of environmental needs and opportunities, the vocabulary goes on developing. Maintenance of the past and addition of the new words in one's vocabulary may continue even upto the period of old age depending upon their reading habits and interests.

In addition to the change in vocabulary and speech, the pattern of giving responses also changes with age. In the early childhood the child's responses are characterized by the "one-word response." Later on, gradually, he begins to use descriptive words like adjectives and adverbs and his responses include a large variety of words and almost every form of sentence structure.

MEMORY GROWTH

Memory is also an important aspect of mental development. At birth, there is little memory, but gradually with maturation and experience, memory increases. The developmental schedule as discussed by Hurlock and Schwartz indicates that "memory of an impressionistic kind appears in the first half of the year and instances of true remembrance appear by the end of the first year. During the first year memory is only aroused by sensory stimuli. With the learning of speech, the child is able to remember additionally by the end of the second year. During the first and second years the memory is stronger for persons and objects than for situations. During early childhood, from 3 to 6 years, situations become significant factors in the child's memory. Also the emotional quality of the impressions influence memory. By 3 years the child can recount the story heard a few days ago and he can also give information about past experiences."

Therefore the child shows signs of memory from the early childhood. The memory which the child possesses in his young age is generally a rote memory. He enjoys repetition and seldom uses logic and a selection process of remembering and forgetting begins to operate. In the later years of childhood memory tends to decrease. But from which age the downfall begins, it is difficult to say with certainty. It varies from individual to individual and generally besides the age and health, the situation and stimuli which are associated with a particular kind of memory affects significantly, in remembrance or forgetting.

Development of Problem-solving Ability

Problem-solving ability is an important constituent of mental development. An individual needs this type of ability in discovering the solution of the problems faced by him. Both thinking and reasoning powers are used in problem-solving. Therefore problem-solving ability depends upon the development of thinking and reasoning. Thinking and reasoning powers begin to grow from as early as two and one half or three years. However reasoning at this stage is confined to concrete and personal things from the child's immediate environment. The younger child deals more easily with the concrete than with the abstract. We cannot expect from him to solve complicated problems which require abstract thinking and more developed reasoning. But gradually, he shows increase in the ability to deal with abstract as he grows in age. He begins to compare and evaluate the ideas and solve the problems through the utilization of verbal symbols and imaginary concepts.

It follows from this discussion that in the beginning children should be provided with the simple realistic problems depending on concrete situations related to their own experiences and environment so that they can store them with insight and understanding. With the increase in age the more complicated problems requiring abstract thinking and widened experiences may be given to them. In this way, gradually, the children should be made to increase their problem-solving ability.

In addition to these aspects, mentioned above the other aspects of mental growth and development include attention, imagination, decision-making, ability of interpretation, etc. Like other aspects they also change, grow and mature with the increase in age due to maturation and learning.

PROGRESS OF MIND: FACTORS

Mental growth and development is controlled by both the hereditary and environmental factors. An individual's mental abilities, at any age of his life, are the products of his heredity and environment. The child is what he gets from his ancestral stock through his immediate parents at the time of conception in terms of mental traits or characteristics and mental apparatus. But the environment which he gets afterwards for the development of those innate abilities is no less significant than the social and cultural experiences, learning opportunities and education which he avails for the developmental process as he advances in age.

In fact, maturation and learning are responsible for controlling the process of mental growth and development which in turn affects the process of mental growth and development. Brain and the nervous system play a significant role in this direction. At birth the brain and the nerves that lead to it, are not fully developed. Their growth and development rapidly increase after birth and get matured in due course. As the nervous system advances towards maturity, the mental powers of the child also go on developing. Therefore, organic growth of the nervous system is the basic factor in mental development.

Learning is a form of experience and education helps the developmental process and in fact intensifies it to reach to its optimum level. It is said to play the same part as exercises play in developing physical skills and power. As Sorenson puts it "A child's legs, arms and body are made stronger by healthful play. We can deduce that the mind with its organic counterpart, the nervous system, improves and becomes better equipped because of use and exercise in the form of reading, calculating, memorizing, speaking, imaging and other mental activities."

INFANCY: PROGRESS OF INTELLECT

Study of intellectual development during infancy is based on approximate guess work. Most of the time of the new born baby is spent with events connected with his immediate bodily needs, *e.g.* hunger, affection, etc... Events like sounds and sights do not have any importance for him. Therefore, through approximate guesses, we try to study the intellectual level of the newborn baby.

When the infant, sometimes after birth, is able to fix at or follow a moving object with his eyes, we mark some early sensory responses. The vision and hearing play an important role in the study of early intellectual development of the child.

ROLE OF WISDOM

The intellectual life of an infant, when he turns his head and follows a person, rings a bell to get amusement out of the sound, displays signs of recognising and remembering certain objects and persons. It has been observed that the infants from birth to twelfth month, show remarkable signs of progress in this discrimination of visual form. At two or three years, they are able to identify differences in position.

DIFFERENT GROWTHS

Experimental evidence shows that at this stage of development, infants develop ability to discriminate colour, sound, weight, time, space, etc. The perception of colour develops rapidly before the child becomes two years old. At the age of four they can discriminate loudness of sounds. After this age, the auditory discrimination becomes more prominent.

AREA OF CONCERN

Infants are capable of paying attention at a very early age. Observation has proved that the beginnings of attention can be seen even during the first week of the life of an infant. During this period his eyes follow bright or moving objects. He develops the ability to watch people before he is three months of age. The infants develop likes and dislikes, interests and preferences during the second year.

MEMORY GROWTH

Intensive observation has revealed that by the third month a baby can recognize his milk bottle. He can also recognize his father and mother even earlier. He can distinguish between a familiar and strange object by the age of six months. An infant can name several objects from seeing pictures at the age of two. At the age of three and four, they can identify pictures correctly, which are mixed up with others.

CREATIVITY IN PROGRESS

The early creative work is the source through which we can study the intellectual growth of the child. The earliest specimen of the creative work of the child is drawing, which most children start. It is the sign of early creative alertness. The choice of lines and colours shown in the drawing of the children, help us to study their intellectual level.

FACULTY OF LOGIC

If we listen to the talk and watch the behaviour of the children we can develop an insight into their power of reasoning and judgement. F.D. Brooks states many interesting cases of reasoning among the infants. A little boy of two was pulling his daddy's hair. The father says: "Don't Danad it hurts daddy". To this, the little boy says "It didn't hurt grandpa".

Another father hurt his hands while working. His three and a half year old daughter told him: "Little girls daddies should not hurt themselves, because little girls love their daddies." Thus, with the increase of age, the power of reasoning and judgement of the infants develop.

GROWTH OF LANGUAGE

Language development is an intellectual process. It involves all types of mental ability like experiencing, perceiving, reproducing, memorizing, associating, etc. We can study the intellectual development of a child through the medium of language. Thus language becomes an important instrument for studying the intellectual life of a child.

During infancy, many children learn to use words. A study made by Smith suggests that active vocabulary at ten months is one word, at twelve months three words; and at fifteen months nineteen words. However, his passive vocabulary, (the words he can understand) is much larger at every stage of language development. When the child becomes 16 months old, he makes varied use of language. He uses words to name people, action and things. He asks questions about things, people and action.

Thus he adds new words, and his active vocabulary becomes 300 words. At this stage of development, the child's language consists of "one word sentences". For example when he says, 'milk', he may mean 'I want milk to drink'. Usually, the words used by him are nouns.

Thus, the infant's achievement in language is the most amazing. The same helpless child, who faces a lot of difficulties to utter a single correct word, uses several thousand words in the later stage of his development. The growth of vocabulary during the first five years of the child is rapid and interesting.

CHILDHOOD AND INTELLECT

The moment the child enters school, his intellectual horizon gets widened. His social contacts and scholastic learning bring further development in language skills. Besides this, he also attains intellectual growth in other fields. Let us now discuss some important aspects of his intellectual development.

When the child grows older, his vocabulary undergoes further development. Intelligent children have a larger vocabulary and greater skill in its use than the backward children. Children, who develop speech at a relatively later stage of growth, are not necessarily sub-normal.

In language development sex plays a very important role. Girls seem to excel boys at the age of the appearance of the first word. They also begin to talk earlier then the boys. Environment and training also contribute considerably in language development.

Children at the beginning of school stage use language for narration more extensively than before. They also express complex thought and reasoning. At this stage, they ask a series of questions on 'What', 'Who' and 'Why' and about fear. They also ask complex questions about God, death and sex. When they become three or four years old they use some 'dirty' words. They like very much the 'toilet' talk.

DIFFERENT LANGUAGES

Some studies done on bilingualism reveal the fact that bilingualism has a retarding influence on the language development of the child. From a study of bilingual children (English and Chinese); it was found that bilingual group had below average vocabulary as compared with monolingual children. A child for instance, in Orissa, who speaks Punjabi, Sindhi, Pushto or Bengali at home, receives school instruction in Oriya or English, faces a lot of difficulties in his linguistic development.

From various studies it has been proved that the development of reading ability in a language other than one's mother tongue is not very difficult to learn. But so far as its pronunciation, grammar, phrases, and idioms are concerned it becomes relatively difficult to master.

DIFFICULTIES IN SPEAKING

The linguistic environment in which the child lives, plays an important role in developing his grasp of context, vocabulary, sentence structure, articulation and grammar. Slow maturation, inadequate learning and emotional tension at times accompany speech defects and disorders. Children may develop incorrect or unintelligible speech habits due to slow maturation or inadequate environmental stimulation. Poor and wrong patterns of spoken and written language should be kept away from his environment from the very beginning of infancy. Expert surgical treatment should be made in case of an organic impairment of speech mechanism like tongue tie, cleft palate, etc. To overcome emotional factors in speech defects, attempts should be made to encourage children to overcome emotional inhibitions impeding the clear and spontaneous use of language.

CHILDHOOD AND REASONING

Throughout childhood, the ability to reason goes on developing. This reasoning process of children functions much in the same way as that of adult, but there are a lot of differences between the children and the adults. Problems faced by the children are related to their own immediate concern. They cannot phrase their thoughts and conclusions like adults. They do not have much experience and relevant information at their disposal to develop thinking and reasoning. They are also less responsive to the demands of the society. Even when they face new problems they usually resort to trial and error. The following are the main differences between the reasoning processes of the child and the adult.

(i) Like the adult a child does not posses the adequate language to phrase his thoughts and conclusions adequately.
(ii) The child lacks the wealth of relevant information and experience that an adult usually possesses.
(iii) The child possesses lesser capacity for sustained attention and lesser power of concentration than an adult.
(iv) He is more pre-occupied with his own immediate environment. Consequently, he is less capable of reasoning about problems that do not directly concern him or are too complex for him.
(v) A child reacts more and arrives at fewer solutions than the adults.

POWER OF IMAGINATION

Beginning from infancy, children remain engaged in imagination. 'Make-believe' plays an important role in the process of development. Imagination helps children to think beyond time and space. When they remain engaged in imaginary activities, they express many of their unfulfilled wishes, and release their emotional problems.

Afterwards, imaginary activities include more adventurous themes. But too much involvement in the world of imagination causes unrealistic ambitions and experience of failure.

CHILD'S MENTAL NOURISHMENT

To provide intellectual diet to the children, books magazines, music, drama, good cinema programmes, and radio programmes play an important role. Therefore, the teachers and parents should try to provide opportunities to their children to use the aforesaid things effectively.

Children should remain away from dangerous comics, sex and terror films, obscene reading materials etc. All these may obstruct the intellectual development of the children.

GROWTH OF INTELLECT IN EDUCATION

To achieve healthy growth, proper intellectual development is very important for the infants, children and the adolescents. Let us now discuss certain educational implications in the following.

(i) *The Problem of Grouping and Classification*: It is commonly an accepted psychological fact that individuals differ from each other in every respect, including the intellectual. It is, therefore, very important for the teachers to group or to classify children into different sections.

It is not wise to classify children merely on the basis of intelligence tests. These tests cannot measure the total intellectual development of the children. For example, a child may have high ability in one field and low in another. Therefore, it is not reasonable to classify children in this manner.

The most reasonable way of classification would be on the basis of maximum homogeneity in intellectual growth. Such scientifically based classification is desirable both for the students and the teachers. Teachers can group children on the basis of homogeneity and facilitate teaching and guidance.

(ii) *Intellectual Growth through Pleasant Instructions*: "Filling the minds of the students with facts is not education." The mind of the child is a growing organism. We cannot pack it ruthlessly with alien ideas. But we should provide knowledge in such a way that it would help to provide natural food for developing intelligence. Hence to make the food of education palatable for children, the method of instruction should be so pleasant that the child feels quite at home in the class. In such a situation, he learns a great deal without a feeling of boredom.

(iii) *Treatment towards Intellectually Handicapped Children*: There are some children, who are intellectually handicapped. Some of them are dull and backward and others suffer form specific backwardness in some school subjects. In our school system, we either ignore them altogether or push them too much. But such attitude towards these children is undesirable. The teachers and parents, therefore, should treat them properly and avoid the load of bookish instruction on them, which is not within their innate capacity.

(iv) *Encouraging Creative Pursuits*: For the growth of intelligence, creative pursuits should be encouraged. Some such pursuits include poetry, drama, literature, radio programmes, journals, magazines, developing cultural association with intellectuals, different hobbies, ideal cinema programme etc. The teachers and parents should encourage the students to take part in these activities.

(v) To Provide Maximum Scope for the Development of Language: The role of language in the development of intelligence is indispensable. Therefore, in the centers of learning maximum opportunities should be provided to the children for language development. Such development could be achieved by giving the child frequent exercises in reading, spelling, writing, etc. Besides this, opportunities should be provided for conversation, listening and repeating stories, participation in debates, discussions, symposia, etc. Teachers and parents should do their best to provide the children with healthy language environment at school and home to facilitate maximum language development.

CHAPTER FOUR

Development and Characteristics of Adolescent

WHAT IS ADOLESCENCE?

The term 'adolescence' is derived from a Latin verb meaning "to grow up." It is defined in the dictionary as the period of life from puberty to maturity. For the biologist, adolescence is a period of a rapid growth. It begins with an accelerated phase that continues until the attainment of sexual maturity, merges into a decelerating phase and terminates when skeletal growth has ended. But at the same time, adolescence is also a social phenomenon. Its duration is determined not only by biological factors but by the way the particular society defines childhood and adulthood. Thus, the sociologist may describe adolescence as a period when society has ceased to regard the young individual as a child, but has not yet accorded him full adulthood status.

Two conflicting themes can easily be detected in these definitions. In one view, 'adolescence is a period of positive attainment, of growth, and of maturation. In the other, it is a period between a stage of transition. This leads us to the issues with which we shall have to deal in trying to understand adolescence. The adolescence is striving toward a goal which, he is in the process of achieving. He behaves like neither a fish nor a fowl. Having left childhood but not yet having achieved adulthood, he is confused about himself, 'as we are often confused about him, as to his entity, *i.e.*, 'who he is'.

A.T. Jersild observes, "Adolescence is that span of years during which boys and girls move from childhood to adulthood mentally, emotionally, socially and physically."

According to Dorthy Rogers, adolescence is "a process rather than a period, a process of achieving the attitudes and beliefs needed for effective participation in society."

The Hadow Report in England has described this stage as, "There is a tide which begins to rise in the veins of youth at the age of eleven or twelve. It is called by the name of adolescence. If the tide can be taken as flood, and a new voyage began in the stream and along the flow of its current, we think it will move on to fortune."

WHO defines adolescence both in terms of age (spanning the ages between 10 and 19 years) and in terms of a phase of life marked by special attributes. These attributes include:

- Rapid physical growth and development
- Physical, social and psychological maturity, but not all at the same time
- Sexual maturity and the onset of sexual activity
- Experimentation
- Development of adult mental processes and adult identity
- Transition from total socio-economic dependence to relative independence

To distinguish adolescents from other similar (and sometimes overlapping) age groupings, which however differ in these special characteristics, WHO has also defined youth and young people.

IS ADOLESCENCE A PROBLEM?

Psychologist, educationists and students of human behaviour have long known that the period of adolescence is probably the most trying in the development of the human being. The period of adolescence—roughly from the age of thirteen to that of twenty—confronts the growing child with severe difficulties. Many adolescents manifest symptoms indicative of great emotional tensions; some develop conditions symptomatic of almost complete defeat. Rebelliousness, defiance, non-conformity, destructiveness and truancy are all symptoms of tension and hostility. Behaviour marked by shyness, seclusiveness, day-dreaming and sometimes bizarre or delusional behaviour are evidence of serious disorganization of the personality.

Children with personality troubles are often unable to cope successfully with the inner conflicts and stresses that develop during the adolescent years. The reasonably stable child encounters troubles, of course, but they are only temporary in nature and he emerges a reasonably well-adjusted young adult. For the emotionally disturbed child, however, the stresses and strains of the adolescent years reactivate the inner conflicts experienced in his early childhood. The new demands made upon him in this period cause him to feel more anxiety and increased tension.

Though the majority of our Indian adolescents remain normal and develop with normal stresses and strains of adolescence, for quite a number of adolescents, life becomes extremely difficult and any new trauma can cause them to become disorganized and reach a breaking point. These disturbed young persons may act out their anxious and hostile feelings in some form of anti-social behaviour. Such patterns of behaviour are known clinically as character disorders and popularly as delinquent or criminal behaviour. Some other adolescents may succumb to the stresses with a psychotic break, in which they lose effective contact with the world of reality. These are the future Schizophrenics. These tragic youngsters have reached the end of the trail, so to speak; whereas the adolescent with a character disorder is at war with society, the adolescent schizophrenic has surrendered and retreated to a world of his own.

As pointed out earlier, the largest number of teenagers with personality troubles continue to cope with the stresses of adolescence without getting progressively worse. These basically maladjusted individuals are able in some fashion to maintain their shabby equilibrium. Although they continue to suffer from inner anxiety and emotional distress, they do not become severely neurotic, anti-social, psychosomatic, or psychotic.

We see that this whole controversy has in two different view points in understanding adolescent behaviour. The psychological viewpoint and the cultural viewpoint. People like Stanley Hall believe that adolescence is a physiological aberration when most of the glands become hyperactive and sex glands start functioning. Excessive energy is released which keeps the adolescent stirred up. Hence problems. Whereas persons like Margaret Mead, the famous anthropologist, believe that adolescence is a cultural invention and in most of societies a bourgeois disease. In support of this cultural viewpoint, she has described the developmental patterns of the mountain-dwelling Arapesh of New Guinea among whom transition from childhood to adulthood is easy as the society is by and large permissive (regarding sex norms) and the adults are mostly affectionate, trusting and Un-aggressive.

ADOLESCENCE PERIOD : GENERAL CHARACTERISTICS

Simply these are more marked and prominent in this period of 13 years to 20 years of age. We shall list a few:

There is an intensification of self-awareness. It starts from the physical and physiological development in the adolescent. There is a disproportionate and enormous body growth. Sex glands start functioning. Other glands too work at a higher pace. As a consequence secondary sex characteristics appear, *e.g.*, growth of pubic hair in both male and female, alongwith development of moustaches and beard, nocturnal falls and hoarsened voice in the male, and menstruation and deposition of fat on the hips and breasts in the female. Also due to the sudden and hyper functioning of the glands, excessive energy is released in the body, physical, mental and sexual. This makes the adolescent very aware of his physique and physiology. That is why we often see them standing before a mirror for too long. Gradually and gradually this physical awareness converts into mental awareness. The process of self-awareness to self-analysis, self-analysis to self-insight and finally from self-insight to self-drive sets in.

The adolescent, during this process, becomes very inquisitive about sex, about society, about the world of work, and about the purpose of life, etc. Hence this is the period to impart correct sex education to orientate them towards social needs, and aspiration, to inculcate in them a balanced pride of their culture, to help them imbibe patriotism, to impart occupational information, and educational and vocational guidance to them, and also to lead them towards subtle topics in metaphysics, ethics and religion. His stepping into so many areas and activities makes him conscious of his rights and duties *vis-a-vis* the authority and society. In a static society, their role was determined at their birth. The son of a merchant would be a merchant. The son of a priest would be a priest. Automatically the adolescent would know his place in the society and would silently accept the role assigned to him. Whatever social mobility obtained, it was all vertical (within the same class, guild or caste) and seldom horizontal (from one class, guild or caste to another). Now in a changing and a dynamic society the adolescent feels lost as to what role he is likely to perform in the society. Hence the need of guidance all the more. There is a caution to be observed at this juncture. Since an adolescent belongs to no 'social group', he develops an intense overboard the social norms and mores. This is precisely what is happening with our Indian youth now since we are changing from an established and static agricultural society to a dynamic and mobile industrial one. We can safely suggest more of such school programmes, may be religion, which may impart some eternal values to our youngsters in a changing society.

There is a great need in adolescents to love and also to be loved. There arises a strong need of acceptance and belongings to a group. As a correlate of this need, adolescents began to search heroes and identify with them so closely that they pick up the characteristics of their heroes through this process of hero-worship. It has been observed that girls find out their heroes more from their immediate environment, whereas the boys go to the far-fetched environment as well. We can also expect more of idealism and less of realism at this stage. The adolescent is in search of a polestar towards which he wants to hitch his wagon. When he is disillusioned, finding no suitable hero in his political, social or religious field, he comes to adjust at an inferior psychic level of identifying with popular film stars and runs amuck and wayward. Precisely, here the teaching of the two great epics like Ramayan and Mahabharat or other such literature is essential. We can easily imagine the differential personality make up of three adolescents, one hero-worshipping Lord Hanuman, the second Lord Buddha and the third a film-actor. Also school has to provide for adequate group mechanism where he feels belonging to some one, and some one belonging to him. The adolescent who fails to learn this process to give and take, the process of emotional sharing in this period in a group, turn so out to be potential neurotic later.

In a study at Hyderabad, where male students from villages beat up girls, it was found out that the urban girls preferred to mix with urban boys more rather than with rural boys due to their peculiar habits. The desire to belong to the group, especially when they were discriminated was too strong in the rural boys.

There are conflicts in motivation hence ambivalence in satisfaction of certain needs, especially on the continuum of dependence—independence. The adolescent feels like a dependent at one time and soon after begins to behave like an independent. He is both a child and an adult. It seems that the

Western adolescents need more of independence, whereas our youth needs more dependence. In a study conducted at the All India Institute of Medial Sciences, New Delhi, the students would feel less anxious and more secure whenever they would visit their parents or local guardians. Also it has been observed that our Indian students get attached to their teachers more in the Western countries than their Western counterparts. The reason offered for this behaviour is "frustration of the desire in early childhood for exclusive-mother relationship due to large or joint family system in India." This seems to be a compensatory viewpoint. We can also say that our Indian students take even their Western teachers to be their parent-replica, and hence depend upon them heavily since they have already learnt to depend upon their parents emotionally. In India, the *Umbilical cord* between the parents and the children is usually not served in the life time. If not economically or physically, the children remain emotionally dependent upon their parents for long.

In adolescents, there is more of creative expression than reasoning. However, the modification of time and reality perspective does take place in this very period. Still their imagination takes an edge over reasoning. Hence their extra ordinary interest in fiction depicting adventure and make-believe sort of stories. This is the time when we should provide them with all facilities to develop their creative powers.

PHYSICAL NEEDS OF THE ADOLESCENTS

Hall has very emphatically observed, "A ton of knowledge, bought at the expense of an ounce of health which is the most ancient and valuable form of wealth and worth costs more than its value." Similar views have been expressed by Carlyle when he writes, "We produce clever devils by the thousand because health is not the object of party politics." Great seer Swami Vivekananda has also stressed the importance of well-built bodies when he remarks, "What India needs today is not the *Bhagwad Gita* but the football field." Our schools must give due importance to this aspect of education. W.M. Ryburn remarked "We need in Indian Education— a general philosophy of physical education—we need a conception of education in which physical education takes its rightful place and in which its vital importance is recognised."

A properly directed physical development programme should result in health, happiness, efficiency and character.

Meaning of Physical Education and Development

Physical education relating to physical development is that field of education which deals with muscle activities and their related responses. Physical development includes the following aspects:

(i) It is growth of nervous system.
(ii) It is growth of muscles.
(iii) It is functioning of glands.
(iv) It is change in height and weight which people normally observe.
(v) It is development of sex.

Physical development and growth include the physical as well as psycho-motor changes in an individual. Physical development also includes qualities like courage, endurance and self-control.

Physical Development at the Adolescent Stage

At the adolescent stage, marked changes take place in the following domains:

(i) Height and weight.
(ii) Bodily proportions.
(iii) Change in voice.
(iv) Increase in motor performance.
(v) Sexual changes.
   1. Boys develop their sex organs.
   2. Sex glands—the gonads—start producing sperms. Boys may suffer from night dreams.
   3. The growth of sex glands among girls is not visible. The first menstrual flow is indicative of their sexual growth.
   4. Growth of public hair around the sex organ,
   5. Hair in the arm pit, legs, arms and the chest,
   6. The growth of beard, and
   7. The tone of the voice deepens.

Among the girls the growth of sex organs is not visible. Other changes are:

(a) The development of breasts,
(b) Increase in the width of hips,

(c) A rounded appearance of body and limbs,
   (d) Growth of public hair, and
   (e) A shrill voice.

Sexual identity includes the expression of sexual needs and feelings and the acceptance or rejection of sex.

Adolescence period is the onset of puberty. Puberty implies a series of physical changes that make the organism capable of reproduction.

Puberty leads to sexual activity, erotic fantasy, experimentation and masturbation.

The period of puberty is a difficult one for most of the adults.

Educational Implications of Physical Growth and Development

A programme of physical growth and development is not confined to the playground but should pervade the class-room and in fact the entire school programme. Physical development in the class-room may take the following forms:

1. Direct instruction emphasising the necessity of having a good physique may be given.
2. Suggestions regarding the maintenance of good health are very helpful.
3. Emphasis on right postures should be laid.
4. Provision of good seating and lighting arrangements in the class-room, thereby impressing upon them the importance of studying under healthy surroundings should be made.
5. Providing ample opportunities to the children for physical activity should be given its due importance.
6. Medical examination of school children by the school doctor should be made at suitable intervals.
7. Physical exercise for every child should be compulsory in the school.
8. Various activities promoting physical development should be well planned and children should be encouraged to take part in these activities.
9. Activities like woodwork, spinning and weaving, book binding, gardening etc. may be introduced in the school as a group project. Such activities will lead to motor development as well as promote co-operation, and emotional adjustment among students.

10. At this stage students also have sexual development. It is necessary for us to impart them sex education.
11. Teachers should be conversant with norms of motor development of the child.
12. A variety of co-curricular activities should be introduced to provide outlets for the development of emotions and instincts which have a close link with physical growth and development.

EMOTIONAL DEVELOPMENTAL NEEDS AND THEIR SATISFACTION

Emotional development is one of the major aspects of adolescence growth and development. Not only adolescent's physical growth and development is linked with his emotional make-up but his aesthetic, intellectual, moral and social development is also controlled by his emotional development. To keep one's emotions under control and be able to conceal them is considered a mark of strong and balanced personality. Therefore, adolescents must be trained to control their emotions and achieve a mental balance and stability which will lead to individual happiness and social efficiency.

The term emotion is derived from the Latin term, 'emovere' which means 'to stir,' 'to agitate,' 'to move' or 'to excite.'

Woodworth, by making use of this explanation defined emotion in the following way: "Emotion is a 'moved' or 'stirred up' state of an organism. It is a stirred up state of feeling—that is the way it appears to the individual himself. It is a disturbed muscular and glandular activity—that is the way it appears to an external observer."

Crow and Crow have defined emotion in the following way: An emotion 'is an affective experience that accompanies generalized inner adjustment and mental and psychological stirred up states in the individual, and that shows itself in his overt behaviour.'

According to Kimball Young, "Emotion is the aroused psychological state of the organism marked by increased bodily activity and strong feelings directed to some subject.

How Emotions Work

All of us observe a large number of persons and objects in the world. We have some feelings for them in our mental make-up. Sometimes our feelings become strong either in favour or against the object or individual or an occasion. This disturbs our mental balance. This disturbance is known as *Emotion*. It not only disturbs our mind, but the entire organism. It is expressed in various movements and expressions of body and it tries to adjust to face the situation.

Features of Emotions

1. We have emotions due to our intensity of feeling. The depth of intensity differs from individual to individual.
2. The expression of emotions is universal in nature, *i.e.,* it is found in all living beings.
3. Every individual has his own outlet of emotions in his own way.
4. Our expressions of emotions are related to a person, object, idea or work.
5. Sometimes the expression of emotion leads to the loss of thinking power.
6. Our emotional expression is related to our instinct.
7. Our emotions persist for sometime and then they disappear.
8. Expression of emotions leads to changes in our behaviour.
9. Emotions rise abruptly but die slowly.

EDUCATIONAL PROVISIONS FOR ADOLESCENTS

As we have seen an adolescent is not an extraordinary specie from the blue or from beneath the earth. He is simply in transition from childhood to adulthood. Looking to his special needs of finding a suitable outlet for excessive energy, creative expression, group belongings, hero-identification, and of discovering himself on the continuum of dependence-independence, the parents, teachers and the society at large should provide for such facilities and conducive environment. Playgrounds to play, magazines and library facilities, excursion, dramatics, and other co-curricular activities, provision of health and sex education (Please refer to the chapter on Sex Education), occupational information programmes, guidance and counseling units, scientific and other hobbies; Literary and political forums and clubs, debates, and declamation contests, self-government, Parent-Teacher Association, Moral and Religious Education, Social Service Camps, mock parliament, sports, dances, etc., are the minimum we should provide for them. Above al what is most needed is "consciousness" on the part of planners, administrators, teachers, parents and other social workers of their psychology. They have not be forced into certain ways and mores, but convinced and gradually moulded through precept. We should remember Coue's Law of Reverse Effects, that you cannot be a dictator or autocratic in the world of emotions. If you coerce or order your mind into a particular way, it may yield for sometime but will again rebound and revolt. It is through concentrated imagination and patient persuasion that one changes. Hence a lot of patience is needed.

In some of studies conducted in India on the phenomenon of suicide, it has been found that there are two peak periods, the teens and thirties, where suicide is maximum. In the Western countries the old age is also equally critical as the teens and thirties, but in India so far the old age is comparatively safer due to Agricultural mores and rural background. In teens, the adolescent needs direction as he has to discover himself and his role in society. It is in the thirties that marriages break up, promising careers disrupted and therefore suicides occur. Having passed the flush of his youth, a person in his mid-thirties often tends to see his early aspiration unfulfilled or his life style becoming a monotonous routine. We also understand that 'thirties' are determined by 'teens', and 'teens' in turn are determined by 'childhood'. Therefore all the more importance of Nursery and School Education.

CHAPTER FIVE

Cultivation as a Discipline

Evolution is a continual process. The study of growth and development helps people understand what life means. That is, one must study the changes that normally occur—in body, thought and behaviour over the course of a life span. Right from the time of conception to death at a ripe age, the human organism runs through various stages of growth; each stage being a ladder-step taking to the final goal of life.

An infant and an adult are paradoxically "like and unlike" each other in very many ways: one is erratic, impulsive and playful and the other seasoned, reasoning and thinking and artful; one is waxing and the other waning, one is like a rising star and the other a setting star.

Biologically, it takes a long span of time for a neonate to become an adult, to become big, to grow in height and acquire weight although all the physical organs are already present at birth. Growth is a natural tendency with all organisms.

UNDERSTANDING PROGRESS

Growth and development are generally used interchangeably though the scientists consider growth to be one aspect of development. Ordinarily the term growth refers to the 'increase' caused by the biological process in which the organism becomes bigger in size, and heavier in weight. Starting his life almost from an invisible dot, the human organism grows to be more than five feet in height and more than 150 pounds in weight. Growth indicates the enlargement of cells, fibres and muscles, elongation of the skeleton and increase in the general volume of the body-parts and organ-systems. Growth brings about perceptible changes in one's structure and form: it is quantitative in the sense that can be measured in inches, points and dynes. Marked structural changes are noticed as the organism advances in age. Day after day and year after year, as the child looks different in appearance, we conclude that the child is growing.

'Development' is a wider term indicating advancement, more unfoldment, a progressive change-a sort of growing forward to a greater maturity; it is a process of qualitative transformation which brings about maturity and functional improvement.

Gessel stresses "Development is more than a concept. It can be observed, appraised and to some extent even 'measured' in three major manifestations: (*a*) anatomic (*b*) physiologic and (*c*) behavioural... Behavioural signs, however, constitute a most comprehensive index of development states and development potential"

Development is growing up characteristically. It is related to growth in as much as that it denotes more specifically the changes in the character and efficiency of the organs, organ-systems. For example, the bones as they grow, they become larger but changes also take place in their ossification, hardness and the ability to bear weight and shocks; elasticity gives way to solidity which gives strength. Similarly the heart grows, becomes bigger and it also undergoes qualitative transformation when it becomes capable of pumping out more blood and thus stand the rigorous of vigorous exercises. Filling up the soft-parts of the brain, elongation of the axons and dendrites of the nerve cells are instances of development in which the internal physiological processes stimulated by them are integrated (or responded to) in a way which enables the individual to master further anew environmental stimulations. The better the child develops, the stronger he becomes to fight knowledge of the environment and the environmental hazards like diseases. Development is an interactive process causing the organism to acquire physiological capacities and psychological capabilities.

DEFINITION OF GROWTH

"Many people use the terms "growth" and "development" interchangeably. In reality they are different, though they are inseparable. Neither takes place alone.

(*i*) The term "growth" is used in purely physical sense. It generally refers to an increase in size, length, height and weight. Changes in the quantitative aspects come into the domain of growth.

(*ii*) Growth is one of the parts of the developmental process. In strict sense development in its quantitative aspect is termed as growth.

(*iii*) Growth may be referred to describe the changes which takes place in particular aspects of the body and behaviour of an organism.

(*iv*) Growth does not continue throughout life. It stops when maturity has been attained.

(*v*) The changes produced by growth are the subject of measurement. They may be quantified and observable in nature.

(*vi*) Growth may or may not bring development. A child may grow (in terms of weight) by becoming fat but growth may not bring any functional improvement (qualitative change) or development.

DEFINITION OF PROGRESS

Development, by contrast, refers to qualitative and quantitative changes. It may be defined as a progressive series of orderly, coherent changes. *The Webster's Dictionary* defines 'development' as "the series of changes which an organism undergoes in passing from an embryonic state to maturity". These changes refer to physical, emotional, intellectual changes which we shall discuss under the following points:

(*i*) Development implies overall changes in shape, form or structure resulting in improved working or functioning. It indicates the charges in the quality or character rather than in quantitative aspects.

(*ii*) Development is a wider and comprehensive term. It refers to overall changes in the individual. Growth is one of its parts.

(*iii*) Development describes the changes in the organism as a whole and does not list the changes in parts.

(*iv*) Development is a continuous process. It goes from womb to tomb. It does not end with the attainment of maturity. The changes, however small they may be, continue through the life span of an individual.

(v) Development, as said earlier, implies improvement in functioning and behaviour and hence brings qualitative changes which are difficult to measure directly. They are assessed through keen observation in behavioural situations.

(vi) Development is also possible without growth as we see in the cases of some children where they do not gain in terms of height, weight or size but they do experience functional improvement or development in physical, social, emotional or intellectual aspects.

Hence when observed in minute details, both growth and development show differentiation. But in a wider and practical sense both terms are used to denote any changes in the organism's physical as well as functional behaviour. These changes which cover physical, emotional, intellectual and social aspects of human life are roughly divided into four major classes by Mrs. Hurlock: (i) Changes in size, (ii) Changes in proportion, (iii) Disappearance of old features, (iv) Acquisition of new features.

All the types of changes have qualitative as well as quantitative aspects and hence generally growth and development go hand in hand. And it is in this sense, that the two terms are to be used collectively. Both, taken together explain the total changes-functional as well as constitutional changes in the body and behaviour of the individual with the lapse of time after the conception.

DEVELOPMENT VS. GROWTH

However, growth and development are so closely linked that at times it is hardly possible to clearly distinguish between the two. Nature has set limits to the extent of growth of every animal and hence no animal would grow beyond those limits. Macy and Kelly declare that "physical development does not necessarily mean increase in size. There are modifications of the body composition taking place constantly. In the body, for example, gain in weight comes partly from increase in neural, glandular, and muscle tissue; in childhood the gain comes principally from bone and muscle tissue; while in adult years, the gain is from an accumulation of fat tissue".

No boundaries are set for development. Normally the growth may stop by the time a boy or a girl crosses further, depending upon one's professional work and labour. Not only does one develop physically but also socially and intellectually. Acquisition of new skills and assimilation of more knowledge constitute those qualitative changes which characterise 'development'. Quantitative measurement of the structure may reveal the pattern of growth a child is following and it is nowadays very easy to find out from the school health records whether the child is growing or not. Similarly tests have been devised to objectively measure strength, an indirect-index of the qualitative change in muscles and bones—and determine the extent of the development.

In the same way, intellectual capacity and ability which are the indices of mental development, can be noticeable in the players and athletes who day after day give better performance in activities involving strength, speed, cardiovascular endurance, etc. Ordinarily when children reveal their motor skills, intellectual ability, etc, differences in their growth and development can be spotted without much difficulty. Physical development is prominent in athletes who regularly take exercise while people with sedentary habits lag behind in this sphere.

Similarly voracious readers show signs of mental development. When athletes behave wonderfully well during play and do not lose mental equilibrium when defeated, we normally say that they have developed emotionally too. Social development is purely qualitative in nature because it reflects one's adjustment in the environment.

STUDY OF GROWTH AND DEVELOPMENT

Regardless of individual background and concerns, it is desirable to examine our purposes in studying growth and development. We want to acquire the following abilities:

1. The ability to recognize individuality. This implies the ability to recognize the uniqueness of each child's traits and view of life.
2. An understanding of the theories and principles of growth and development so that one can understand development in terms of the varied hereditary, environment and self influences usually involved.
3. An increased effectiveness in observing and interpreting the pattern of individual behaviour.

4. The ability to differentiate and evaluate the effectiveness of varying points of view in child study.
5. The development of a point of view and set of principles basic to guiding children more effectively in the learning and adjustment processes.

Thus, the student of child development should be involved not merely with learning a number of facts, but also with developing skills which can help him both personally and professionally throughout his life. This necessitates the continuing and purposeful observation of children in action, to supplement regular class study. As time goes on, he will be able to apply his knowledge and experience to interact more effectively with children.

CONCEPTS OF PROGRESS

Development psychologists believe that an accurate picture of the principles of growth and development is essential for the teacher. They are as follows:

1. *Growth in Some Direction is Inevitable:* All living organisms have to grow come what may. Propensity to grow is inherent in the organism. Because of malnutrition or some other environmental factors, the functional capacity of the child may not improve. Yet he has to grow and become bigger to the extent to which his heredity has set limits. It has been found that mental development is not much affected by malnutrition in childhood, provided the child received normal diet later on and that unfavourable conditions are not allowed to continue. All persons gain normal height even if they are not subjected to any special diet and physical exercises. Only those who exercise shall have better physical functional ability. There is, in each individual, an urge to grow and become bigger. Some individuals strive to grow into athletes, others into Mathematicians. The inner urge for growth will certainly take some form or direction.
2. *Mental Growth is Dependent upon the Changed Structure:* Along with increase in child's physical proportions, his ability to experience things enhances because physical growth and mental activity go hand in hand. When a child is found to be poor at perception and comprehension, it is because various organs of perception are not fully developed to

receive cues from the environment and he is not in a position to sift the wrong from the right. Gradually the brain also becomes capable of accumulating experiences. A child and an adult differ from each other in physical as well as mental growth. Perception and execution of complex motor skills involving a very high degree of neuro-muscular coordination is beyond the mental limits of the child while an adult having richer experience of years, takes little time in picking up hints and behaving accordingly. Qualitative mental activity is not possible without proper growth of the nervous system.

3. *Characteristically, Children are Ego-centric and Adults Socio-centric:* A child's behaviour is motivated by the intra-organismic drives which lead to the achievement of biological ends. When the needs connected with this process are not satisfied, the child revolts. As the child matures, he also learns to consider "other things" before his self. Much of his instinctive behaviour gets modified because the society demands certain norms, standards, customs and traditions as well as etiquettes to be observed and followed in the manner of walking, talking, dressing up, eating and the like. The adult behaviour is guided more by social norms and standards. Childhood, in fact, is a state of animal-hood. The child does what pleases him and what strengthens his ego. In infancy, for example, all activities of the child, including play, are individualistic in nature. Childhood is not bound by the shackles of social norms and standards.

4. *Growth is a Creative Process:* Right from the time of conception to adulthood marked differences in structure and form appear-thus resulting in behavioural variability. Transforming a infinitesimal zygote into a child, is the nature's highest form of creativity. As a child advances in age, year by year marked changes become visible in his behaviour. Instinctive behaviour which hitherto was more or less fixed, starts giving way to variability. Behaviourally what a child is at the age of one year, he would not be so at the age of five and the child at the age of fourteen is entirely different from the one at five. The process of growth creates novel, cognitive, conceptual and motor forms of behaviour as the child marches ahead in time.

5. *Heredity Sets Limits for Development in Terms of Potential:* Even if environmental factors such as food, air, exercise, etc, are abundantly available, the organism would never grow beyond the limits nature has already set on various animals and their respective species. Even twins may differ on anatomical characteristics. Certain races are tall while others are short statured.

   Similarly short children born of short parents would not gain height despite the best nutritional facilities and physical exercise. No teacher of physical education and sports should hope to increase the height/size of the individual which is already determined and demarcated by his hereditary forces. Many parents and teachers still erroneously believe that certain physical exercises can help children gain height. The teacher of physical education has to take special note of this fact. The activity programme has to be framed keeping in view these facts concerning the anatomical structure and its developments. Similarly many other hereditary traits cannot be developed beyond a certain limit. A born imbecile will never become a genius despite all efforts. Effects of certain congenital defects and deformities might be attenuated. Yet the total cure is impossible.

6. *Different Aspects of Growth, Develop at Different Rates:* Some children start toddling earlier than they start babbling; some start articulating sounds before they step into the phase of upright locomotion. Parents often worry when there is some delay in the appearance of a particular trait or characteristic at a particular period of time. Children characteristically speak three to five words at twelve months of age but in the next three or four months they seldom use words and often even forget the ones they knew. Language growth slows down for the time being because the child's physical energy and enthusiasm for learning are thoroughly occupied with the thrills of upright locomotion. Physical growth proceeds rapidly during puberty. Children probably learn more new things in the first five years of life than at any comparable period during the rest of their lives. In most of the children there is no synchronization between the physical and the mental growth. Some children become psychologically mature earlier while some excel mentally earlier than others. Ultimately all aspects of growth catch up by the time maturity is reached.

7. *Various Organs of the Body Grow at Different Rates:* Each organ reaches its maximum extent or dimension at different times. But within this chaos, a definite order has been found by the researchers. They speed up first reaching their peak growth rate only after about three months after the adolescence spurt has begun. In other six months, it is the turn of the calf muscles. Four months later, the hips and chest begin to broaden at an accelerated rate followed by the shoulders. In both sexes, the length of the trunk and the depth of the chest reach peak growth last of all.
8. *Growth is Characterised by Fluctuation:* Many factors may be held responsible for fluctuation in growth. Generally infancy or pre-school years are periods of accelerated growth while later childhood and late adolescence are periods of slackness. They are, in fact, periods of consolidation. After adolescence, the growth tapers off. Some psychologists have found certain individuals still growing-though imperceptibly-even at forty. Nutrition, physical and mental stresses and strains and other environmental factors influence the rate of growth. Some time, with all other factors there is still fluctuation in growth with certain children. For this, some internal and external factors may be responsible. Fluctuation in growth is not a drawback but an internal law and can easily be spotted if periodic check-up is made and proper records are kept. A month-to-month and year-to-year study, through psychometrical and ability tests, can reveal fluctuation.
9. *Any Breaks in the Continuity of Development will Generally be due to Environmental Factors:* Given an adequate environment, development will ordinarily take place in a relatively predictable way. Infants will grow physically as do most other children in the culture. They will learn to crawl before they walk. By the age of two they will have a rough working knowledge of the language that surrounds them; and toward the end of childhood they will experience rapid physical changes culminating in sexual maturity and adulthood. Motor, or intellectual development may be impeded in cases of severe childhood diseases or as a result of certain maternal diseases while the child is still in embryo. In much the same way, diet, drugs, and illness can affect children directly at various stages of their development and stunt both physical and intellectual growth. And, according to a principle

already stated, the effects of these conditions will be most pronounced during the period of most rapid growth.

10. *Correlation and not Compensation is the Rule in Development:* It has often been assumed by grandmothers that nature makes up for deficiencies in some areas by compensating for them in others. Thus, children who develop with frail and uncoordinated bodies, will most likely be given exceptional minds to make up for it. Only rarely will mother nature give the same individual both a superior body and a superior mind.

   In reality, mother nature is probably not responsible for such events. Striking incidents of compensation that can be gleaned from personal experience or anecdotal evidence are probably most often the result of considerable direct effect on the part of the individuals concerned. Because all individuals have a need for acceptance by others. Children who are unsuited for the competitive aggressive sports of their peers because they are significantly smaller, may naturally become more interested in intellectual or other matters. The point is that the compensation is not a natural phenomenon, but results instead from the individual's activities motivated by whatever needs are predominant at that time. That correlation rather than compensation is the rule is supported by evidence from a number of studies of gifted children.

11. *Development usually Proceeds at the Rate at which it Started:* Children who learn to walk and talk at an early age are likely to be advanced in all areas of development throughout their childhood. This does not mean, of course, that they are more intelligent and better developed physically than children who mature more slowly. Although their biological clocks may be faster, they are not necessarily programmed for more superior development.

12. *Development is a Life Long Process:* Generally growth and development go hand in hand. When the boy or an individual child grows in structure it also develops in function. But it is not the universal truth. A time may come when he may grow but does not develop or he may develop but does, not grow. Again growth may stop at a particular period, but development continues after growth has ceased. Development thus, is a continuous process. An individual

changes both physically and psychologically and encounters new adjustment problems throughout his life.

13. *Development Involves Changes:* The life of an individual is dynamic in nature. It is never static. From the moment of conception to the time of death, it undergoes changes. At each stage of human development, changes take place, whether for good or bad, as a result of accumulation of experience. The aim of such developmental changes are achievement of genetic potentials or self-actualization.

14. *Early Development is more Critical than Later Development:* Milton, the world famous poet once said, "The childhood shows the man, as morning shows the day." Right from the beginning of the early childhood, one can predict the future of an individual. Freud, in his study about personality maladjustment emphasises on the significance of early years of life. Erikson also opines that "childhood is the science of man's beginning as man". Thus, most educationists and the psychologists feel that the early development of the child is very critical. Early pattern of life is relatively unchanged as time goes on. The early impression of the child remains for all times to come. Therefore, the first five years of the child have been called "critical period". From this age onwards the foundations are laid for future life. The environment in which the child lives during this period has strong impact on his hereditary patterns. Hence guidance is most needed in the early stage of life.

15. *From Infancy to Childhood each Individual has his Own Rate of Growth:* The rate of development varies from individual to individual. While some develop rapidly others develop slowly. Dull children continue to be dull and the bright children maintain their brightness. Children having mental defects stop growing at an early age in comparison to the normal children from physical point of view, a child who is tall and heavy for his age, will continue to be tall and heavy to his age, and a child who is weak for his age, will continue to be so. Such rate of growth is a tendency and it may be influenced by environment.

16. *The Pattern of Growth is Continuous and Gradual:* Behaviour of an individual does not become mature and perfect soon after birth. It is a slow continuous and gradual process. To enter into a stage or level, it takes time. Early childhood lays

the foundation for later childhood and later childhood for adolescence. Therefore, it is not possible to demarcate sharply the different stages of development. It is a continuous process. Physical growth and mental and social development is also a continuous process. The process of continuity is maintained even in the development of traits.

17. *Growth is a Process of both Differentiation and Integration:* People vary in their behaviour because of differences in their genetic constitutions. From birth till the end of life man's behaviour changes at each progressive stage. This change in behaviour pattern occurs due to new discrimination and generalisation of different factors. Now we shall discuss how the child discriminates and generalizes mental processes.

The complex mental processes are the combinations of simple processes like sensations, feelings and images. Behaviourist also build complex behaviour patterns from simple reflexes. At the first stage of life the child is in a state of confusion but gradually according to his age and mental ability he is able to discriminate things properly. For example, when the child utters the words mummy, daddy, etc, he may use the same word 'mummy' for every woman. But when his intellect develops properly he uses the same word for one person only. At first the child does not know the actual relationship with different people. But gradually he learns to distinguish between them. Again another example may be stated that in early infancy emotions begin as undifferentiated generalized excitement. But day by day anger, fear, love, and delight begin to be distinguished from each other. In the social development the child also selects his friends, peer groups, and companions through the process of discrimination.

In growth and development integration and co-ordination of different physical parts, mental activities are more important as differentiation because the growth and development of every individual is a process of integration. Staging a drama, appearing at a competitive examination, playing cricket, giving a lecture, writing an essay, organising a social function are seen as simple unitary responses but all the activities require some mental and physical capacities in an integrated way. For example, we expect more achievement from a three or four year old child when he starts his first alphabet learning. But until the proper movement of his hand, and proper mental development he cannot write a single letter. Therefore without proper integration and co-ordination among different organs, no success is possible.

From the above discussion it has been found out that growth is both differentiation and integration. These two processes happen together. Both are important and fundamental aspects of growth and learning. Thus, we must keep these two in mind while framing the curriculum and selecting methods of teaching.

18. *The Effect of Training Varies with the Stage of Maturation:* In the process of growth and development the role of maturation is more important. But what do we mean by maturation? It is appropriate inner growth which develops readiness for learning. Without proper development of inner organs of the body, the child is unable to acquire new skill by guidance or training or education. Therefore training and teaching will not be fruitful unless actual maturation has taken place. But from our day to day experience we have seen that many parents don't have any knowledge about this inner growth. They lay much emphasis on education and training and expect notable results. Now psychologists have conducted many investigations upon this factor of growth and development. The outcomes of their studies indicate that the teacher or the parent cannot put new things into the child until he is mature for that. Real matured child can learn easily. Therefore proper training or instruction should be given at the right level of maturation and that may produce right results. In the process of teaching the subject matter for curriculum, and evaluation procedure, the level of maturation of the child must be taken into consideration.

19. *There are Wide Individual Differences in Growth Pattern:* Individuals differ in respect of their physical appearance, mental ability, school achievement, height, and weight, habit and skills, temperament etc. This individual difference occurs due to genetic factors, environmental influence and many other reasons. But in the process of growth and development children vary in their rate of growth. It implies wide individual variations both in their rates and pattern of growth. From our modern research it has been found that

growth is a creative force which results in new experience and ability. According to one's own intelligence and ability, and influence of his own environment he is capable of making a unique pattern of growth. Thus, this variation occurs spontaneously in growth pattern.

20. *Both Rate and Pattern of Growth can be Modified:* Both rate and pattern of growth can be modified by the conditions within and without the body. Although the patterns of growth are family definite for all children yet 'some' modifications can be envisaged. When environment does not offer equal opportunity to all, the natural flow of growth is modified. Amount of activity, psychological challenges, learning facilities, security, affection, discipline, etc, are a few factors which determine how fast and to what extent the potentialities of the child will have opportunity to develop. Children living under abject poverty and constant mental strains when freed, will show positively modified growth patterns. Growth brings differentiation as well as integration in behaviour. The processes are closely knit. It is impossible to understand the 'physical' child without understanding, at the same time, the 'thinking', the feeling and the 'impulsive' child. Likewise it is impossible to understand a mentally 'matured' child without evaluating his social development. There is a close relationship, for example between his total adjustment at school and his emotional growth, his physical health and his intellectual adequacy; his intellect is related to his physical health and his intellectual adequacy; his intellect is related to his physical well being: his physical growth and health are deeply affected by his emotional development; his emotions are influenced by the school success or failure, by his physical health and by his intellectual growth. His growth—physical, intellectual and social—is a product of his family history, his personal history and his current satisfactions and strains. Differentiation is a marked sign of growth; each organ, each aspect of the child's personality reaches its fullness by the process of differentiation; integration aims at synthesising all aspects to give the individual a sort of uniqueness and "wholeness".

21. *Developmental Process and Education:* Opportunity for good education and learning help developmental processes-being

an inextricable aspect of an individual's personality. Acquisition of knowledge, experience and motor skills clearly point out the direction and the pattern of an individuals growth. Gesell claims that innate capacity for growth "is a gist of nature. It can be guided, but it cannot be transcended by an educational agency". The patterns of behaviour which develop through learning, clearly indicate the cultural influences. Generally, children studying in public and convent schools seem to be maturer than children studying in ordinary schools. Urban children seem to behave in a more mature manner in the field of sports than do the children from rural areas.

The above generalizations about growth and development serve as a sort of directive principles of programme-planning in educational setting. Generality may solve a great number of problems of education and yet 'individuality' may always pose itself as the biggest problem to the educationist and the psychologist alike.

IMPORTANCE OF PROGRESS

Developmental changes are continuous and gradual. The importance of these continuous changes among children has been highlighted by research in the field of child psychology and child education. Because of these developmental changes certain characteristics emerge in the life of an individual, which put a permanent stamp on his whole life.

Besides these, the ultimate success or failure of his life are determined largely by the way he happened to have spent his early infancy and childhood period. It is the real period of learning. During this period, the most significant patterns of thought and behaviour are formed. Therefore, the study of early infancy and childhood in human development is the most significant.

DEVELOPMENT: PHASES

Life begins at the moment of conception, when the ovum (the female reproductive cell) is fertilized by the sperm (the male reproductive cell). Not only before birth, but also after birth for many years the child is a helpless organism until and unless he is helped by the continuous process of growth and development and attains maturity.

When one attains maturity he ceases to be an adolescent and labelled as an adult member of the society. He is supposed to play a responsible role in the society. Before being called as adolescent, he is named as child or infant, etc. All of these names—infant, child, adolescent and adult, etc, are linked with various stages of growth and development through which the child passes from birth to death.

There are certain common developmental or practical characteristics belonging to each stage. The human organism shows peculiar quantitative and qualitative changes in his body and behaviour with the help of which we can say at what particular age an individual belongs to which definite stage of his life.

The life span of an individual can be divided into the following stages.

Name of the Stage	Period and Approximate Age
1. Prenatal (pre-birth) stage	From conception to birth.
2. Stage of infancy	From birth to five years.
3. Childhood stage	From 6th to 12 years or in strict sense up to the onset of puberty.
4. Adolescent	From the onset of puberty to the age of maturity (generally from 13 to 19 years).
5. Adulthood.	From 20 years and beyond or from the age of attaining maturity till death.

Psychologists studying child behaviour tend to discern distinctive phases in the development of the child, and they conceptualize the whole development process as consisting of certain identifiable stages. Though logical objections against stage concepts are strong, the concepts may be useful for practical purposes.

There is no single scheme of stages of development. Depending upon the aspects of behaviour studies, and the investigators frame of reference, there are different schemes of developmental stages. It is not possible to discuss here all the schemes of development stages.

Dr. Earnest Jones has divided human development into four phases.

1. Infancy   (1 to 5 years)
2. Late childhood   (6 to 12 years)
3. Adolescence   (12 to 18 years)
4. Maturity   (18 years onward)

James Ross deviated a bit from the above divisions. Instead of four, he says, the stages of development are five in number.

1. Infancy   (Birth to 3 years)
2. Early childhood (3 to 6 years)
3. Later childhood (6 to 12 years)
4. Adolescence   (12 to 18 years)
5. Adulthood   (18 years onward)

Dr. Earnest Jones tells us that we grow up twice achieving a pseudo-maturity before puberty. At this age. "nature seems to undo most of her pioneer work and begin again the process of building up and consolidating." In his opinion adolescence and adulthood are recapitulations of infancy and late childhood respectively. Before adolescence, each year of growth brings rapid changes and each year itself is a separate stage of development. Reckoning the span of each developmental stage is more a matter of convenience than a rule.

FACTORS AFFECTING PROGRESS

Since we all have similar beginnings, it is interesting to ask what makes us all so different as we grow older. One answer is that, except in the case of identical twins, we have different heredity. Another answer is that we have different environments. There is further more a constant interplay between heredity and environmental influences and our physical and mental characteristics are the complex results of both factors.

STARTING OF LIFE

Each of us begin life at the moment of conception. Conception is the moment when the ovum (the female reproductive cell) is fertilized by spermatozoan (the male reproductive cell). Thus a single cell smaller than the head of a pin, later multiplies and become many cells.

This cell results from the fertilization of a female's ovum by a male's sperm. Heredity is determined by complex organizations of chemical materials within the nucleus of the fertilized cell. These chemical materials are contained in nuclear structures which are known as chromosomes or coloured bodies.

Microscopic studies have shown that there are forty six chromosomes in every body cell. Within each sex cell whether male or female, there are 23 pairs of chromosomes before the maturational process takes place. Within each chromosome there are strings of microscopically small particles, the genes. The genes are the physical substances passed on from parent to offspring. Those are the carriers of hereditary traits. The moment of conception is regarded as one of the most important moments in the life of an individual for the following reasons.

(i) The first important reason is that at the moment of conception, when the ovum is fertilized by the sperm, is the determination of the newly born child's hereditary endowment.

(ii) Whether the child will be male or female is determined once and for all at the moment of conception only. Nothing after this moment can change the sex of the child.

(iii) The third important condition determined at the time of conception is whether the child will be single or multiple. Thus number of offsprings is also determined at this moment.

(iv) The fourth condition determined at this moment is the ordinal position in the family; whether the child will be first born, second born in the family has a lifelong influence on the behaviour pattern of the child and his personality development.

ROLE OF HEREDITY

Since the combination of genes an individual receives from his two parents is a matter of chance, only in rare situations will two children get identical combinations and hence identical heredity. This is only possible in case of identical twins (or identical triplets, identical quadruplets, and so on).

Identical twins develop from the same, zygote. If a zygote divides into two cells, each separately goes to form a new individual...... Since each cell has the same genes as the zygote, the heredity of the two individuals will be identical. These are known as identical twins; they are always of the same sex and are identical in many other respects.

Not all twins, however are identical. Host twins are fraternal twins; they develop from two separate eggs of the mother and hence begin as two zygotes formed independent by the union of two different sperms with two different ova. Fraternal twins are no more alike genetically than ordinary brothers and sisters (siblings) born at different times. Fraternal twins may or may not be of the same sex.

From the foregoing, we come to know that we have different heredity. Therefore, we differ from each other.

The Atmosphere

Like heredity, environment also plays an important role in growth and development of an individual. It is everything, other than heredity, that influences an individual's growth and development. It starts from the period of gestation in the mother's womb. Of course, it must be pointed out at this juncture that it is a mere superstition that everything the mother does affects the unborn foetus. Some ladies spend the months of pregnancy visiting art galleries in the belief that they are improving the child's mind. While malnutrition of the mother or disease or any such factor can affect the uterine environment of the foetus, external factors like visit to beautiful places or listening to music cannot have any direct effect.

The environment influences an individual all through his life from "womb to tomb". Environment refers not only to the physical surroundings but even to the thoughts and attitudes of others which exert an influence on the individual. It is very difficult to study the environment because it is also unique to each individual. Let us take the case of two brothers playing in a room.

Though the physical environment is the same for both, the psychological environment is not the same. One boy is older and is playing with a younger brother while the latter is playing with an older brother. Their past experiences too cannot be identical and therefore their reactions to the situation are also different. Hence psychologists are faced with many problems when studying the effect of the environment because it is impossible to keep it constant and introduce a few variables.

Heredity and environment influence human development. For example, differences in eye colour are hereditary, differences in social attitudes are largely environmental, and differences in intelligence have both hereditary and environmental origins except in the case of identical twins, where they are purely environmental.

Hereditary and environment in interaction with one another, produce the wide range of individual differences observed among people. Heredity gives a predisposition for high intelligence of activity level, but the extent to which the potential becomes a reality is determined by the interaction of genetic endorsement.

NOURISHMENT BY NATURE

Nature and nurture are jointly responsible for the development of personality characteristics, abilities and skills of an individual. In this connection we shouldn't treat nature and nurture separately in determining their contribution to particular type of behaviour. Therefore the issue in Nature versus. Nurture should not be raised. Nurture, or the environment, seems to determine whether the potentialities will be realised. For instance, a person has the genetic potentiality to be educated, but his potentiality may fail to be expressed because of poverty or illness which comprise the environment. The potentiality always acts through the environment and the result of the joint of nature and nurture is the behaviour of the persons as seen by others. The greater the potentiality and the more favourable the environment, greater will be the result of the joint action. Thus an individual is the product of an interaction between nature and nurture.

GENETICS AND ATMOSPHERE

There is always a controversy between the psychologists, biologists and educationists whether heredity or environment is a more important factor for growth and development of an individual. This controversial issue is very significant for the teachers.

If we say that heredity is responsible for the growth and development of an individual, then the teacher has nothing to do. He has simply to watch how the innate potentiality of the child gets unfolded. If, on the other hand, we consider environment to be responsible, for the growth and development of the child, then the role of teacher becomes very important. When he becomes the sole moulder of the students according to his own ideals, he can shape or pattern the life of the students in the way he likes. Thus, he occupies a pivotal place in the process of growth and development.

Role of heredity and environment in the process of growth and development from the external point of view is not at all desirable. Those who support heredity to be the only factor responsible for growth and development argue that nothing can be done to improve the individual beyond the limits laid down by heredity. On the other hand, those who support the role of environment to be the most important factor are guilty of exaggerated optimism that there are no limits to the growth and development of an individual.

But it is not possible to have a watertight compartment between the two factors of heredity and development to work for the growth and development of the child. It is not possible to point out the traits which are exclusive hereditary or environmental. Besides this, most of the modern psychologists are of the opinion that because of the interaction between the energies inherited by an organism and development of an individual, it is impossible to estimate the amount of contribution made by heredity and environment for the growth and development of an individual.

Nor is it possible to have watertight compartments between the two factors. From the moment the child is conceived in its mother's womb, the two factors work hand in hand and continue to play their roles throughout his life. A study of both the points of view brings us to the conclusion that heredity or environment alone cannot be the sole determinants of the status of an individual. The combination of the two factors in obvious and implicit ways makes the individual what he is.

A child is purely a product of heredity at the time of conception. He receives this heredity from his father and mother, who are having different traits, qualities and characteristics. Each of them contributes to the heredity of the child through genes.

A child becomes a distinct individual with distinct characteristics of his own because of the interaction of genes. Hence the teacher cannot change the influence of heredity on the child. A child who has inherited poor intelligence cannot replace it with superior intelligence by the help of a teacher. A teacher can only help in the development of his intelligence within the given limits.

The influence of heredity of the child begins from the very beginning of life. Soon after conception, the organism comes in contact with the environment. The effect of this contact becomes apparent only after the birth of a child.

Cultivation as a Discipline ■ 123

It becomes very easy to understand the influence of environmental factors because of the marks left by the forces operating in the environment in which the children live. Being influenced by environment they learn different attitudes, values, etc. Malnutrition for a long period and poor hygienic conditions develop certain functional deformities and diseases which leave a permanent mark in the life of an individual.

The teacher plays an important role in moulding the environment of the child. In order to become a successful teacher, he needs to understand the concepts and role of heredity and environment in the life of a child.

GROWTH AND DEVELOPMENT: DIFFERENT FACTORS

Maturation is considered as the chief competitor of learning as a modifier of behaviour. Maturation is regarded as those stages of growth and development which takes place from within the subject without the help of any special training, practice, experience or stimulation.

For example, at a particular stage, a child starts crawling or sitting or standing or walking. At a particular stage of its development, a tadpole starts swimming and a bird starts flying. All these changes in behaviour are the result of maturation. But the ability to talk by a parrot, the ability to drive a motor cycle or to swim in a river, etc, are the products of learning.

Learning sometimes depends upon maturation. A child can learn a thing better, only when he reaches a particular maturational level. For example, during the age from 1 to 5 a child can learn the language better, a stimulus response function. All our sense organs are bombarded by the stimuli of the environment and we respond to them.

The sense organs help us to understand and to interpret the environment, to discriminate between good and bad stimulus, to decide to welcome which stimulus and to avoid which one. All these are stages or processes of learning activity.

Different senses contribute differently to the learning process. This is illustrated by an interesting experiment by C.H. Hongik. A number of white races were divided into 5 groups to learn a maze. Some learnt it with all senses intact. Others learnt after being blinded by operation, some others after being blinded and deafened.

Another group after being blinded and rendered anosmic (made intensive to adore). The last group was deprived of all these senses.

ROLE OF LEARNING

Learning to an extent is also a function of maturation. One cannot teach a new born baby to walk or to pick up tiny objects with his four fingers, however much one may try Before anything is learnt by a person, his sensory-motor and also the nervous system including brain must reach a certain level of maturity.

The predetermined sequential stages of maturity of the sensory-motor and nervous system of an individual comprise the "critical time" for that learning. Similarly there is critical time for other important tasks like toilet training, reading, learning socially approved behaviour, etc. If a child is taught a behaviour before the critical time *i.e.* before he attains the maturational level for the task, he fails to do so. If he is taught that task after the critical time, he also fails to master it effectively as is proved from the language problems of the wolf-children.

IMPACT OF EDUCATION ON GROWTH

To be successful in the teaching-crafts, a teacher, therefore, must have a thorough knowledge of the process of child development. A mere bookish knowledge of child life, however, will not be of much help to a school teacher. Descriptions and researches contained in the literature on child development are, of course, very enlightening for a teacher. But unless supplemented by concrete observations of and experimentation with children, a mere bookish reading will be of little value in actual school or home situations.

A sound knowledge of various characteristic features of child development through infancy, childhood and adolescence is indispensable for the teacher owing mainly to the following reasons.

1. It gives him the most authentic knowledge regarding the human staff that he deals with the children.
   It enables him to understand the root causes of their good and bad behaviour.

2. It helps him to match his teaching techniques and standards with the developmental level that a child has actually attained. He is thus enabled to avoid being too difficult, too easy or too common place in the classroom.
3. By enabling him to understand his own infancy and childhood periods it facilitates him to understand his own self This self-understanding proves immensely helpful for him in becoming a better teacher and a better person.

CHAPTER SIX

Significance of Individual

Through the centuries, personality has been regarded as a practical force in determining success or failure in life. If the person has some socially undesirable traits, he inherited them from his parents, if he is stingy and sullen, he can't become generous and cheerful any more than he can change his eye colour, his stature, or the size of his ears. The implication is that neither training nor desire to improve will be of any avail. The person is a prisoner of his genes, the acceptance of this belief discourages any motivation to try to improve the personality. The person with red hair has a fiery temper or the person with a high forehead is a 'brain'.

The implication is that, since the physical traits are inherited and thus not subject to change, the personality traits that accompany them are similarly implacable to change. A third widely held belief is that personality changes automatically accompany body changes. Since body changes are a part of the developmental sequence over which the individual has no control, it is assumed that the accompanying personality changes are likewise uncontrollable.

According to tradition, radical physical changes are accompanied by equally radical personality changes at two times during the life span; first, at puberty, when the child's body is transformed into that of an adult, and second at old age when pronounced physical changes throughout the body parallel the loss of the reproductive capacity. Good personality traits are balanced by undesirable ones, thus producing the 'average' person. The harm in accepting this traditional belief is obvious. If a person believes that nature will provide him with desirable traits to compensate for the undesirable, he will have little motivation to take the initiative in personality improvement. The traditional belief that physical and personality characteristics go hand in hand is so widely held that physical characteristics are commonly used to judge personality.

SOME SYMBOLS

Some of the symbols most commonly used to judge personality are analysed. These include such important symbols of self as clothing, speech, names, use of leisure time, and reputation. Many traditional beliefs imply that the kind of personality a person develops as well as the outstanding traits in his personality pattern are determined by his genetic make up by what his parents were before him. Acceptance of this premise weakens any motivation the person might otherwise have to improve his personality.

It also weakens the motivation of parents and teachers to try to guide and direct the development of personality in children during the early formative years of their lives. As early as the days of Hypocrites in ancient Greece, it was observed that some personality changes were man made, that they resulted from changes in the environment and in the person's general health condition at times other than puberty and middle or old age.

DEFINITION OF PERSONALITY

When psychologists define "Personality", they tend to refer to qualities within a person, characteristics of a person's behaviour, or both. In a now famous definition, psychologist Gordon Allport (1937) mentioned both inner and external qualities of behaviour, but he emphasized the inner qualities; "personality is the dynamic organization within the individual of those psychological systems that determine his unique adjustments to his environment".

In a more recent definition, psychologist Walter Mischel (1976) "mentioned both inner process and behaviour but emphasized behaviour. Personality, he wrote, consists of the distinctive patterns of behaviour including thoughts and emotions that characterize each individual adaptation to the situations of his or her life". No single definition of personality is acceptable to all psychologists. However, most agree that personality includes the behaviour patterns a person shows across situations or the psychological characteristics of the person that lead to that behaviour pattern.

Theories

Personality has been studied in a number of different ways. Some have developed broad theories to explain the origin and make-up of personality. Others have focused only on one or two issues, such as the influence of heredity on personality.

The first approach theory construction, was popular for many years. As a result, we have many broad personality theories with focus on them. Most of these broad theories can be grouped into four categories:

> Type and trait theories of personality both focus on people's personal characteristics. However, various *Type* theorists and *Trait* theorists differ in the ways they use those characteristics to describe people. We will begin to examine these differences by returning briefly to George and Crystal and considering what "types" of people they are.

Of the first type theories that we know of was proposed about 400 B.C. by Hippocratism, a Greek physician now known as the Father of Medicine. He grouped people into four temperament types: sanguine (cheerful, vigorous, confidently optimistic); melancholic (depressed, morose); choleric (hot tempered) and phlegmatic (slow moving, calm, unexcitable).

What are these types that we put together to form typologies? A type is simply a class of individuals said to share a common collection of characteristics. For example, "introverts" could be described as people who share characteristics such as shyness, social withdrawal, and a tendency not to talk much; while extroverts share a tendency to be out going, friendly and talkative. Usually, sharp typologies do not work well scientifically.

Eysenk's Hierarchical Theory

Eysenk (1967) identified the major component of personality as a small number of personality types. Each type is made up of a set of personality characteristics. For example, people who fit Eysenk's extroverted type are said to have such characteristics as sociability, liveliness, and excitability. Each one of these characteristics, according to Eysenk, can be broken down into certain habitual-response patterns that apply to several situations; each of these habitual-response patterns can be broken down further into specific responses within specific situations. This progression from broad, global type down to specific situations-bound responses is what makes Eysenk's approach a hierarchical theory.

Allport's Theory

G. Allport counted about 18,000 trait like terms in English language-terms that designated "distinctive and personal form of behaviour"

These terms, mostly adjectives, describe how people act, think, perceive and feel. Allport (1961) believed that this rich collection of trait like terms provided a way of capturing the uniqueness of each individual. He believed that this uniqueness could be described well in terms of the individual's traits or "personal disposition", at three levels of generality.

Cardinal traits — were defined as those which are so dominant that nearly all of the individual's actions can be traced back to them.

Central traits — were described as characterizing an individual's behaviour to some extent but not in such a complete way as cardinal traits.

Secondary traits — These traits are such as "likes chocolate" or "prefers foreign cars" — traits that are influential but within a narrow range of situations. Allport also used ideographic approach.

Single Trait Research

Some try to focus carefully on one single trait. For example, many have studied "locus of control" — the degree to which we believe that we cause or control, events in our lives. If we believe that we are the cause of most events, we have a highly internal locus of control.

PERSONALITY FACTORS

Freud's question reveals a tendency for which dynamic theorists are often criticized: a tendency to over interpret — that is to attribute deeper meaning behaviour than the behaviour really warrants. A related criticism is that dynamic theorists often make claims about personality process without testing them scientifically.

Both criticisms are often applied to Freud's theory, which remain in some respects one of the least substantiated of the major personality theories. However, Freud's is also the most influential and the most comprehensive theory of personality. It has had a major impact on psychology, sociology, anthropology and literature — indeed, on western thought in general. Currently its influence and popularity have faded somewhat among some psychologists, partly because there is so little hard, scientific evidence to support the theory. Dynamic approaches involve a research for the process by which needs, motives, and impulses are studied.

Freud's Psychoanalytic Theory

Freud's approach with a look at the raw material he used to shape his theory: the thoughts and recollection of his patients. As "Frau Emmy's" recollection spilled out, Freud's mind was churning, piecing together a complex psychological puzzle.

Freud's psychoanalysis became both theory of personality and a method of psychotherapy. Psychoanalytic theory has three major parts:

1. A theory of the structure of personality, in which the Id, Ego, and Super-ego are the principal parts;
2. A theory of personality dynamics, in which there is a conscious role; and
3. A theory of psychosexual development, in which different motives and body regions influence the child at different stages of growth, with effects persisting in the form of adult personality traits.

Personality Structure

(Id, Ego, and Superego):

(i) *Id:* The Id, the most primitive part, can be thought of as a sort of store house of biologically based urges: the urge to eat, drink, eliminate, and especially, to be sexually stimulated. The sexual energy that underlies, these urges are called the Libido. The Id operates according to what Freud called the pleasure principle.

(ii) *Ego:* It has big importance in this theory.

(iii) *Super-ego:* It controls our anger.

Jung's Analytical Psychology

C.G. Jung (pronounced "Yoong") was at one time, considered by Freud to be his heir apparent. Analytical psychology (Jung, 1928), differed from psychoanalysis in some very significant ways, and Freud's affection for Jung faded. One of the main differences between the theorists was that Jung thought childhood psychosexual development to be not nearly so important to adult adjustment as Freud did. Jung placed much less emphasis than Freud on aggressive impulses arising from past conflicts and much more emphasis on people's future oriented goals, hopes and plans.

Jung believed to be a part of unconscious mind that went beyond the personal experiences of the individual. The collective unconscious mind he said, grows out of the past experiences of the human race. In addition to the collective unconscious, Jung credited each individual's conscious experience that had been repressed.

A major contribution of the dynamic approach has been the concepts of defence mechanisms, which are used to cope with anxiety. Among these defence mechanisms are:

1. *Repression:* In Freud's theory, people use to allay anxiety caused by conflicts.
2. *Reaction Formation by Conflicts:* People attempt to cope with conflict.
3. *Projection:* Blaming others, or projection
4. *Rationalization:* An acceptable conscious motive for an unacceptable unconscious one.
5. *Intellectualization:* Related to rationalization is intellectualization.
6. *Displacement:* The person substitutes a different goal object for the original one.
7. *Regression:* Retreated to an earlier pattern of adaptation, possibly a childish or primitive one.
8. *Sublimation:* The highest level of egodefence.

CONCEPT OF LEARNING

Learning and conditioning in classical, instrumental and cognitive forms—are highly relevant to personality and its development. Dollard and Miller used animal experiments to develop and test selected Freudian notions for example, conflict and repression. Thus, advancing early social learning theory, Bandura and Walters extended social learning theory into the domain and observational learning. Skinner's radical behaviourism used instrumental conditioning principles to explain the way in which environmental conditions influence people's behaviour.

Learning and behavioural theorists have been accused of diminishing the person in personality, but many value their approaches for their clarity and their experimental 'test-ability'.

HUMANISTIC CONCEPT

Humanistic theories emphasize the importance of people's subjective attitudes, feelings, and beliefs, especially with regard to the self. Carl Rogers theory focuses on the impact of disparity between a person's ideal self and perceived real self. Maslow focuses on the significance of self-actualizations. Theories of this type are often criticized for their heavy reliance on subjective self-report data.

The person-situation controversy revolves around a key question. Are people's behaviour determined primarily by such "personal" factors as traits or primarily by the situations people find themselves in? Recent research suggests an answer: "It depends". Some people are strongly influenced by some traits that do not greatly influence other people. Moreover, some situations are "powerful" involving less structures and thus "weak" they permit personality traits to have a stronger influence on people's behaviour.

EVOLUTION OF PERSONALITY

Watson opines that personality is everything that we do.

Guthrie has defined personality as "those habits and habit systems of social importance that are stable and resistant to change". But this definition is incomplete as it does not tell us about those habits which are not socially important. Habit of "posing" is not of social importance, but is certainly a clue for personality. Guthrie's phrase "of social importance" is presumably equivalent to "which determine the impression we make on others." Another 'objection' is that a person does not behave in the same manner twice towards the same stimulus.

Kempt has defined personality as "the habitual mode of adjustment which the organism effects between its own egocentric drives and the exigencies of the environment."

May and Harishorn stressed social aspect, according to them "personality is that which makes one effective and gives influence over others."

Garden Allport states "personality is the dynamic organization within the individual of those psychophysical systems that determine his unique adjustment to his environment". It recognizes the changing nature of personality, "a dynamic organization". It focuses on the inner aspect rather than on superficial manifestations, but it establishes the basis for social stimulus value of personality (unique adjustment to the environment).

Symonds has defined personality as "the portrait on landscape of the organism working together in all its phases".

Linton, "Personality is the organized aggregate of psychological processes and states pertaining to the individual".

Psychologists of Gestalt School define personality "as a pattern or configuration produced by the integrated functioning of an individual".

Cruze defines personality as "an organized and integrated unity consisting of many elements that work together as a functioning whole."

Kimble Young "Personality refers to the more or less organized body of ideas, attitudes, traits, values and habits which an individual has built into roles and status for dealing with others and with himself."

Woodworth and Marquis define personality as "the total quality of an individual's behaviour as it is revealed in his characteristic habits of thought and expression, his attitudes, interests, his manners of acting, and his own philosophy of life.

G.W. Hartman: "Personality is integrated organization of all the pervasive characteristics of an individual as it manifests itself in focal distinctiveness to other."

Fredenburgh: "Personality is a stable system of complex characteristics by which the life pattern of the individual may be identified."

J.P Guilford: "An individual's personality, then is his unique pattern of traits....... A trait is any distinguishable, relatively enduring way in which one individual differs from another."

A man's real personality includes what he wishes to be, how he wishes to appear, how he appears to others, and how he appears to himself. It involves his evaluation of his environment of other people, and himself. "Personality, indeed, is truly an abstraction, inferred from behaviour, rather than anything tangible and measurable".

Worren: "Personality is the entire mental organization of a human being at any stage of his development".

METHODS OF EVALUATION

There is no single set of concepts that all clinical psychologists subscribe to. The kinds of information and the kinds of test particular clinical psychologist use to understand personality depend upon his theoretical orientation. In any case, the problem is enormously complicated and the discipline devoted to understanding individuals and making predictions about their behaviour in future situations is only beginning to achieve scientific status.

The methods that clinical psychologists use will be described briefly under the following headings: the interview, the questionnaire, projective techniques, observational methods, and behavioural techniques. The methods will be described generally with only a brief illustration of specific instruments.

Interview

The techniques of interviewing can be broken down into three broad methods. The first of these is: (1) free interviewing, (2) directed interview, (3) structural interview.

Free Interview

In this technique, the interviewer says as little as possible, simply asking open or leading questions, such as, "could you tell me something about your family"? or "Could you tell me why you have come to the clinic?" This technique usually is less threatening or disturbing to the patient than direct and specific questions and allows the interviewer to see readily what is important to the patient. If the method is used exclusively, however, it may be a long time before certain kinds of important information are brought up directly by the patient.

Direct Interview

In the second type, the interviewer knows that he wished to cover certain kinds of information and will ask many more direct questions. It may also make a patient feel that his role is only to answer the questions asked and consequently, to neglect talking about some painful subject that he feels is important but the interview neglects to touch on in his more direct question.

Structured Interview

Here the interviewer sets up a standard condition for all interviewers. He is required to ask the same questions generally in the same orders, and to use a standard procedure for follow-up questions. Generally a psychologist uses a structured interview when he desires to obtain a rating or a numerical score for assessing some specific characteristic.

Of course, all three techniques can be combined in a single interview with a patient. The interviewer beginning more or less with the free technique rounds up his information with more direct questions and possibly includes a brief structured interview to measure some particular variable at the end of his clinical interview.

Questionnaire

The questionnaire played a prominent role in the early attempts to measure personality in the United States. Generally, a subject is confronted with a series of statements and asked to indicate whether the statements are true or false about himself, or whether he cannot decide or does not know.

In other types of questionnaire the subject has to state which of two alternatives is more true of him. This is called the forced-choice method, and the choice are generally arranged so that the statements are equally positive or negative.

Projective Techniques

There are many different kinds of projective tests, most of them have all or some of the characteristics listed below:

The Method is Indirect

Compared with the questionnaires, it is more and more difficult for a subject who wished consciously to distort to know what represents a "good" versus a "bad" answer or a right versus a wrong answer. The all projective techniques are completely true than other questionnaires.

Freedom of Response

Freedom of response is the second important characteristic of some of the projective methods.

Word Association Test (W.A.T.)

The most common projective test still used in several clinics is the word-association test. Subjects are given a stimulus word and asked to tell as quickly as possible the first word that comes to mind as an association. Jung an early colleague of Freud, added the idea that the association process could reveal unconscious, repressed ideas to serve as a method of discovering "unconscious complex".

The Rorchach Test (R.B.T.)

The Rorchach Test is one of the most widely used and known projective techniques. In this test, the subject is presented with a series of ink-blots and is asked to tell what they suggest to him. There are no correct or incorrect responses, but what the subject sees in the ink blots presumably reflects his own personality.

Thematic Apperception Test (T.A.T.)

It being important to measure the needs that are significant variables in the theory of personality, Murray and his co-workers developed a series of tests of the projective type. Murray assumed that the subject was not usually aware of his own needs and that some instrument to reveal his unconscious thought would provide a better understanding than tests that depended on self-report. He felt that fantasy provided such a means of obtaining unconscious motives and devised a series of techniques in which the patient told his fantasies when he was listening to music, or completing incomplete stories, or when telling stories about pictures. The latter instrument, in which the subject was asked to tell a story about a picture, became the most widely used of the techniques.

Sentence Completion Method

In the sentence completion method, the subject is asked to complete a sentence, the first word or words of which are given by an examiner. In some way this method is related to the word association techniques, the major differences being in the length of the stimulus. Some applications of the method, however, demand only a single or brief response. Many types are used and incomplete sentences tests have been devised to measure a variety of variables.

SITUATIONAL CONTACT

Person-situation interaction controversy revolves around a key question. Is the behaviour of a person determined only by personal factor or situation in which they are placed? The latest research says that it depends. Some are influenced by some traits that influence people. In some cases the situations are powerful.

IMPORTANCE OF IDENTITY

Identification

It has been pointed out that identification, the second important molding technique, is often called 'learning by imitation'. More correctly defined, identification is the process by which a person takes over the values of another by imitation. It is the 'tendency to view oneself as one with another person and to act accordingly'. Imitation is more limited than identification. In identification, the individual tries to duplicate in his own life the ideas, attitudes, and behaviour of the person he is imitating.

Identification may accompany child training in which the person learns through guidance and control. When a child identifies with an adult he learns to do what the adult does as well as what the adult tells him to do. Learning by identification in absence of child training however, occurs when a person identifies with popular hero or someone who has no control over him and no responsibility for training him. Child training accompanied by identification is far more effective in personality development than training or identification alone. This is especially true in the case of young children.

Sex Appropriate Patterns

From what has been said above, it is apparent that identification often plays a more important role in moulding the personality pattern than child training. Identification is more important, for example, in learning appropriate sex roles; the young person can learn more from imitating a good model than from direct teaching. By identifying with an adult outside the home who conforms to the socially approved pattern of sex appropriateness, the young person learns the sex-appropriate pattern that is so essential to good social adjustments.

As was stressed earlier, however, a combination of child training and identification is better than either alone because learning by one method is reinforced by the other. Equally important, identification provides motivation to learn, which is often lacking or weak when child training is used alone.

In conclusion, the following observations show how important a role identification plays in moulding the personality pattern.

- If a child lives with criticism, he learns to condemn.
- If he lives with hostility, he learns to fight.
- If he lives with fear, he learns to be apprehensive.
- If he lives with pity, he learns to feel sorry for himself.
- If he lives with jealousy, he learns to feel guilty.
- If he lives with encouragement, he learns to be confident.
- If he lives with tolerance, he learns to be patient.

- If he lives with praise, he learns to be appreciative.
- If he lives with acceptance, he learns to love.
- If he lives with approval, he learns to like himself.
- If he lives with recognition, he learns to have a goal.
- If he lives with fairness, he learns to value justice.
- If he lives with honesty, he learns the virtue of truth.
- If he lives with security, he learns to have faith in himself and others.
- If he lives with friendliness, he learns that the world is a good place in which to live.

CHAPTER SEVEN

Perception of Learning

TRADITIONAL CONDITIONING

Very early some classical experiments were conducted in 1890s by I.P. Pavlov, and the name classical conditioning was given to those situations of experiments. Pavlov was a Russian Physiologist. He established principles of this basic form of conditioning. Another name given to this conditioning is Pavlovian Conditioning. Some have also called this as 'Respondent Conditioning'.

The term "stimulus" comes from the Latin word for "good" or "prod", and thus in psychology, the term is sometimes used to refer to events which evoke, or call forth, a response the individual is "goaded into action." A more general meaning of the term stimulus is anything in the environment that can be detected by the senses.

One of the stimuli in classical conditioning is called the conditioned stimulus (CS.) The other stimulus is known as the unconditioned stimulus (US).

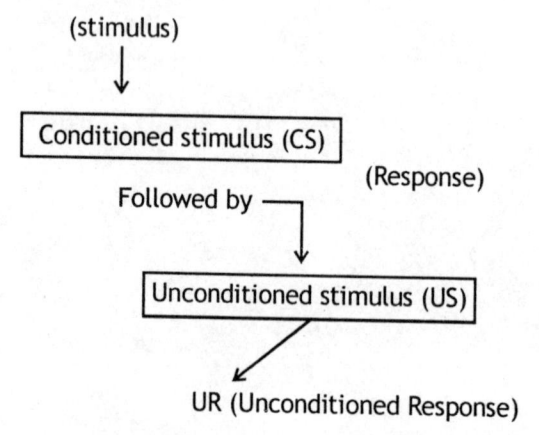

(stimulus)
↓
┌─────────────────────────────┐
│ Conditioned stimulus (CS)   │
└─────────────────────────────┘
     Followed by ──┐   (Response)
                   ↓
        ┌─────────────────────────────┐
        │ Unconditioned stimulus (US) │
        └─────────────────────────────┘
              ↙
        UR (Unconditioned Response)

In classical conditioning, a neutral stimulus (CS) regularly precedes an unconditioned stimulus (US) that evokes an unconditioned response (UR).

As a result of this pairing, the previously neutral conditioned stimulus now begins to evoke a response. This is what is learned in classical conditioning. The response evoked by the conditioned stimulus after learning is known as the conditioned response (CR).

Current Theories

Current theories of classical conditioning process take the viewpoint that the conditioned stimulus becomes a signal for unconditioned stimulus.

Thus, when the conditioned stimulus is presented, the unconditioned stimulus is expected and the learner responds in accordance with this expectation.

Extinction Theory

Extinction in classical conditioning is the process of presenting the conditioned stimulus alone without the unconditioned stimulus for a number of trials.

Stimulus Generalization Theory

Stimulus generalization is the tendency to give conditioned responses to stimuli that are similar in some way to the conditioned stimulus but have never been paired with the unconditioned stimulus.

The greater the similarity of these stimuli to the original conditioned stimulus, the greater the amount of generalization.

LEARNING OF INSTRUMENTS

In instrumental conditioning, also known as "Operant conditioning", an action of the learner is instrumental in bringing about a change in the environment that makes the action more or less likely to occur in future.

An environmental event that is the consequence of an instrumental response that makes the response more likely to occur is known as a reinforcer.

Positive Reinforcenment

A positive reinforcer is a stimulus or event which, when it is contingent on a response, increases the likelihood at the response will be made again.

Negative Reinforcement

A negative reinforcer is a stimulus or event which, when its cessation or termination is contingent on a response, increases the likelihood that the response will occur again.

Primary Reinforcement

Primary reinforcers in instrumental conditioning are reinforcers that are effective without any previous beneficial training; they work "naturally" to increase the likelihood of a response when they are made contingent on it. On the other hand, the ability conditioned, the secondary, reinforcers to influence the likelihood of a response depends upon learning. Stimuli become conditioned reinforcers on being paired with primary reinforcers.

Human Learning

Human Learning goes far beyond animal learning. Man is more skillful when compared to animals and the variety of tasks he learns and perform are quite numerous and complex. The tasks may range from the simple cases like learning to typewrite to the complex cases such as flying a jet plane or operating a computer.

Human Learning comprises of his ability to acquire (motor) skill and more than that the highly developed unique ability to use words meaningful in such activities as speaking, reading, writing etc.

LEARNING OF MOTOR

Motor learning refers to the acquisition of skills involving movement. Such skills of movement are found in activities like typewriting, dancing and playing games like football. Generally the skill means competence and efficiency of an, individual in a given kind of task. Here, our interest will be on motor skills. Such skills involve not only movements, but may also involve utilization of perpetual processes for controlling movements (in such instances, the learning processes involved are called perceptual-motor learning). Motor learning may be influenced both by external stimuli such as visual or auditory stimuli and by internal stimuli such as kinesthetic stimuli.

It has been pointed out that the changes that take place in learning a motor skill. For instance, learning to use typewriter involve many processes such as locating the various keys, moving the fingers to the appropriate keys, the processes of pressing the keys with optimum pressure, using the space bar and other controls properly. When one starts to learn typewriting he makes numerous errors, is slow and clumsy in his performance and also takes quite an amount of time to perform a given bit of typewriting. Though in an irregular manner, with constant and continued learning, we find this state of affairs being replaced by an ability to typerwrite in a smooth manner with fewer or no mistakes and relatively within a shorter span of time.

THE STYLE

The process of learning takes place in a particular pattern or follows a sequence. The rate of learning or the progress of acquisition can be graphically represented plotting performance as a function of time or of trials. These representations are called the learning curves. In a learning curve, usually the performance is plotted on the Y axis and the amount of time taken or the practice period is plotted on the 'X' axis. Such curves are of three kinds namely (1) positively accelerated learning curve (2) negatively accelerated learning curve and (3) the S-shaped learning curve. An example of these learning curves are given below. In a positively accelerated learning curve the initial progress is small and progress at the terminal point is rapid. In a negatively accelerated learning curve, we find that gains are striking at initial stages and minimal at later stages. In a S-shaped learning curve the rate of progress is irregular.

In the S-shaped learning curve, we find a 'flatterned out' stage during which there is no apparent improvement in learning. This is called a 'Plateau'. The plateau is preceded and followed by period of improvement in performance. Positively accelerated learning curve is characteristic of tasks involving memorization of simple materials. Negatively accelerated learning curves occur when the tasks involved are difficult and when the tasks to be learnt is similar to the tasks already learnt and when the subject lacks adequate motivation. In S-Shaped learning curves, the task is of uniform difficulty, where fast and slow learning alternates.

THE DIFFERENCE

Discrimination is developed in instrumental or operant, conditioning when differences in reinforcement accompany different stimuli. For example, a person or animal may learn to respond to a positive stimulus (the S+ or S+) present when responses are being reinforced and not a negative stimulus (S+ or S+) are not being reinforced that is during extinctioning. Stimulus discrimination in instrumental, or operant, conditioning is also referred to as the stimulus control of behaviour.

Avoidance Learning

The learned response is made before the onset of a noxious event and thus prevents the learner from being exposed to the noxious event: the noxious event is therefore avoided. Avoidance learning is explained in terms of the concepts of species-typical defence reactions and safety signals. Extinction of avoidance learning is often quite slow.

COGNITIVE CONCEPTS

Cognitive learning refers to changes in the way informations is processed as a result of experience a person or an animal has had. Cognitive maps, latent learning, insight learning and imitation are described as examples of cognitive learning. Cognitive-learning interpretations of classical and instrumental conditioning are discussed.

Latent Learning

The word "latent" means "hidden" and thus "latent learning" is learning that occurs but is not evident in behaviour until later, when conditions for its appearance are favourable. Latent learning is said to occur without reinforcement of particular responses and seems to involve changes in the way information is proposed.

Insight Learning

In a typical insight situation, a problem is posed, a period follows during which no apparent progress is made and then the solution comes suddenly.

Imitation

Another cognitive learning situation—one that is very important in human learning—occurs when we imitate another individuals, or model our behaviour on that of someone else. We might formally define "imitation" as a response that is like the stimulus triggering the response.

OVAL KNOWLEDGE

It is concerned with acquisition and retention of verbal habits. Ebbinghaus gave the classical ideas in the field. He devised nonsense syllable which were consonant vowel-consonant combination which had no dictionary meaning. He also used these as units of learning in his famous experiments which have enhanced understanding of the processes of verbal learning.

In recent times activity in the field of verbal learning has also shifted to research in languages and in psycholinguistics. This includes the role of natural language habits in the analysis of verbal learning.

The same can be said of the steps involved in learning to move one's body around. The development of walking, in particular, involves a predictable series of milestones. The order of events is quite consistent, but the age at which each milestone will be reached is hard to predict for a given child.

The use of the hands or tools, shows another predictable development sequence. It begins with infants thrusting their hands in the direction of a target object, essentially "taking a swipe" at the object. This is followed by crude grasping involving only the palm of the hand. Then there is a sequence of increasingly well coordinated finger and thumb movements. In the first year of life, the infants can combine thumb and finger action into a pincer motion that allows them to pick up a single chocolate chip from a table top.

GOADING OF KNOWLEDGE

Social motives such as need for achievement, need for power, and human aggression, are learning motives that involve other people. They are measured by projective tests, pencil and paper questionnaires, or by inferences made from actual behaviour in certain situations designed to bring out the expression of these motives.

These might be described as the "push theories of motivation," behaviour is "pushed" towards goals by driving states within the person or animal. Freud (1940-49) for example based his ideas about personality on innate, or inborn, sexual and aggressive urges, or drives. In general, drive theories say the following: When an internal driving state is aroused, the individual is pushed to engage in behaviour which will lead to a goal that reduces the intensity of the driving state. In human beings, at least, reaching the appropriate goal which reduce the drive state is pleasurable and satisfying. Thus, motivation is said to consist of (1) a driving state, (2) the goal directed behaviour initiated by the driving state, (3) the attainment of an appropriate goal, and (4) the reduction of the driving state the subjective satisfaction and relief when the goal is reached. After a time, the driving state build up again to push behaviour towards the appropriate goal. The sequence of events just described is sometimes called the motivational cycle.

Drive theories differ on the source of the driving state which impels people and animals to action. Some theorists, Freud included, conceived of driving state as being inborn or instructive. The important notes on learning are as under:

1. Learning can be defined as any relatively permanent change in behaviour that occurs as a result of practice or experience. This definition has three elements.
   (a) Learning is a change in behaviour, for better or worse.
   (b) It is a change that takes place through experience; due to growth or maturation are not learning. This part of the definition distinguishes learning from innately controlled species-typical behaviour.
   (c) Before it can be called learning, the change must be relatively permanent; it must last a fairly long time. Exactly how long cannot be specified, but we usually think of learned changes in behaviour as lasting for days, months, or years, unlike the temporary behavioural effects of factors such as alertness or fatigue.
2. If we could understand the learning process and apply our general understanding of it to a particular person's life, we could go a long way towards explaining many of the things that a person does. If we could understand some of the principles of learning, we would have a better idea of how to change behaviour when (as in child rearing and psychological therapy) we want to change it.

3. Usage of words which forms the basic for verbal learning is a behaviour that is unique to human beings. Verbal learning involves many steps, the first being that of simply learning to utter a word. Subsequently other words can be learned indicating common characteristics of objects such as 'soft' for example. Finally, the ability to arrange words in a meaningful sequence to form a sentence is the one to occur.
4. As human beings belong to the specific species using words for communication purposes experimentation on human learning is predominantly on verbal learning. Investigations on verbal learning are popular because experimentally verbal materials are easier to work with and verbal learning situations lead to the study of complex human behaviour and thinking. Human thought, in other words, can be explained through the analysis of his verbal behaviour.
5. Enquiries into human learning and memory was pioneered by Herman Ebbinghaus in late 1888. He worked with what he called the nonsense syllables. Nonsense syllables are meaningless verbal material, three lettered consisting of two consonants, one on either sider and having a vowel in the middle-for example TEB, FOZ, BAG etc. These were used by him because they were devoid of meaning and help the study of learning process from its earliest stages.
6. The major kind of verbal learning tasks to be studied are: (*a*) free recall, (*b*) serial and (*c*) paired associate.

Free Recall Learning

In this kind of learning task, the subject is required to memorize a list of verbal material which may consist of words, sentences or nonsense syllables. The subject is asked to study the items and is asked to reproduce. This procedure is adopted for a number of times, probably until the subject is able to reproduce the entire list. The subject has the freedom to reproduce the lists in any order. But, usually the subject follows a particular sequence of reproduction which is referred to as subjective organization.

Subjective organization is important because: (1) it shows that learning is an active process since the subject has to participate; (2) it indicates the limitations on our memories; usually we are able to retain seven items in immediate memory; (3) that organising the material in 'units' or chunks aids remembrance.

Serial Learning

In this method, a list of verbal material is presented in a particular order. The subject will be required to learn the list by going through it in the same order. The list would have taken to have been learnt, through this method only if the list is reproduced by the subject in the same order. Suppose the following list of numbers are given 182, 264, 98, 109, 8, the correct sequence of numbers should be reproduced beginning with 182, and going through 264, 98, 109 and 8.

Paired Associate Learning

In this kind of learning, a particular stimulus is associated with or linked to a particular response. The subject must be able to give out the correct response on being given the stimulus concerned. For example, in a paired-associate task, numbers might be used as stimuli and nonsense syllables may be used as responses thus 182-ZOF, 264-LAF, 98-REK, 109-TUS, 8-PIB.

Subject should learn the appropriate pairs and give the correct responses. For example, they should be able to give the response of TUS when given the stimulus 109 and LAF to 264 etc.

Meaningfulness of Material

In the process of learning, we are able to learn with ease and quickly those materials which are meaningful than those that are meaningless. For example, it is easier to learn a word like BOY than a nonsense syllable like TUX. Generally, when learning materials have the following characteristics they are said to be meaningful. Greater similarity of an item to an English word makes that item more meaningful.

ROLE OF NEUROPHYSIOLOGY

It shall be profitable to note the following which shall enable you to answer the MCQS quickly:

1. The Physiological and mental growth of humans and animals needs systematic studies. Body structure and behaviour help animals and human to adjust in environment and they also help in learning. The studies of instincts have contributed to the Physiology of behaviour.
2. Nervous system is divided into two parts seriously: Central nervous system and a peripheral nervous system.

3. The nervous system both in its structure and function is complex. The nervous system is distinguished as central nervous system and peripheral nervous system. The central nervous system comprises of the brain and the spinal cord which are encased in the skull and the spine. Those that are found outside the case constitute the peripheral nervous system.
4. It may be pointed out that both fibers of sensory and motor neurons form part of the peripheral nervous system. The fibers of the peripheral nervous system have two important divisions namely the autonomic and the somatic system. Autonomic system refers to a division of the nervous system which serves the endocrine glands and the smooth muscles. During emotional states such as anger and fear, it controls the internal changes in the body. Besides, it is activated for purposes or maintaining internal balance of the body. The autonomic system consists of two parts each of which is functionally opposed to one another. The part of the autonomic system known as the sympathetic system swings into action to prepare the body to meet emergencies in such conditions as frightened emotional states. This system mobilises the energies of the body for an emergency and stress. The bodily reactions under such situations such as increased blood pressure, increased heart beat and pulse rate, profuse perspiration and inhibition of salivary responses, etc. are due to the functions of the sympathetic system; on the other hand the para sympathetic system functions to conserve the resources of the body for purposes of health and growth. During periods of rest and relaxation this system slows down heart beat, reduces blood pressure and produces all the other visceral responses.

ROLE OF NERVOUS SYSTEM

The central nervous system consists of two important parts namely the spinal cord and the brain. The spinal cord is situated in the spinal column and the brain is encased in the skull. The functions of the spinal cord are two fold. Firstly, it acts as the conduction part to and from the brain; it serves as a communication centre.

If there is a "governing" organ of the body, then certainly it is the central nervous system. Ultimately, it is this complex structure which controls our overt behaviour, regulates the internal working of our bodies, and serves as the basis for all our mental processes. As we have noted, the central nervous system consists of two major parts, the spinal cord and the brain.

IMPORTANCE OF SPINAL CORD

Basically, the spinal cord may be viewed as having two major functions. First, it carries sensory information from receptors throughout the body to the brain, and conducts information from the brain to effectors (muscles and glands). Thus, in this respect, it may be viewed as a major channel in our internal communication system. Secondly, it plays an important role in various "reflexes". As you are already aware there are seemingly autonomic actions which are evoked in a very rapid manner by a particular stimuli. Some common examples involve withdrawing a hand from hot objects and the familiar knee-jerk reaction tested by your family doctor during a routine check-up. Such reflexes involve neutral circuits in which information from various receptors is carried to the spinal cord, where it stimulates other neurons. These then transmit information to muscle cells thus producing the reflex actions. Although this may sound relatively simple, we should note that the mechanisms involved in even basic reflexes are quite complex. Actually, thousands of Neorons play a role and input from the portion of brain is also involved.

BRAIN FORMATION

The structure of the brain consists of three parts: Forebrain, Midbrain, and Hindbrain.

Forebrain

The forebrain is by far the largest of the three divisions of the brain. That part of it which lies immediately over the midbrain is known as the "diencephalon". In several ways, it is one of the most intriguing sites we shall consider, for it is here that many of our appetites and motives appear to be controlled. The two most important structures in the diencephalon are the "thalamus" and "hypothalamus." The hypothalmus, which lies immediately above the midbrain, is a relatively small structure. However, it exerts many important effects. For example, it seems to play a major role in the regulation of the autonomic nervous system, in the integration of reflexes, and in the regulation of important glands with the body,

Midbrain

The countrylike divisions within the continent of the midbrain are the *Thalamus and hypothalamus* (blue area). Within them, are state-sized regions, and within those regions are the specific places, or collections of even smaller organized structures. Specific *thalamic fields* and nuclei serve as relay stations for almost all of the information coming into and out of the forebrain.

Specific *hypothalamic fields* and *nuclei* serve as relay stations for the internal regulatory systems, monitoring information coming in from the autonomic nervous system and commanding the body through those nerves and the pituitary.

Hindbrain

The major countries of the hindbrain are the pons (bridge), the *medulla oblongata*, the *brainstem*, and the *cerebellum* (the small cerebrum) purples area). The structures within the pons, medulla, brainstem, and cerebellum generally interact with forebrain structures by relays through the midbrain, with some exceptions. The pons and the brainstem are the major routes by which the forebrain sends and receives signals to and from the spinal cord and the peripheral nervous system. The *field* and *nuclei* of the pons and brainstem, which control respiration and heart rhythms, are critical to survival. The attachment of the cerebellum to the roof of the hindbrain has been interpreted to mean that it receives and modifies information related to body and limb position before that information makes its way to the thalamus and cortex. The cerebellum stores the basic repertoire of learned motor responses which the motor cortex may request.

Alliances

Individual people living in different places around the world often join together to achieve a specific objective—doctors, space scientists, or people against nuclear weapons, for example. Certain individual brain cells, or neurons, also link up to achieve collective purposes. These purposes are given functional names, such as the "sensory system" or the "motor system." These names signify the places that are active when the brain performs these functions.

We also find in the brain's organization an analogy to the political alliances formed when a number of countries, representing many individuals work together for a common purpose. One such major alliance of brain structures is the limbic system, so named because it is linked around the inside edges of the cortex (*limbus*, in Latin, means "border") This group of structures helps in regulating emotional state.

FUNCTIONS OF BRAIN

Through direct observation of the growing brains of animals and through pathological examinations of human embryos who die during their development, we can specify in some detail the large changes that the brain undergoes while the human embryo is developing. Understanding these large-scale developmental events should help you remember the major subdivisions of the brain and their structural details. This summarizes the stages of human brain self-assembly.

Early in the course of development, a flat plate of cells, known as the *emorynic disk,* assembles in the middle of the rapidly growing hollow embryo. This sheet of cell is formed from one of the three major embryonic cell lines, called the ectoderm, which will also give rise to the skin. Shortly after it assembles, the embryonic thickens and builds up along its midline.

ROLE OF ENDOCRINE SYSTEM

Earlier we noted that the hypothalamus plays an important role in regulating certain glands. These are the endocrine glands-that secrete hormones (special chemical messengers) directly into the blood stream. The relationship between these glands and both the hypothalamus and autonomic nervous system are complete Basically, the hypothalamus influences the endocrine system through its impact upon the pituitary gland.

Pituitary Gland

This gland is located just below the hypothalamus. One part of it (the posterior pituitary) is closely connected to the hypothalamus, while another (the anterior pituitary) is linked to it indirectly by a system of tiny blood vessels.

Adrenal Glands

Adrenal medulla, produces epinephrine and norepinephrine. These play an important role in preparing the body for stress or emergencies. For example they produce such effects as speeding the heart beat, raising blood pressure and constricting blood vessels in the stomach and intestines.

Adrenal cortex, produces several hormones which promote the release of sugar stored in the liver into the blood. These also help to regulate and maintain the chemical balance within cells of the body.

Gonads (Sex Glands)

Gonads-produce male and female sex hormones. These are responsible for the appearance of secondary sexual characteristics such as facial hair in male and breast development in females. In addition, they also play a role in both sexual and maternal behaviour.

Thyroid Gland

Thyroid gland produces "Thyroxin" which controls the rate of metabolism. (It also regulates growth prior to adulthood).

Parathyroid Gland

Parathyroid gland produces hormones which regulates level of calcium and phosphate in the body. These substances play an important role in the functioning of the nervous system. As mentioned here, the endocrine glands produce or release hormones which regulate a very wide range of bodily processes.

Before concluding, we should note that some of the endocrine glands are stimulated in a direct manner by the autonomic nervous system. For example, when stimulated by the sympathetic nervous system, a portion of the adrenal glands (the adrenal medulla) releases two hormones, epinephrine (adrenalin) and norepinephrine (noradrenalin). These produce such effects as raising blood pressure, speeding the heart beat, and increasing nervous prespiration. Thus, they help prepare the body for dealing with stress and emergencies.

As we have already noted, the link between the hypothalamus, endocrine gland and autonomic nervous system are quite complex. In general, they all function together in an integrated manner to adjust and control our internal bodily state.

(a) Given the extremely "tight" schedule under which the nervous system constructs itself, the logistical supports for the process are vitally important. During the formation of the embryo, for example, maternal physiology is adapted to furnish all possible needed supplies to the growing foetus, regardless of the mother's own needs. Obviously, adequate nutrition is essential. The developing nervous system is also critically susceptible to maternal infections and other physiological "insults." Certain viruses, or drugs used by the mother, may send confusing chemical signals to the rapidly growing and modifying nervous system of the embryo. The nature and severity of birth defects usually correlates with when and for how long such problems existed.

(b) *A Central Dogma:* The lessons of this book are founded on one assumption—that all of the normal functions of the healthy brain and the disorders of the diseased brain, no matter how complex, are ultimately explainable in terms of the basic structural components of the brain. We can call this statement our "central dogma." Now, let us examine that dogma more carefully.

(c) Everything that the brain does when it works properly and when it does not, rests upon the events taking place in specific, definable parts of the brain. By "parts," we mean the region or structure of the brain. By "events," we mean the actions those parts perform together.

(d) However, many of these actions are extremely complicated and for many, if not most of them, scientists do not yet know exactly which parts of the brain are most critically involved or exactly what it is that these parts do. Yet compared with the almost total ignorance of these subjects that persisted well into this century, we now have a considerable amount of very critical information about them. The basic pieces of information about how the brain is organized and how it functions form the principles of neuroscience, and extending these principles so that the more complex acts of the brain can eventually be understood is the basic goal of the very exciting brain research now going on.

(e) Before we look at those principles, however, we need to dig out a controversial concept buried within our dogma. What does the phrase "everything the brain does" mean? It certainly means moving, sensing, eating, drinking, breathing, talking, sleeping. But does it also include mental acts—thoughts and dreams, musings and insights, hopes and aspirations? In previous eras, those "mental acts" have been separated from the functions of the brain and placed in a much more non-material and private place called "the mind."

(f) The cerebrospinal fluid fills space continuing from the outer surfaces of the brain and spinal cord to its inner spaces, the *cerebral ventricles*, received the lion's share of attention from the ancient students of the brain. The ependymal cells lining these inner ventricular spaces are also specialized, and, except for certain key spots that we need not consider further, their edges are sealed together tightly, apparently to limit passage of anything across this lining layer. The cerebrospinal fluid itself is produced by specialized blood vessels, the *choroid plexus*, which filters out the blood cells. The choroid plexus is attached to certain parts of the ventricular system, and the fluid that its cells yield circulates from the inner ventricles up over the surface of the cortex and cerebellum and down into the space around the spinal cord.

(g) The function of this internal circulation of spinal fluid is not known, but physicians make use of it when trying to diagnose infections of the nervous system—bacterial meningitis, for example. When infection is present, the spinal fluid exhibits white blood cells and a protein content that is much higher than normal. Because the spinal fluid also contains some of byproducts of synaptic transmission, diagnosticians and researchers frequently examine its content as they try to piece together chemical clues to the unsolved mysteries of brain disorders. The possibility that the cerebrospinal fluid might transport chemical signs of brain abnormality almost brings us back full circle to the view of the Greeks and Romans who considered the ventricles and their plumbing functions to be of premier importance.

WHAT BRAIN DOES?

All of these facts about cells and circuits have been organized around a skeleton outline of the cellular organization and function of the brain's machinery. Let us review those general statements now that they have been explained to some degree.

1. The basic operating elements of the nervous system are the individual nerve cells, or neurons.
2. Neurons share certain universal cellular features with all the other cells in the body.
3. But they vary considerably from other body cells in their configurations, connections, and styles of operation, as well as their names.
4. The activity of neurons is regulated by the properties of the nerve cell membrane.
5. Synaptic transmitters alter the membrane properties of neurons.
6. Each of the basic biological functions of a neuron can be modified to meet functional demands.
7. The basic wiring patterns of the brain are genetically specified.
8. Three basic patterns of neural circuitry emerge from genetic specifications: hierarchical circuits, local circuits, and single source/ divergent circuits.
9. Genetically specified circuitry patterns can be modified locally by activity.
10. The nervous system also contains cells other than neurons: glial cells, and those of the vascular system and the connective tissues.

ROLE OF THE CEREBELLUM

As its name implies, the *cerebellum*—the word is a dimunitive form of cerebrum—is indeed a small brain. It has an extremely regular structure, the surface of which is greatly expanded relative to its volume by virtue of its many folds. Sliced and viewed from the side, its individual small, folded lobes, which look something like leaves, are called "folia." An identical four-layered cellular structure curves through every folium. One of the two most prominent layers of this structure contains very large neurons, the *Purkinje cells,* which form a single layer. Another layer contains *granule-cell neurons* that cluster, several cells deep, just beneath the Purkinje neurons.

Information comes to the cerebellum from the cerebral cortex, from the brainstem, and from the spinal cord. The spinal cord carries up information about the position of the limbs, trunk, head, neck, and eyes, all of which is integrated by the Purkinje cells. Purkinje neurons seem to fire very rapidly and inbursts much of the time, perhaps indicating their constant surveillance of trunk, limb, and head location and position. The Purkinje neurons then send their output to the villagelike *deep cerebellar nuclei* of large neurons buried deep within the depths of the cerebellum. Information from these nuclei modifies the activity of neurons in the motor cortex.

Despite its elegant structure and its very well worked out cellular circuitry, the exact role of the cerebellum in motor function is far from understood. Coarse experiments on subjects in whom the cerebellum is either injured or stimulated suggest the importance of this structure in controlling the muscle tone needed to hold a posture. The brain has thus parts that help in learning of all kinds of intellectual and language learning.

CHAPTER EIGHT

Mental Fitness

We can not overestimate the importance of mental health. Fortunately, a great deal of attention has been given in recent years to this important aspect of the individual's total personality. Not only has the school become much more conscious of its responsibility in this connection, but the community at large has also demonstrated its interest in the problem through very active mental health groups composed of lay persons as well as professional medical, clinical, and teaching personnel.

SCOPE OF THE PROBLEM

From the days of Adam and Eve—or at least from the days of Cain—problems of mental ill-health have been with us. These, then as well as now, ranged from the mild problems that occasionally bother the most serene and calm person, to the drastic disturbances that characterise the psychotic. It is only recently, however, that mental-health problems have gotten understood and accepted for what they are, namely, a state of ill-health in the mental field comparable to similar conditions in the field of physical health. Thus, until recently, psychotic persons were considered to be possessed of the devil and were burned at the stake or hidden at home or pushed out into the street so that neighbours would not know of the existence of such a person in the family. Mental institutions, or asylums as they were called, kept the insane much like beasts, often in chains, and floggings were not uncommon. Today, on the other hand, it is not uncommon for people to visit a psychologist or a counselor in connection with personality difficulties in much the same way as a person sees a physician for a checkup or for minor treatment.

Mental illness is not only our number one health problem but its incidence is actually on the increase. Whether this implies that people are more maladjusted than they were years ago is a matter of conjecture. It can be argued that the complex age in which we live with its urbanization and its resulting crowded areas, lack of responsibility on the part of children, lack of satisfaction out of one's job resulting from monotonous machine tending, and other social ills is conducive to mental illness. On the other hand, the higher recorded incidence of mental illness may reflect nothing more than a greater awareness of mental-health problems, a greater ability to detect them, and a greater willingness to admit their existence. And, of course, the fact that people live longer also contributes to an increase in the mental problems connected with old age.

Statistics on the prevalence of mental disorders are difficult to appraise. Figures from the National Association for Mental Health indicate that, in the area of the psychoses alone, there are in the United States about three quarters of a million patients in institutions for the insane and that a quarter of a million new patients are admitted each year (in addition to the one hundred thousand readmissions) but this does not include the many patients who are cared for by relatives or are placed in special homes. The White House Conference on Child Health and Protection (1930) estimated that some 2,5 million American children (*i.e.*, over 10 percent) displayed well-defined behaviour problems. Likewise, Cobb estimates that some seven million Americans suffer from various mental disorders while the National Association for Mental Health places at nine million the number of Americans who suffer from mental illness and other personality disorders—the discrepancy being due, of course, to the degree of severity of the disorder used in the criterion.

In the area of the neuroses, it is estimated that over half of the clientele of the average medical practitioner suffers from illness of psychogenic rather than organic origin. During the last war, some 900 thousand young American men were rejected from military service because of personality problems and 460 thousand were discharged for mental illness (about 36 percent of the total medical discharges) and another quarter million were discharged for neuropsychiatric reasons. Many developed hysterical or other symptoms which not only precluded further military service but also caused them to be hospitalised at considerable cost to the taxpayer. In the same way, the cost of goods purchased incorporates a sizable markup resulting from wages paid to absentee workers—

at home, because of migraine headaches and other neurotic dysfunctions—or on strike, because of rigidity that prevents labour and management from agreeing on what is fair and what is right.

Mental ill-health also underlies many of the social problems that confront us daily. The fact that some three out of every four marriages end in divorce is evidence of the emotional instability of many 'adults.' Misbehaviour ranging from minor classroom problems to juvenile delinquency and adult crime, graft, corruption, even on the part of trusted officials, is further evidence of the same lack of adjustment. It is also true that people lose their jobs or at least miss out on promotions very often not for lack of competence in vocational skills but rather because of inability to get along with others. In fact, what is probably the greatest single weakness of the average person, namely, inability to inspire others to give their best in the attainment of desirable goals—which is quite evident in the failure of many leaders whether in school, business, industry, government, sports, or even club work—is very often due to some personality quirk that antagonises would-be cooperators and followers. And not least in this connection is the distrust that currently characterises human relations at the personal, national, and international levels.

The cost to society of the problems just mentioned is impossible to estimate but there is no doubt that it is high. In the area of crime, there are well over a half million Americans over eighteen years of age supported at taxpayer's expense in jails and prisons at any one time. The cost of hospitalisation of psychotic patients in state institutions alone is approximately a billion dollars a year (exclusive of the loss in earning power of the patients). And, of course, the monetary cost would be a relatively minor consideration by comparison to the cost in terms of the unhappiness and the disruption in the lives of the patients and their relatives.

Thus, as summarised by Griffin, Laycock, and Line in 1940, out of a hundred elementary school children selected at random, four or five will spend part of their lives in mental hospitals, four or five will develop serious mental illness but will be cared for in special institutions, one or two will commit some major crime and will spend time in a jail or penitentiary, three or four will be so handicapped by retarded or stunted mental development that they will have difficulty in becoming useful and productive citizens.

Of the remainder, it is estimated that from thirty to fifty will fail to reach the maximum efficiency and happiness in life possible for them because of unwholesome emotional habits and personality traits. A more up-to-date—but hardly more encouraging—report was given by William Meaninger in 1948:

... half of our hospital beds in America are devoted to mental illness. That fact is often amazing to laymen. Statistically about 50 per cent of all patients who go to doctors have emotional problems. These are expressed not only in attitudes and behaviour but in physical symptoms—in the heart, in the limbs, the stomach, or the aching back. There are many, many evidences we live in a sick world. We have hit an all-time record of crime which is costing us about ten billion dollars a year in this country. We have an increasing amount of delinquency in every community in the country. We know that our divorces have doubled inside of six years....

CLASSROOM AND HYGIENE

These rather frightening statistics suggest that something needs to be done to minimise the acuteness of the problem and, once again, the school is elected as the agency in the best position to deal with it. This is perhaps as it should be since the school gets the child rather early in life before too much harm has been done, and since the school is itself a major factor in the degree of mental health the individual attains. Furthermore, the school needs to be concerned with the child's adjustment if for no other reason than that emotional disturbances will make relatively impossible the attainment of even academic goals.

As an organised programme, mental hygiene has three main purposes:

(a) the prevention of mental disorders through an understanding of the principles of adjustment;
(b) the preservation and development of mental health; and
(c) the removal of maladjustment by means of psychotherapy and other measures.

As it applies to the classroom, mental hygiene is not a matter of the teacher struggling desperately to keep children from going insane or to cure those who are already in difficulty: on the contrary, mental hygiene in the classroom is a positive programme oriented toward the promotion of adjustment on the part of each and every child. Thus, mental hygiene is not a body of specialised procedures such as might be involved in a clinical situation but is part and parcel of the teaching process or, as stated by Redl and Wattenberg, the very core of good mental hygiene in schools is the way in which the learning activities are guided. The same point is made by Rivlin in the following quotation:

> Mental hygiene is not a discrete scheme of psychiatric procedures, nor is it a distinct body of facts. It is rather an attitude and a point of view that should influence everything the teacher does professionally: her method of asking questions as well as her manner of accepting answers; the procedure followed in administering tests and that governing the supervision of playground activities; the appeals by which she stimulates the pupil's desire to participate in classroom activities and the measures to which she resorts to bring the unruly into line, her attitude toward the asocial child, such as the young thief or the bully, and that toward the unsocial pupil whose timidity prevents him from mingling with others. Far from being a distinct group of skills and facts, mental hygiene in the classroom takes on significance only when it is bound so inextricably with all the teacher does that careful analysis alone can reveal its exact influence. There is no opposition between sound educational procedures and mental hygiene principles; both are concerned with the adjustment of the present child and of the adult he will become.

Thus, the aims of education and of mental hygiene are one and the same, namely, the promotion of the all-round development of the child. Mental hygiene is not a new fad, an outgrowth of a soft psychology; it is, on the contrary, the very essence of modern educational philosophy which stresses such objectives as self-realisation, happy human relationships, economic efficiency, and civic responsibility. In fact, far from being a misguided fad of educationists, mental hygiene deals with the very core of human welfare and pervades all fields of human relations. It is something that has always been done but which needs to be emphasised in these days of mass education and parents-in-a-hurry where no one has time to consider the child as an individual.

Mental hygiene was but slowly introduced into the school. This may have been partially due to the relative lack of orientation of teachers toward the clinical aspects of the child's growth and development. It was no doubt directly related to the older view of the school as a place where teachers taught and pupils learned. In fact, there are even today rugged individualists who object to babying the child and to the teacher having become a nurse, social worker, minister, doctor, psychiatrist, despite the fact that he is probably qualified only as a teacher. Also involved is the fact that schools are always being pressured into adding extra programmes and the first impulse is to resist such additions, particularly when extra cost in money and teacher time and energy is involved. However, as teachers found that, in the long run, attention to the principles of mental hygiene was a wise investment from the standpoint of pupil growth as well as of teacher-satisfaction, mental hygiene became progressively more accepted although even today many teachers are operating in more or less direct defiance of its principles.

If the school is to be effective in fostering the mental health of children, it is necessary that it define clearly what it can and what it cannot do. Thus, the teacher needs to recognise that his training does not enable him to deal with the therapeutic or corrective aspects of mental hygiene. This is one area where love and good intentions are not enough: all that the teacher can do in advanced cases is to detect them, to have them referred to competent authorities, and to cooperate with recommendations for treatment as they apply to the classroom. Actually, the teacher's greatest contribution to the mental health of the children in his class lies in the area of good teaching, *i.e.*, it lies in providing individual children with meaningful experiences and opportunities for satisfying needs and in creating an atmosphere of acceptance for all children no matter what they do or who they are.

In other words, the teacher's greatest contribution to the mental health of the child lies in being a good teacher rather than in attempting to be a second-rate psychologist or psychiatrist. It may even be that teacher-training institutions should emphasise good teaching rather than place emphasis on mental hygiene as if it were something over and above good teaching.

Teachers need to recognise that, for a number of reasons, they cannot function in the role of clinical psychologists. First, whereas the clinician is dealing with only one person at a time and can, therefore, be as permissive as the occasion demands, the teacher has a class full of children and the need to be accepting and permissive with one child may be negated by the needs and rights of the other children. Even though the teacher can usually build up a feeling of trust on the part of the class so that he can deal with individual children without disturbing his relationship with the group, there are limits to which one child can be a disturbing influence on the class as a whole, especially since some of the other children may also have problems of their own.

Furthermore, the clinician does not have such other concerns as having to grade the child, to report his progress to parents, and get him ready for the next grade—all of which are likely to complicate the relationship between pupil and teacher beyond that of the clinician and patient. The teacher must also accept the fact that, while the child's view of the clinician may be neutral (on par with a physician or dentist), his notion of the teacher includes a great deal of carry-over from his experiences with other teachers, much of which may be unfavourable.

Whereas the teacher is not qualified to deal with the corrective aspects of mental hygiene, he needs to make it one of his primary responsibilities to acquaint himself with the symptoms of maladjustment so that he can recognise its existence early and make a referral of the child to a competent clinician. Unfortunately, teachers are not too well trained in recognising danger signals and sometimes consider as a model the quiet retiring child who never gives a bit of trouble and consider the troublemaker as ready to be institutionalised, whereas actually the former is probably in greater danger from a mental health point of view than is the latter.

The relative incompetence of teachers in judging the severity from a mental-health standpoint of various behaviour problems was brought out by Wickman's well-known study in which he found teachers to rate fifty behaviour problems in somewhat the reverse order of the ratings of trained clinicians. Actually, the study contained a number of flaws and more recent and better studies have shown much closer agreement between teachers and clinicians. Thus, Schrupp and Gjerde, in a repetition of Wickman's study using the same set of directions for both groups, found a correlation of 86 in the ratings of teachers and clinicians (as opposed to a correlation of. 04 found by Wickman). Whether one needs to be disturbed about the discrepancy in outlook that still exists between teachers and clinicians is a matter of opinion and it is possible that, in view of the difference in their function, certain differences in their views are to be expected. On the other hand, there is perhaps still a need for a further shift in teacher orientation from a concern over breaches of classroom decorum to a more objective consideration of behaviour from the standpoint of the long-term development of the whole child.

Mental Health Factors in the Classroom

Since nearly all of the child's experiences during the formative years are connected with first the home and then the school, it follows that these two agencies are more than any other responsible for the child's (and the adult's) mental health. This has been substantiated by such studies as that of Kaplan and O'Dea, the results of whose investigation of the mental hazards of school children are listed in the following table.

By its very nature, the classroom incorporates many features which may constitute definite hazards to the mental health of children—and particularly of certain children, *e.g.*, those of limited mental ability. Thus, the fact that the school has primary responsibilities in the area of promoting academic learning can, unless care is exercised, mean frustration, perhaps even continuous frustration, for some children.

This can be particularly devastating to the child inasmuch as, since he cannot easily withdraw from the situation, he may be faced with a situation very similar to that which leads to experimental neurosis in laboratory experiments. On the premise that prevention is a more constructive approach to the problem of mental health than is correction after the harm has been done, the teacher needs, therefore, to evaluate carefully from a mental hygiene point of view each and every classroom procedure. The following is a partial list of the more obvious factors that have a direct bearing upon the mental health of the school child.

> The wide range of individual differences to be found in the classroom makes it difficult for the teacher to provide meaningful experiences for each child and to have each attain at least a minimum of satisfaction for his needs. This problem is, of course, accentuated by an emphasis upon examinations and competition which may result in continuous failure and frustration on the part of a few children.

The Mental Health Hazards of School Children As Reported by Teachers

Mental Health Hazards	Percent
Unsatisfactory home conditions	91
Failure of traditional curriculum to meet the need of many children	62
Overcrowded classrooms	51
Fear to participate orally in class due to insecurity	51
Failure of schools to realise and satisfy individual differences and achievement	50
Inadequate playground facilities	48
Failure to be accepted into desired clique	48
Parents unhappily married	44
Inability to participate in all desired school activities due to financial difficulties	44
Failure of report card to give adequate description of child's potentialities	44
Inadequate clothing and spending money	43
Lack of parental cooperation with the school	42
Labeling students as delinquents	39
Teachers using degrading remarks before other students	39
Conflicting personalities of pupils	39
Shyness	37

Since the matter has been discussed in a previous chapter, the student is urged to review the various solutions suggested in terms of their likely effect upon the mental health of the child. Thus, in the case of examinations, a child should welcome an opportunity to evaluate where he stands—or where the group stands—as a prelude to planning the next step; but, when examinations take on the flavour of Judgment Day together with the definite possibility of being found inadequate, examinations can do far more harm from the standpoint of the child's total growth than the good, if any, which they promote from an academic point of view.

Disciplinary Measures Used by Elementary Teachers

Disciplinary Measure	Frequency
Constructive assistance (creating opportunity for successful participation, conference with parents, special responsibility.)	31%

(Contd.)

(Contd.)

Disciplinary Measure	Frequency
Verbal appeal (reasoning, requested cessation)	25%
Censure (scolded, shamed, warned, embarrassed, sarcasm, soaped mouth)	11%
Deprivation (deprived recreation time, isolated, removed from class, changed seat, etc.)	10%
Searched for reason for misbehaviour	6%
Ignored or did nothing	5%
Overtime or extra work	5%
Other	7%

Discipline is a necessary aspect of growth and, as such, is part and parcel of mental hygiene. Thus, when approached in a constructive way, discipline embodies the principles of mental hygiene, and hence can be an important force in promoting mental health on the part of the child. Fortunately, a very definite trend has developed in recent years toward the use of more positive discipline in our schools. Nevertheless, as noted in the tabulation of disciplinary measures used by some three hundred elementary teachers shown in the following table, some teachers in their attempt to maintain classroom discipline still resort to such potentially harmful procedures as sarcasm, ridicule, and punishment.

While it is encouraging to note, for instance, that the majority of the cases reported involved measures that are positive and sound from the standpoint of mental hygiene, the results also show that even in the middle of the twentieth century there is still an unnecessary incidence of punitive and psychologically destructive measures being used by teachers who ought to know better.

Note, for example, that various forms of censure were used in 11 per cent of the cases. In fact, a breakdown of the last category shows that physical force was used in one percent of the cases on an over-all basis which would imply that, since most teachers rarely, if ever, use force, some teachers must be placing considerable reliance upon such measures.

Of even greater importance than discipline from the standpoint of mental hygiene is the emotional climate of the classroom. In fact, emotional climate is relatively synonymous with the concept of mental hygiene, once the therapeutic aspects of the latter are excluded from discussion. When the atmosphere of the classroom is one of permissiveness and acceptance, the child is free to use his capacities for maximum self-realisation. The role of the teacher with respect to mental hygiene is crucial for it is he who is responsible for the emotional tone of the classroom and for translating the principles of mental hygiene into effective classroom living. This calls for a number of characteristics and abilities on his part, of which none is more important than that of sensitivity to the needs and feelings of others which would prevent him from subjecting the child to unfair and excessive competition, to an unsuitable curriculum, or to unrealistic demands. Teachers are not qualified to treat severe adjustment problems but they can show a little understanding and friendliness to the child who is left out, who has a trying home situation, and make it possible for him to taste occasional success and recognition. To do this is particularly important inasmuch as not all children can be referred to a professional counselor and many will have to rely on the teacher for whatever help he can give. Furthermore, if our concern is to be with the developmental aspects of mental health, whatever help is given the vast majority of children will have to come at the hands of the teacher.

The academic work of the classroom should be meaningful to the child in terms of his abilities, purposes, and interests. When the child finds that he can get satisfaction for his needs through doing the work of the school, he will not only be happy but he will also work as hard as his abilities permit so that there will be no need to rely on punishment, nor for the teacher to appoint himself inspector of pupil shortcomings. Under these conditions, he will set his own pace and excessive pushing will only cause frustration and interfere with his growth. Such a curriculum can certainly do more for the mental health and the growth of the child than any programme of guidance or special help superimposed upon a rigid programme of instruction supervised by inflexible and authoritarian teachers.

A number of other aspects of the classroom situation could be singled out for similar considerations. Suffice it to say that everything the teacher does as it relates to the child—homework, grouping, reporting to parents, promoting or retaining—has implications for better or for worse from the standpoint of his mental health. The teacher needs to be fully aware of the grave responsibility this places upon his shoulders.

MENTAL HEALTH: GUIDELINES

Guidance, mental hygiene, and, in fact, education in the modern sense, all have the same purpose, namely, the promoting of the maximum self-realisation of the child. They differ, however, in approach and in scope.

Education tends to be oriented toward promoting the child's all-round growth (perhaps with special emphasis on the academic).

Guidance and mental hygiene, on the other hand, function largely in the field of personal and social growth although the adjustment which they promote certainly has implications for the other phases of his over-all development. From the standpoint of promoting personal and social adjustment, mental hygiene is probably more basic and generally more effective than guidance since it permeates everything that goes on in the classroom and is, therefore, likely to have a greater influence on the child than are the infrequent contacts he has with the counselor.

Furthermore, mental hygiene, in its broad sense, includes all that is generally incorporated under guidance. The distinction is essentially that which distinguishes pupil-personnel work in the elementary school, where the mental health activities are integrated with the total programme, from that in the high school where a formal guidance programme is superimposed upon the curricular programme but very often is not too closely integrated with the work of the classroom.

In some high schools, for example, the counselor may see the student for a 15-minute interview per semester—usually more often in the case of the troublemakers—in an attempt to provide understanding and friendliness, while, all along classroom teachers continue to put through their academic paces each day some 150 students whom they barely know.

It seems clear that counsellors, even at best, can only be a supplement to the teacher in this matter of promoting the adjustment and growth of the children in his classes and that, at all times, the teacher will have to bear the brunt of the guidance of these children. The guidance programme can probably serve its best function in helping the teacher to do his job in the classroom through providing a central agency for collecting data on all children and through providing a referral service for some of the more difficult cases. Unfortunately, as a part of this service, the average counselor is hardly qualified as a competent clinician; in fact, many counsellors are just classroom teachers with relatively little training in psychology—a situation which can be dangerous, for, as pointed out by Woodruff, there are no expendable personalities to practice on by would-be counsellors who, although they may feel endowed by nature with a special gift for helping others, nevertheless do not have adequate technical preparation.

TEACHER'S MENTAL HEALTH

Whereas the focus in the modern school should be upon the child, his growth, and his adjustment—the mental health of the teacher is certainly no less important. In fact, when we consider the influence from the standpoint of both adjustment and achievement he can have over a vast number of children, the adjustment of the teacher assumes even greater importance than the adjustment of any other single person in the classroom.

Maladjustment is not unknown among teachers. Whereas research findings vary, estimates based on such studies as those of Fenton and Hicks would suggest that some 20 per cent of teachers in the field are in need of psychiatric help. Altman, for instance, found 4 per cent of the 35000 New York teachers in his sample to be mental cases. At the more normal level, research has shown worry, disturbed sleep, shyness, indecision, absent-mindedness, fatigue, and headaches to be (in order) the most frequent symptoms of nervous instability among teachers. How this would compare with any other occupational group is debatable: it may well be that the strain of teaching brings out neurotic trends, or that such trends in a teacher would cause alarm while the same problems in the average layman would go unnoticed or, at least, cause no apprehension. Even such studies as that of Smith and Hightower showing teachers with a greater incidence of neurotic symptoms than any other group of patients at the Mayo Clinic would have to be interpreted cautiously since the samples involved may not be representative of the various occupational groups listed.

However, comparison with other groups is essentially irrelevant; the fact remains that there is a high incidence of maladjustment among teachers. But whether this is a result of the strain and stress of the classroom creating an adjustment problem too severe for all but the most stable, or whether teaching attracts individuals with various forms of maladjustment has not been determined. It may be, for example, that teaching attracts individuals with strong feelings of hostility who see the classroom as a place where they can vent their aggressions against defenseless children and who feel that freedom to browbeat children is an aspect of academic freedom. It is no doubt possible to cite examples of persons who have gone into teaching apparently for the purpose—perhaps among others—of bossing children around or of satisfying a neurotic need to be loved.

Although the evidence is not entirely clear, maladjusted teachers tend to have maladjusted pupils. Boynton and his co-workers, for instance, found that adjusted teachers have pupils who are more stable than do teachers who are considered maladjusted.

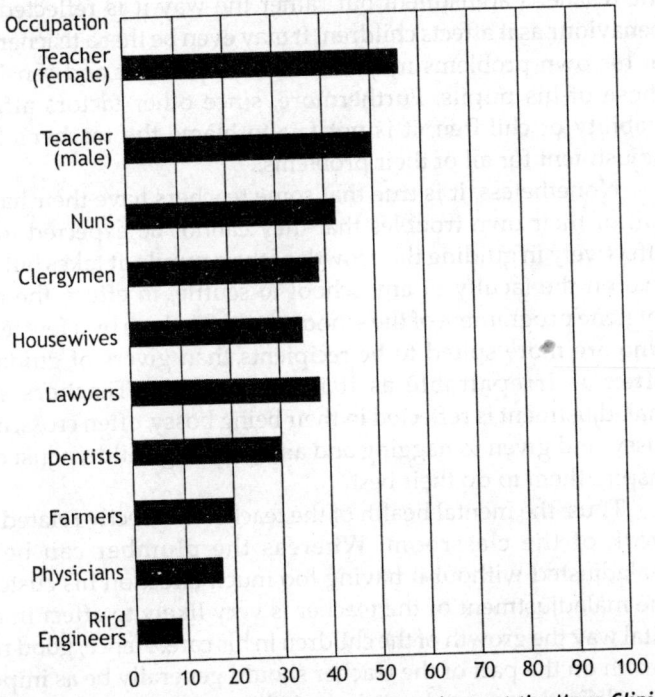

Occupation	
Teacher (female)	~55
Teacher (male)	~50
Nuns	~40
Clergymen	~35
Housewives	~35
Lawyers	~40
Dentists	~30
Farmers	~25
Physicians	~18
Rird Engineers	~8

Incidence of neurotic symptoms among patients at the Mayo Clinic

Similar results were obtained by Baxter. And, of course, the average person can recall instances of a frustrated teacher who had negative effects upon students who, in turn, vented their annoyance by making it miserable for him, thereby complicating his adjustment problems. The very strong stand against the presence of maladjusted teachers in the classroom taken by the American Association of School Administrators is reflected in the following quotations from their 1942 yearbook:

...the emotionally unstable teacher exerts such a detrimental influence on children that she should not be allowed to remain in

Mental Fitness ■ 171

the classroom.... Such teachers need help, but while they are being helped they should be out of classrooms so their pupils may be freed from the psychic injury, repression, and fear which their presence creates.

On the other hand, the fact that Ash found no correlation between the teacher's adjustment and the emotional and social behaviour of his pupils may suggest that the important thing is not the teacher's adjustment but rather the way it is reflected in his behaviour as it affects children. It may even be that a teacher aware of his own problems may be more sympathetic and sensitive to those of his pupils. Furthermore, since other factors affect the stability of children, it is not fair to blame the teacher's lack of adjustment for all of their problems.

Nonetheless, it is true that some teachers have their hands so full of their own troubles that they cannot be expected to work effectively in guiding the growth of their pupils. It takes but one or two on the faculty of any school to scuttle, in effect, the mental hygiene programme of the school: the harm done by a few teachers who are more suited to be recipients than givers of guidance is often as irreparable as it is inexcusable. Teachers whose maladjustment is reflected in their being bossy, often cross, always fussy, and given to nagging and antagonising children just cannot inspire them to do their best.

Thus, the mental health of the teacher is directly related to the work of the classroom. Whereas the plumber can be most maladjusted without it having too much effect on his customers, the maladjustment of the teacher is very likely to affect in a very vital way the growth of the children in his care. Hence, good mental health on the part of the teacher should generally be as important a qualification as academic knowledge or a valid teacher's license. This would be of particular importance in the grade school where children may be stuck with the same teacher day in and day out for a whole year.

TEACHER'S HEALTH: REASONS

Much of the material of this text has direct bearing on the mental health of the teacher and he should be able to apply the principles we have discussed to his situation as well as to that of his pupils. Thus, for example, he needs to appreciate the fact that, like any other human being, he must derive certain satisfactions from his job if he is to remain a contented and integrated individual; and that he is not promoting his own adjustment nor that of his pupils when he attempts to satisfy his needs at the expense of the children in his class. Teaching, like any other profession, involves both favourable and unfavourable mental hygiene factors. Among the former we might mention the following:

(*a*) Teaching includes ample possibilities for satisfying the needs of the teacher. The teacher doing a good job has the satisfaction of seeing children grow, of feeling their affection and respect, and of obtaining recognition by parents and the community. This is probably the greatest satisfaction to be derived from teaching. But it tends to be restricted to those who enjoy their teaching sufficiently to be good teachers. The poor teacher very often reaps nothing but pupil and parental hostility, if not contempt.

Teaching involves a variety of work and a constant challenge for the person who is interested in children and their growth. Every child is unique and presents unique problems that call for the highest level of professional competence. Although the teacher will not always be successful in solving these problems, there will certainly be no lack of opportunity to use all of his skills, initiative, and ingenuity for the benefit of children and his own self-satisfaction. When the teacher becomes sensitive to the needs of children and attempts to make the classroom a pleasant place for them, he soon finds that they, in turn, help satisfy his needs, so that teaching becomes rewarding.

(*b*) Teaching offers steady employment with rather good pay, steady increases, a reasonably short day, and numerous vacations throughout the year. This advantage is, of course, lost when teachers become straddled with heavy co-curricular responsibilities, when they have to attend university classes, or when they feel compelled to take on an extra job to supplement their salary.

(*c*) Among other advantages might be mentioned association with educated persons of like interests, clear work, and contact with youth whose enthusiasm and vitality will never let the teacher grow old—unless he grows sour—in which case, it will be remarkably effective in hastening the process.

For some teachers, the major hazard in teaching is monotony. Using the same methods, the same outlines, the same illustrations, the same audio-visual aids, eating the same meals at the same restaurant, wearing the same style of clothes—all of these things down to the same bridge partners every Friday and the same pew in church every Sunday are typical of the lives of some teachers. They are in a rut! Presenting the same material year after year—and repeating it for the benefit of the slower children for good measure—is bound to get boring. It is like presenting the same play over and over again. Actually, good teaching can never be routine: it calls for improvement in method, for changes in content depending on the interests, needs and purposes of the children; and, above all, it calls for teaching children, and not subject matter. On the other hand, it is true that teaching is sometimes frustrating because the results of one's work are not immediately observable. This is especially so in the area of pupil adjustment where a teacher may work for months—apparently in vain—trying to straighten out a child. It is also true that some teachers by trying too hard and expecting too much disappoint themselves and become discouraged.

Teaching can involve a great deal of nervous strain. Not only are numerous emotionally charged situations likely to occur during the course of the day, but, even at best, children are full of pep and vinegar and they can be irritating even to the calmest teacher. When the teacher is unstable to begin with, the strain on teacher and pupils alike can become unbearable. Such a teacher should probably be guided out of the profession, whenever possible.

The teacher needs time to collect his wits and his energy. A free period when he can take a minute to relax without having children under foot, perhaps time for a cup of coffee on days that have been particularly trying will often do wonders in terms of setting the ship back on an even keel. Teaching may actually involve considerable fatigue on the part of the teacher depending on the size of the classes taught, the nature of the pupils and of the subject taught, and, of course, the physical stamina of the teacher. Teachers, especially those in the smaller schools, are often loaded down with co-curricular assignments, committee meetings, various other assignments, unending reports and other clerical—if not Janitorial—duties in addition, of course, to a full teaching load. Thus, to quote Bowl by:

...the problem of extra curricular duties is really enough to take your time, your health, and your breath away. Every teacher is expected to serve as a class advisor as well as sponsor of two or more activities, plus a little coaching or dramatic work on the side. Three-in-one oil is modest in its numerical claims when compared to the small-high-school teacher who is expected to be a seven-in-one paragon—guidance expert, advisor, teacher, clerk, and assistant janitor, plus football and basketball coach.

Likewise, in the Kaplan and O'Dea study, the results of which are shown below, many of the mental hazards listed by teachers are in the category of unsatisfactory work conditions. Yet generally it is the frustration resulting from things undone and problems unsolved as well as from boredom, rather than good hard work, that leads to fatigue. Once the strain starts to accumulate, tension piles up and teachers get to nagging, overemphasise the unimportant and the trivial, and become unable to organise their work on an effective basis. The result is general annoyance and shortness of temper which soon leads to animosity on the part of pupils and, thus, to a vicious cycle.

Mental Health Hazards of Classroom Teachers

Mental Health Hazards	Frequency
Teacher load too heavy	64%
Overcrowded classrooms	51%
Inadequate housing	50%
University work carried concurrently with teaching	49%
Failure of report card to give adequate description of child's potentialities	48%
Lack of parental cooperation with the school	44%
Teachers performing secretarial duties	42%
Insufficient supplies and equipment	40%
Failure of school to realise and satisfy individual differences	39%
Lack of school funds to operate efficiently	37%

Closely connected with the matter of nervous strain as an unfavourable feature of teaching are the frequent conflicts that arise during a school day. The maintenance of discipline, for example, often poses a problem for the teacher who wants to be loved and appreciated and yet does not know how to be permissive without having students take advantage of him. He may feel that he has to choose between bedlam and resulting censure from the principal, or autocratic control and pupil antagonism. Of course, such things as defiance and hostility on the part of students are much more common in some communities and at certain grade levels than others, but again it seems that some teachers are always running from one conflict to another while others never have trouble. When such conflicts occur too frequently, the teacher might well ask himself whether he is bringing these problems upon himself by such things as rigidity of personality or insensitivity and incompetence in adjusting the curriculum to the needs and purposes of the pupils. On the other hand, teachers sometimes run into a problem when their need to be loved and to avoid pupil hostility makes it difficult for them to maintain discipline and insist on a certain amount of work. This often leads them to compromise some of their values with resulting feelings of guilt and anxiety.

Generally, when a relationship of mutual understanding exists between teacher and pupils, when the teacher has earned the respect of students and they are convinced that he has their interests and welfare at heart such conflicts are likely to be rare and of a minor variety, especially when he is proficient in adapting the curriculum to student needs and purposes. He must also give the child feelings of status and recognition and thus make it unnecessary for the latter to become a behaviour problem in order to get attention. He should be sure to provide legitimate outlets for the release of emotional tension so that it is drained off before it reaches explosive proportions.

The teacher needs to understand not only children and what causes them to behave as they do but he also needs to understand his own behaviour. The secure teacher should be able to accept defiance and other irritations without being unduly upset and certainly a teacher who enjoys children can understand that their buoyancy and high vitality is bound to get them in trouble once in a while. Therefore, when he finds himself unduly provoked at the child's behaviour, he might well ask himself what in his background causes him to be so disturbed at this kind of behaviour.

Some teachers feel that the way to handle conflicts with students is to point out in no uncertain terms who is boss. Unfortunately, this generally restores order and it gives the teacher the illusion that he has solved the problem whereas, in reality, he has only dealt with superficial behaviour and actually aggravated the problem through increasing inner tensions and frustrations of which the misbehaviour is but a symptom. In general, tough disciplinarians create more problems than they solve: by increasing resentment and hostility they create misconduct while, at the same time, causing conflict and maladjustment on the part of the child. Such conduct also precludes the building of respect and acceptance on the part of pupils and denies teachers the satisfactions they so definitely need. In short order, besieged by pupil and parental hostility and rejection, such teachers are forced to depend more and more on autocratic control and punitive measures which, sooner or later, rebound against them.

Conflicts also arise out of poor teacher-principal relationships. Just as some teachers are misguided in their dealings with pupils, so some principals and administrators consider pupils and teachers as mere cogs in the pedagogical machine. And just as children suffer from repressive autocratic control at the hand of teachers, so do teachers often suffer from the same sort of control at the hands of the administration. Many teachers feel they are forced to contend with unrealistic standards, rigid requirements, and petty politics. They sometimes feel that they are prevented from doing their best for the child by administrative restrictions, oversize classes, constant interruptions, and endless clerical details. Some principals have outdated ideas as to such things as classroom management and expect teachers—who feel they know better—to act accordingly. And, of course, conflicts arise from the opposite situation, *e.g.*, when the teacher, exasperated at the behaviour of youngster, sends him to the principal only to be told by the latter that perhaps if he were a little more understanding of children he would have fewer problems.

The communication system between teachers and administrators sometimes breaks down to the point where, while each blames and complains about the other, they never get to dealing constructively with their differences. Teachers often complain about the principal to each other but in front of him blame the pupils and the parents. In the meantime, the frustration and hostility of both the principal and, especially, the teacher are directed toward the child as the scapegoat in the situation, while apathy and poor school morale bounce from teacher to pupil and back again. The emotional as well as the academic tone of the school — and eventually of the classroom — revolve around the work of the principal. However, his responsibilities cause him to be interested in the whole school rather than in individual teachers and occasionally the teacher may feel cheated out of deserved recognition, especially when favouritism and petty politics are present.

Conflicts also arise when parents do not see eye to eye with the teacher on such matters as discipline, homework, curriculum, or teaching methods. Parental and community reactions sometimes pickup momentum and concentrated attacks, such as the recent wave of criticism of the school stemming from American lag in the missile race, result. The poor teacher often finds it difficult to agree simultaneously with the mother of the gifted child who wants rigid grading and a highly technical curriculum and with the mother of the duller child who has a different problem, or with the mother of the well-behaved child whose jacket was torn by one of the more uncontrollable children of the school and with the mother of the latter child, with the parent who wants more homework and the parent who wants less — all of which he is expected to do while at the same time complying with administrative regulations on the subject. Pressures are even applied to win sports events whatever the cost in terms of harm to individual children and of the violation of the teacher's basic values of sportsmanship. It must be noted in this connection that the parent is generally well-meaning; he simply wants the best for his child, a reaction which is both understandable and commendable; and the parent may be right except that his child is only one of the thirty or more with whom the teacher has to contend! At any rate, all these demands made upon him to be everything, top everybody at once leaves the poor teacher confused and often demoralized. And for, the same lack of communication that sometimes characterises teacher-principal relationships is also to be found at times in the dealings of teachers and parents so that the teacher may feel 'without a friend in the world.'

A fourth source of difficulty connected with teaching which is, fortunately, being relaxed in recent years concerns the isolation of the teacher resulting from unnecessary community restrictions on his personal life. That the imposition of a few restrictions is psychologically sound has been mentioned before. Teachers have by their own choice set themselves in a position where children are likely to identify with them, where they become their heroes to be copied. They can, therefore, not allow themselves to become involved in scandals or even minor episodes that might go relatively unnoticed in a lesser position. If a teacher is not willing to accept the fact that his life is not his to live after school hours, he is in the wrong field. For the clergyman, the mayor, the principal, or any other person in a position of public responsibility to be found drunk in the gutter is not 'his own business'!

Nevertheless, certain restrictions are unnecessary: the community cannot put restrictions on such things as smoking, participation in civic groups, courtship and marriage, and other activities to which the teacher, as a member of a democratic community, is entitled, without in the long run destroying his effectiveness. In some communities, for example, the teacher—and particularly, the woman teacher—is never fully accepted on an equal basis by parents and other adults and, even in social situations, she is not Jane Smith but Miss Smith, Joan's teacher. The community often places her on a pedestal and, thereby, denies her such basic rights as the right to innocent fun, courtship, and privacy. Many women teachers, for instance, are rather frustrated at the thought of becoming 'old maids', for not only do they find the male teachers with whom they associate in the school to be married but they are also restricted in husband-hunting in the community. Perhaps all these restrictions are a carry-over from the mixed feelings about teachers which a number of people carry with them from their school days but, whatever the reason, they make it difficult for the teacher to lead a normal life and enjoy the satisfactions of the usual social contacts. These restrictions are, of course, more rigid in small communities than in large cities where the teacher may be residing in an entirely different section than that in which he teaches. The solution probably lies in the direction of having the teacher convince himself of his rights as a citizen and his duty as a public servant and leader of youth and to insist on these rights—provided, of course, these rights do not interfere with his responsibility as a teacher. It might, for instance, be pointed out that taking sides in a controversial issue, regardless of the merits of the teacher's stand, might easily jeopardise his effectiveness with a certain group of pupils (and their parents) who have deep-seated convictions from the opposite viewpoint. The question of racial integration might be an illustration of this point.

Salary is also a point of contention for some teachers, although generally the salary issue comes up only when morale is low and other grievances are present. Thus, some teachers sometimes feel that they are not understood and appreciated, that there are no extra rewards for effort and effectiveness, that all the administration and the community does is pile them with extra chores but never a word of recognition. Some teachers may feel that lack of professional help in the form of academic consultants and clinically trained workers, forces them to struggle with problems they are not able to solve. Thus, the question of low salary is generally tied to a general discontent and, often to lack of adjustment on the part of the teacher to teaching as a career.

The salary of teachers does not compare with that of other professions like medicine, dentistry, law, or engineering, but it is reasonably free from operating expenses and is not subject to risk. Besides salaries have come up and will maintain this rise as teachers continue to provide competent professional service. Teachers must remember that they are in the profession to provide a service, not to get out of it all the traffic will bear. If a teacher feels that he is underpaid, such a feeling is likely to lead to frustration, to a lack of enthusiasm and initiative which can do great harm if transmitted to children and, by preventing him from doing his best job, engenders endless difficulties and frustrations. For that reason an underpaid teacher is rarely worth what he is getting and for the good of all, including himself, he should look for a position elsewhere. Teaching has certain attractions and certain drawbacks and it draws a particular group of people who are content to operate within such a framework. A person who is not happy to work under these conditions owes it to all concerned to get out. The welfare of children is at stake.

TEACHER'S HEALTH: ENCOURAGEMENT

Teaching is not without its mental health hazards which, as we have seen, take their toll among teachers. The fact that some teachers and not others display signs of maladjustment, however, apparently points to differences either in the stability of teachers as they enter the profession or in the conditions which they encounter after they become teachers. The two sets of factors are, of course, closely interrelated: well adjusted teachers are likely to deal with whatever conditions they encounter with effectiveness and improve them. The unstable teacher is likely to find himself in the middle of a vicious circle, for the unfavourable factors involved in teaching are magnified in the case of the unfit, with resulting harm to himself as well as to children.

The writer is fully convinced that the most effective way of improving the mental health of the teaching profession (and succeeding generations of youngsters) is to select as prospective teachers individuals who are emotionally stable and who go into teaching because of an interest and a mature liking for children.

This places a great responsibility upon the shoulders of teacher-training institutions, especially since the factors that are involved in teacher-success are not only relatively unknown—in the 143 studies of effective teachers summarised by Barr, no single teacher characteristic or factor stands out—but also relatively difficult to appraise.

Nevertheless, from a psychological standpoint, the following teacher characteristics and qualities may be considered as conducive to effectiveness in promoting mental health on the part of the child: (*a*) emotional security, stability, and relative freedom from anxiety; (*b*) ability to identify with children and include them within their sphere of enlightened self-interest; (*c*) a cooperative democratic orientation; and (*d*) a balanced and positive outlook on life. Appraising the presence of these traits in prospective teachers is obviously difficult in the setting of the usual lecture-type college classroom situation.

An approach that combines classroom participation, pre-internship contacts with children in the field, and the use of such standardised instruments as the Minnesota Teacher Attitude Inventory and even the Minnesota Multiphasic Personality Inventory as a means of determining suitability for teaching tend to be more fruitful but even then we can more successfully identify those individuals whose characteristics will tend to prevent them from becoming good teachers than those who will be successful. Thus, such procedures and instruments may permit the identification of teacher candidates who are so engrossed in their own difficulties that they are not likely to be in any position to understand and help children with the problems of growing up. On the other hand, the relative absence of negative traits does not automatically guarantee success in teaching.

The principal has a particular responsibility not only in choosing good teachers for his school but also in promoting and maintaining morale and school efficiency at a high level, for, just as the teacher sets the tone of the classroom, so in a more general way the principal sets the tone for the school. Implied in the above statement are: (*a*) a democratic organisation and operation of the school, including a discussion (and not a dictation) of policies, constructive supervision, and group action on school problems; (*b*) adequate salaries, equipment, and other facilities that befit the dignity of the teaching profession; and (*c*) cordial relations among administrators, teachers, pupils, and parents, each aware of his responsibilities and of the need for cooperation.

The teacher himself has the primary responsibility for his own mental health. Granted a liking for children, he still needs to acquaint himself with the principles of psychology so that he can understand children better. He must be fully sold on teaching as an opportunity to be of service to children and must be fully convinced that whatever promotes their adjustment will also be conducive to his own happiness and mental health. In fact, he should concentrate on developing positive relationships with pupils, fellow teachers, parents, and administrators through developing sensitivity to the needs of people and resourcefulness in dealing effectively with others. He also needs to understand and accept himself, for only as he has accepted his own shortcomings is he in a position to accept those of others. Furthermore, since competence is conducive to a feeling of security, he should strive to develop competence in both his subject area and in teaching methods so that he can guide more effectively the growth of children along worthwhile and meaningful lines. Nothing gives a teacher a lift as much as does pride and confidence in his ability to do the job and to earn the respect and gratitude of pupils, parents, fellow teachers, and administrators.

As he grows in ability to consolidate children into a functional cohesive group bent on the pursuit of common goals, he finds troubles disappear. Furthermore, as he grows in security, he finds it easier to be tolerant, to look upon annoying behaviour on the part of other as something to analyse from the standpoint of causation rather than as a personal affront. Then the child's misbehaviour becomes a challenge just as the principal's criticisms serve as the basis for improvement rather than as a cause for resentment. Under such conditions he can see things in perspective, he can distinguish the important from the trivial and petty, he needs no longer to be on the defensive. Furthermore, as he becomes freed from having to worry about his security, he finds more time to plan, to routinise what should be on a routine basis, and thus, he preserves his energies for constructing more meaningful classroom experiences.

The teacher should cultivate wide interests and associate with people outside the narrow circle of the classroom so that he does not have to be so dependent upon his students for the satisfaction of his needs. He can then be more objective in dealing with students and be of greater help to them. He should also be aware that all work and no play makes Jack a dull boy and should have separate time for both. This is particularly true of the woman teacher with a family who, unless she plans it carefully, may find that her attempt to be a wife, a mother, and a teacher will result in her being a failure in all three.

The teacher needs to keep in good physical health and, although some teachers, perhaps because of their relative freedom from unnecessary tension and their ability to put work on an efficient basis, seem full of energy, others definitely need their weekends and their vacations to recuperate. It follows that the teacher should not take pupil assignments home for grading unless he is sure there is no better way and that the time and energy so spent could not be put to more constructive use. This is not to be construed as an endorsement of laziness: the writer is merely suggesting that the effectiveness of a teacher is probably more closely proportional to the planning and the imagination he brings to the classroom than to the number of hours he keeps his nose to the grindstone.

Yet, despite all the constructive planning of which the teacher is capable, there will be days when everything will go wrong, when he will feel like crawling in a hole in the ground. If this occurs frequently, he might well be in the wrong field and, despite all the glory that attends the virtue of persistence, it is an even greater virtue to know when to quit. Yet, he shouldn't waste every ounce of the energy he should be spending in teaching worrying about his effectiveness. He should do the best job he can—and let us not forget the words of Redl and Wattenberg:

There are not enough saints to fill all the teaching positions, so imperfect human beings must do the bulk of the instruction of youth—What counts is not your virtues or your vices but what you do to children with them.

Summing up

Mental illness is America's number one health problem today. Fortunately, it has received considerable attention in recent years in both lay and professional circles and extensive research into the cause and cure of mental disorders is being conducted. Nevertheless, it is probably true that no other institution is in as good a position to deal with the problem as is the school: not only does it have contact with the child from early in life through the formative years but, since so much of the child's life centers around the work of the school, his school experiences are bound to have a profound influence upon his mental health. The following are among the more important concepts of mental health as they apply to the classroom:

(a) Mental hygiene in the classroom is not a fad nor a body of clinical techniques; on the contrary, it is part-and-parcel of the teaching process by means of which the child's maximum self-realisation is promoted.
(b) Mental hygiene has three main purposes:
   (i) the prevention of mental illness;
   (ii) the development of mental health; and
   (iii) the correction of mental disorders.
(c) It is by means of good teaching that the teacher can do most to promote the mental health of the child. Because of the nature of the situation in which the teacher operates and the nature of the training he has received, his efforts in the direction of the therapeutic aspects of mental hygiene should be restricted to early detection of danger signs, to referral to a competent clinician, and to cooperation with his recommendations.
(d) A number of factors in the classroom constitute potential mental health hazards. Amongst these might be mentioned the demands of the curriculum, discipline, the emotional climate of the classroom, examinations, and reporting.
(e) Regardless of the availability of clinical and guidance services, the brunt of the guidance of the child and the promotion of his mental health will have to be borne by the classroom teacher.
(f) The mental health of the teacher is of primary importance in view of the effect his personality can have upon a large number of children. Unfortunately, research has shown considerable maladjustment among teachers and, although the same can be said about any other occupational group,

maladjustment among teachers is more closely related to their work than is the case in other occupations.

(g) Teaching, just as other occupations, has both its favourable and its unfavourable features and it usually attracts persons who can find happiness within such a framework. For the right person, teaching can be a source of satisfaction and self-fulfillment whereas for the misfit the satisfactions are minimised and the drawbacks are correspondingly magnified. The latter should be guided out of the teaching profession for the good of all concerned.

(h) The most effective way of improving the mental health of the teaching profession is to select, as prospective teachers, individuals who are well adjusted and who have a mature liking for children.

(i) Administrators need to do all they can to make the work of the classroom teacher pleasant. In the final analysis, however, the teacher needs to assume responsibility for his own mental health, to attempt to understand and accept himself, to develop competence in dealing with children, and to cultivate a sense of perspective that will prevent him from becoming unduly upset at minor irritations.

CHAPTER NINE

Instincts and Habits

It is a matter of common observation that the lower animals perform many activities without any previous training on the part of the individual. These activities apparently are performed in a definite and uniform manner by all members of the species. Among typical illustrations we may cite the beaver building its dam when of a certain age, at a certain time of the year, and in a tolerably definite manner. The wild-goose migrates southward every year, and again in the spring its well-known honk may be heard as the flock seeks northern latitudes. Honeybees build their comb in an apparently invariable way from year to year; wasps, bumblebees, yellow-jackets, hornets, each have characteristic ways of constructing their nests and of gathering food.

Birds of a given species build nests peculiar to themselves; dogs bury bones; hyenas are ever vigilant; cats play with captured mice; cattle, deer, and other animals, are afraid of red objects, etc. Many animals possess at birth, or almost immediately after, fully developed reactions for food-getting, and many exhibit very early attempts at self-protection from supposed foes. The foregoing activities are denominated as instinctive, and instinct may be defined in a preliminary way as follows: Instinct is an inborn tendency on the part of a given individual to act in a certain way under given stimuli without any foresight necessarily of the end to be accomplished, and without any previous education on the part of the individual.

Marshall has given the following discriminating definition: "Instincts are forces within us which are organic, which appear in us because we are organisms; which lead us to undertake, without forethought, actions of a very complex nature involving the movement of many parts of the body in relations which are more or less fixed, actions which, as the biologists say, are more or less thoroughly co-ordinated."

He illumined the question still further by saying that, "Our instincts are springs of action which exist within the organism: our instinct actions occur because we are organisms, and because as organisms we inherit with our organic structure habits of action which lead to the attainment of certain ends which have significance for the organism; and we inherit these habits in general because our ancestors have become better adapted to their environment in consequence of the recurrence of these tendencies to act in certain specific ways upon the appearance of appropriate stimuli."

Paulsen wrote of instinct: "The bee knows nothing of the brood of winter, and has no insight into the processes of nutrition; she is guided in all her activity, in her search for blossoms, the construction of her cells, the feeding of her offspring, by perceptions and traces of recollection, which are represented physiologically as nervous processes and dispositions." In other words, instincts are race habits, impulses, or tendencies toward activity in a given direction because of ancestral experience which has become so implanted in the race as to make its appearance in the individual a matter wholly reflex in character.

The animal acts in a given way because its nervous mechanism functions in a predetermined manner.

Not Individual Education or Prevision

It is a popular notion that animals which exhibit instincts possess a clear foresight of the ends to be accomplished. "If the bee did not know that it must store up honey for a certain purpose, why should it be so diligent?" "Why should the beaver build its dam if not for definite self-protection and for protection of the expected young?" "Why should the ant store up food except for the long winter?" (It is not because the ant is lethargic all winter and needs no food.) Apparently common sense has a case against us.

But we could cite much evidence to show that the same animals perform instinctive actions when there is absolutely no possibility of such foresight. Among cases which show the utter irrationality of instinctive actions, the following are typical: Well-fed domesticated dogs will bury bones, old shoes, etc., when no necessity exists for providing against future contingencies.

They will do these things without having had a chance to imitate other dogs. As all farmers know, hens will often spend much valuable time in sitting for weeks upon a rude nest with a china egg and acting as important and cross as if the mother of a brood of a dozen. Hens hatched in incubators and without opportunity to imitate the act will perform it just as certainly and naturally as if such opportunity had existed. Now, were the act rational and not reflex, no hen would exhibit such stupidity. Its organism was simply keyed in a certain manner and it had to act in harmony with such demands.

Lloyd Morgan cites the case of the Yucca moth, which performs certain activities but once in a lifetime and those without any possibility of education. The insects emerge from their chrysalis-cases just when the flower opens, each for a single night. From the anthers of one of these flowers the female moth collects the golden pollen and in the pistil of another deposits her eggs among the ovules. The action seems to be the result of fore knowledge. This fertilization of the flower is as necessary as the fertilization of clover blossoms by bumblebees. "These marvellously adaptive instinctive activities of the Yucca moth are performed but once in her life, and that without instruction, with no opportunities of learning by imitation, and, apparently, without pre-vision of what will be the outcome of her behaviour; for she has no experience of the subsequent fate of the eggs she lays, and cannot be credited with any knowledge of the effect of the pollen upon the ovules." There are numberless cases of insects which pass through various metamorphoses, that perform perfectly and almost invariably certain activities, although none of a given generation have ever seen any of a preceding generation.

STUDY OF INSTINCTS

A habit is a resultant of the education of the individual, while instincts are the resultants of accumulated race experiences. These experiences are conserved and accumulated through natural and artificial selection and, according to eminent authorities like Romanes, through the transmission of acquired characters. This last view is as strongly denied by able men like Weismann. To produce a habit the individual must repeat a given series of actions a sufficient number of times to establish an easy path-way of discharge in the nervous system. Instinctive tendencies often have a marked influence in facilitating the formation of some habits.

Reflex action is non-voluntary and usually controlled by lower centres of the nervous system and not by the higher brain centres. I touch a hot stove. An impulse is sent toward the cortex, but when it reaches the spinal cord a current there generated innervates the muscle, causing me to withdraw my hand. In reflective, voluntary action, the higher brain centres are brought into requisition. In a reflex the response to a stimulus is indefinite. The reaction may be for the good of the individual or it may not. It may or may not accomplish an apparently determined end, as in winking to avoid injury to the eye. The line of demarcation between the two is not sharply drawn. Undoubtedly many apparently purely individual reflexes have much of the instinctive elements in them, and all instinctive actions are of the reflex type.

Spencer has denominated instinct as compound reflex action. According to this interpretation the difference may be explained in the words of Lloyd Morgan: "Reflex acts are local responses due to specialised stimuli, while instinctive activities are matters of more general behaviour and usually involving a larger measure of central (as opposed to merely local or ganglionic) coordination and due to the more widely spread effects of stimuli in which both external and internal factors co-operate."

"It would seem, therefore, that, whereas a reflex act—such, for example, as the winking of the eye when an object is seen to approach it rapidly—is a restricted and localised response, involving a particular organ or a definite group of muscles, and is initiated by a more or less specialised external stimulus; an instinctive activity is a response of the organism as a whole, and involves the co-operation of several organs and many groups of muscles. Initiated by an external stimulus or a group of stimuli, it is, at any rate in many cases, determined also in greater degree than reflex action by an internal factor which causes uneasiness or distress, more or less marked, if it do not find its normal instinctive satisfaction."

VARIABILITY OF INSTINCTS

It has been a popular notion that instincts are fixed and invariable in a given species in all its individuals and through successive generations. Nothing could be further from the truth. Instead of coming ready-made once for all, we find that they are products of evolutionary forces. They come into existence, are subject to modifications, and may atrophy or decay, leaving only vestigial evidence or none whatsoever of their existence.

Marshall says that: "The definiteness and the invariability of the co-ordination of these actions are relative definiteness and relative invariability only." This became evident when it was noted that the efficiency of many instincts even of the lower types depends upon the trend of the activities they induce even where there is a certain degree of variation in circumstances of stimulation, or in the stimuli themselves, and consequently in the reactions to these stimuli. The reader will remember that we illustrated this fact by recalling to his mind the variations of action and co-ordination noted in the young chick in its instinctive search for food supply; the general end being reached through slightly varying co-ordinations of action.

"It will also be remembered that as we studied instincts of a higher type we found less definiteness and invariability of reaction, and a marked preponderance of cases where the guidance of our actions to the production of certain ends is attained by the strengthening of trends of action which come to persist through many differences of stimulation and through many variations of reaction."

Genesis of Instincts

Instincts are impulses resulting from the conservation of habits through heredity. Any memory implies habit in the making. The fact of the preservation of a tendency to react at a subsequent time in a way that the organism has acted before is the beginning of a habit. If the activities are repeated a sufficient number of times a genuine habit is formed. This habit means a reflex tendency to react in a similar way at subsequent times on similar occasions. If the habit becomes thoroughly ingrained and children are born subsequent to its formation, the tendency is transmitted. This hereditary tendency or impulse is an instinct. If the given habit becomes widespread in the species and important to their existence, it comes in time to be a race habit, or, as it has been denominated, an instinct. All habits are in fact pseudo-instincts, as Marshall has termed them.

It is not necessary that habits become universal in a species in order to become instinctive, although the universality of possession of a habit is a general criterion of an instinct. There are what may be termed race, national and family instincts. These are characteristics sufficiently universalised to produce the hereditary tendencies in a given line of descent. We speak with perfect psychological propriety of the phlegmatic German, the emotional Frenchman, the stoic Indian, etc. Similarly we may recognise instinctive family tendencies. These are often so strong as to mark a given family in a striking manner. Because of the origin of instincts it follows, even, that each individual has some instinctive tendencies peculiar to himself. The streams of heredity have united in such a way as to make the resultants peculiar to each individual. In fact, no two individuals are exactly alike. Their instincts function at varying times, in different degrees of power, are modified by education in different ways; in fact, present manifold un-uniformities.

INSTINCTS UNDER CHANGE

Although the functioning of instincts is primarily dependent upon the maturity of the organism which causes at the proper time impulsive promptings to action, yet the influence of environment must not be overlooked. The time of building the honeycomb, the time when the beaver builds its dam, the time when the wild-goose will fly northward, the time when the parental instincts are to manifest themselves, are mainly inherent within the organisms themselves. The organisms are in a measure like machines with time alarms. When development has reached a certain point, when the springs have been compressed to a certain tension, release is sure to occur. However, environment may hasten, retard, or even entirely inhibit functioning. The kind of weather, altitude, latitude, amount of sunlight, moisture, etc., all affect the time of flowering and the fruiting periods of plants. Climate, latitude, and conditions of nutrition affect the time of maturity in animals and human beings. It is well known that people in torrid zones mature and decline earlier than in temperate zones.

The difference between the ordinary worker bees and the queen of the hive is largely one of nutrition. All the workers possess potentialities which if nourished would have caused them to develop into maternal bees. Within the first eight days of existence the larvae destined to become workers could by such feeding as the queen larvae receive, be developed into sexually-perfect queens, capable of reproduction. When a queen dies, the workers by royal feeding develop a queen from worker larvae. The potentialities of either worker or queen are inherited, and the particular development is determined by a little more or less nourishment.

House martens now build their nests beneath the eaves of houses while formerly they lived in rocky haunts. Barn swallows also build their mud abodes beneath the eaves of barns. This they cannot have done long because barns are a modern invention. Chimney swallows must have had a different method of nest-building before the invention of chimneys. Domestic ducks in Ceylon have lost their former natural love for water and are entirely terrestrial in their habits, while some other ducks have been known to forsake their marshy haunts and build their nests in trees, bringing their young to the water on their backs. Certain species of Australian parrots that were honey-feeders have become fat-feeders since the development of the sheep industry which enables them to prey upon the carcasses of dead sheep. They have learned to select unerringly certain portions of the carcass which afford the choicest morsels. The polar bear has learned to bite its prey instead of hugging as other bears do. Many transformations in process in whales, seals, dolphins, etc., were alluded to in a former section.

Darwin said apropos of this: "Hardly any animal is more difficult to tame than the young of the wild rabbit; scarcely any animal is tamer than the young of the tame rabbit; but I can hardly suppose that domestic rabbits have often been selected for tameness alone; so that we must attribute at least the greater part of the inherited change from extreme wildness to extreme tameness, to habit and long-continued close confinement."

Modification of Instincts Through Education

The domestication of wild animals affords a vast array of most important illustrations of the transformation of habits, instincts, and even of structure. The testimony should be very suggestive of the possibilities of race transformation in the human-species. Domestic horses have lost most of their primitive wildness and the new instincts of docility render them of inestimable service to man.

The cat in its wild state is one of the fiercest and most untamable of creatures, but once domesticated it is one of the gentlest, and most attached to man. It is a far cry from the fierceness and restlessness of the wolf and the jackal to the domestic dog, but the ancestry of the latter can easily be traced to the former. Contrast the sneaking, ferocious denizens of the forest with well-bred shepherd or Newfoundland dogs which display such affection, fidelity, and sagacity in protecting the interests of their masters. Even among domestic dogs we find great elasticity and variability of instincts and structure—all the result of definite attempts to produce and conserve desirable characteristics. Think of the special instincts of the Newfoundland as compared with the greyhound; those of the Collie with pointers and setters; and each of these as compared with pugs, poodles, and terriers. Each shows the results of generations of education, conservation, and selection.

Should there be any tendency to raise objections that many of these special characteristics are the result of individual training rather than instinct, it must be emphasised again that the special tendencies of different breeds show themselves unfailingly even when the dogs are isolated from all others when young. Romanes shows conclusively how young Coach-dogs will spontaneously run around and bark at horses, how Pointers will point, and Setters will set. He even shows how special traits come to be inherited in particular families of dogs. He quotes from Darwin's MSS, the following: "The Rev. W. Darwin Fox tells me that he had a Skye terrier which when begging rapidly moved her paws in a way very different from that of any other dog which he had ever seen; her puppy, which never could have seen her mother beg, now when full grown performs the same peculiar movement exactly in the same way." In speaking of the tumbling instinct peculiar to certain pigeons, he remarks much to the point: "It would be as impossible to teach one kind of pigeon to tumble as to teach another kind to inflate its crop to the enormous size which the pouter pigeon habitually does." In time the world will come to understand that functions, and among them instinctive functions, are as distinctly heritable as structures, and moreover, that they begin, grow, and develop in precisely the same way.

ANIMAL'S INSTINCTS

Although the lower animals possess a large number of ready-made instinctive reactions which they utilise in their life activities, yet it must not be concluded that all their actions are blind and that nothing of rationality is manifested. Instincts are the fundamental guiding powers, but intelligence, often of a high degree, modifies and to some extent determines the particular direction in which the action shall issue. Even the lowest animals add to instinct through education which the vicissitudes of environment make necessary. This education further lays hold of and, to some degree, controls the instincts. Of course, the types of reaction are determined by latent potentialities, but the details often exhibit great inhibition and control. Romanes's entire volume on animal intelligence is a forceful argument against the theory of blind instinct dominating the life of the lower animals. Many marvellous adaptations which could only result from intelligence are recorded by Romanes, Sir John Lubbock, Lloyd Morgan, and many other writers of reputation. Even in man shall we not say that the types of reaction are largely predetermined by race habits? The applications, however, become so controlled by the life of reason and the directions so complex as to obscure their origins.

To show that the instincts of lower animals may be supplemented by intelligence, I quote from some of the observations and experiments of Huber on bees which are cited by Eimer: "Once the bees had made on a wooden surface the beginning of two combs, one to the right, the other to the left, in such a way that the latter should support an anterior, the former a posterior comb, and the two when finished should be separated by the usual distance between two combs in a hive. But the bees found that they had not allowed sufficient distance. What did they do in order to avoid losing the work already done? They joined the beginnings of the two combs into one. The curvature necessarily produced was in the continuation of the comb completely levelled, so that the lower part of the comb became as regular as one properly commenced."

Eimer says further that: "The skill of the garden spider in building her web no doubt depends on instinct, but only with regard to the main process: here also reflection is exercised on many points. In the mere choice of the place where the net is to be spread the spider needs to take many things into consideration: direction of wind, sunlight, abundance of insects, and, above all, the assurance that the web will be safe from disturbance in the place selected, require a host of intelligent conclusions—the question of security from disturbance alone requires a number. And yet how correctly the spiders usually judge in this very respect."

Wallace is authority for the statement that migrating birds do not fly unerringly to desirable regions. He says: "Thousands annually fly out to sea and perish, showing that the instinct to migrate is imperfect, and is not a good substitute for reason and observation." Romanes remarks that: "Instincts are not rigidly fixed, but are plastic, and their plasticity renders them capable of improvement or of alternation, according as intelligent observation requires." "Thus we see that the oldest and most important instincts in bees and birds admit of being greatly modified, both in the individual and in the race, by intelligent adaptation to changed conditions of life; and therefore we can scarcely doubt that the principle of lapsing intelligence must be of much assistance to that of natural selection in the origination and development of instincts." Conversely it must not be supposed that man acts without instinctive impulses and solely from intelligent guidance. The next paragraph shows very clearly the part played by instinct in man.

INSTINCTS EVERYWHERE

Instincts are ascribed by the uneducated only to animals. Because man comes into the world a very helpless creature and remains so for such a long period, it is thought that human beings possess no instincts. These traits are thought to be special provisions for the guidance of the animals lower than man. But although man is not limited to habitual reactions, either racial or individually acquired, he possesses even more instincts than other animals. The reason we do not recognise instinctive traits in man is because they are exceedingly complex, rendered so through modification by each other, by habits, and by education.

James has said that man possesses all the instincts of the lower animals and many more. This is not literally true. Even though man were a direct descendant of all the lower animals, we should have to remember that recapitulation is not complete. Many organs and functions have been exercised in the course of evolution. Old instincts have died out and new ones have been born. It would, however, be correct to say that man possesses as many instincts as the lower animals and vastly more. Instincts are simply potencies or impulses which cause the individual to act in particular directions. Abilities in music or mathematics are just as truly instincts as the phenomena of nest-building by birds or the spinning of webs by spiders. Wundt says that "the human being is permeated through and through with instinctive action, determined in part, however, by intelligence and volition."

INSTINCTS OF MAN

Among the most readily apparent human instincts the following are typical: Sucking, biting, clasping with fingers or toes, carrying objects to the mouth in childhood, crying, smiling, protrusion of the lips, frowning, gesturing, holding the head erect, sitting up, standing, creeping, walking, climbing, imitation, talking, emulation, rivalry, pugnacity, anger, resentment, sympathy, the hunting instinct, migration; a great many fears or phobias, as of high places, dark places, strange objects; acquisitiveness, constructiveness, play, curiosity, gregariousness, bashfulness, cleanliness, modesty, shame, love, parental feelings, home-making, jealousy, pity.

The list might be made vastly longer. In fact, man is a great complex of tendencies to acting, feeling and thinking in a great variety of directions. These impulses are all instincts. Should some one argue that such a phenomenon as speech is not instinctive, but a result of imitation, I would make the rejoinder "Then why does not my dog learn to speak the same as my child?" They both have the opportunity of hearing and imitating. The very fact that my child learns to speak while my dog does not is evidence that my child possesses a potentiality which my dog does not possess. This tendency or impulse is an instinct. Why is it possible for the cat carried miles away in a bag to find its way back unerringly? Or why can the homing pigeon and the bee fly in 'bee lines', while we human beings make such sorry mistakes concerning directions? Because the cat, the pigeon, and the bee have potentialities which we do not possess.

Any activities or tendencies to action which are universally possessed by a race or species,—which do not have to be learned by the individuals, or which are learned by individuals with great readiness, may be considered as instincts.

FEATURES OF HUMAN INSTINCTS

After having shown how universal and fundamental are instinctive tendencies, an attempt will now be made to indicate something of their educational significance. A few typical instincts will be discussed in detail, but the educational bearings must necessarily be on broad general lines.

Among the earliest human instincts to be exhibited are those of sucking and swallowing. These are absolutely necessary for self-preservation and are about as deep-seated as the automatic cardiac movements, the respiratory and intestinal movements. Some children have been observed to suck the thumb within three minutes after birth. To be sure, sucking and swallowing await the action of a stimulus. Until there is excitation of the proper organs there is no manifestation of the instinctive activity. But this is not the same of pulmonary action, of heart and vascular action, and of intestinal action? The pulmonary muscles and the cardiac muscles do not begin to act until stimulated. Purely physical forces cause the air to fill the vacuum in the nose, mouth, bronchial tubes, and lungs. Thus stimulated, the mechanism, functionally mature, is set in motion. The circulation awaited similar stimulation (about the fifth month of foetal life). Thus the new life once set in motion beats on and on, and a prolonged cessation means death. So the apparatus of sucking, functionally mature, awaited the proper stimulus to make it available for self-preservation.

Grasping

Grasping with fingers and toes is another activity ready to function at birth. New-born infants grasp objects with the hand, and sometimes even with the toes. The ability to grasp with the toes almost dies out through disuse, but the ability to grasp objects with the hand develops because of its great importance as a means of self-preservation, Educationally it is also an important means of knowledge-getting. During the first weeks and months of the child's life he is enabled to get a great many ideas of the various qualities of objects: tastes, hardness, roughness, smoothness, shapes, etc. Distances and sizes are measured by the experience gained in reaching, which is a part of grasping, and in touching. The experiences thus gained are fundamental in all later knowledge of the world of things. The child should be provided with objects whereby this instinct may be exercised. While he is learning to seize more accurately and to grasp more firmly and accurately he is learning many ideas that are basal in later concepts. The sucking instinct and the instinct for putting everything in the mouth, although detrimental in many instances, still aid the little one in his exploration of the material qualities of things. I have noticed a child of seven months exercise much care in carrying a rough pine stick to his mouth. As soon as he begins normally to grasp after things he should be supplied with various objects to handle. This is especially true when he begins to sit alone.

Locomotion

The instinct for locomotion prompts the child to execute movements which are destined to multiply indefinitely his range of explorations. First by creeping, crawling, rolling, or sliding he manages to propel himself about his limited world. This is, of course, one of those deferred, instincts which manifest themselves only when functional maturity of the centres involved becomes complete. Through a fear that the child will soil his clothes by creeping, many mothers very injudiciously discourage all efforts at creeping or any other means of locomotion other than walking. Besides being a potent means of strengthening chest-muscles, lungs, arms, and other parts of the body, creeping is an absolutely necessary means of education. No greater sin could be committed against the child than by curtailing his infantile efforts at personal locomotion. By locomotion the child not only acquires accurate knowledge of hundreds of objects and their qualities, but all the senses are receiving definite training and development.

The two requisites for the development of the senses, as noted elsewhere, are proper nutriment and stimulation. If either be lacking or in excess, the results are detrimental. It would, of course, be absurd to try to force upon the child's notice a multitude of sensory impressions. Over-stimulation, such as may be produced by too much playing with children, keeping them up at unreasonable hours, arousing from sleep to exhibit to admiring friends, etc., is positively harmful. It may produce precocity, but the final outcome may be unstrung nerves or arrested development. Too often the baby is played with, in reality to amuse the elders, under the pretext or the mistaken idea that the baby needs amusement. The rule should be to furnish the child sufficient materials to satisfy his capricious interests, but to let the child be the pacemaker. When it is hard work to amuse the baby, something besides amusement is needed. The little nerves are probably already overwrought, and rest and quiet, possibly sleep, are needed.

As soon as the child begins to walk, his ideas begin to expand wonderfully. Whereas his sense perceptions were confined mainly to the house through the creeping stage, he now, if properly treated, begins to explore the region round about, sometimes to the annoyance of the neighbours and the embarrassment of his parents. But the only way to understand the world is to travel. The one, child or adult, who sticks by the home fireside always remains provincial and circumscribed in ideas. Children's vocabularies are good indexes of the extent of their explorations. The children who have not seen rivers, hills, trees, birds, cows, and other animals; trains, engines, and mills, do not have these words in their vocabularies. A city child of even three years old increases its vocabulary and its stock of ideas amazingly by being taken into the country. The country child undergoes the same change by going into city environment. Thus the instinct for locomotion is a most important means to advantageous educational ends.

Expression

Children often invent gesture language. Deaf-mutes also do so, even when isolated from speaking people. Ribot quotes Gerando as saying that: "Children of about seven years old who have not yet been educated, make use of an astonishing number of gestures.... in communicating with each other." As a further illustration of this spontaneous, natural language, he says that: "Gerando and others after him remarked that deaf-mutes in their native state communicate easily with one another. He enumerates a long series of ideas which they express in their mimicry and gestures, and many of these expressions are identical in all countries."

This instinct for expression should receive proper attention. As soon as the child manifests a desire to communicate his ideas in speech, his crude, spontaneous, and more deliberative attempts should be encouraged. Instead of mimicking the child in his baby expressions and helping to fix the wrong form in his mind, one should repeat for him the correct form distinctly and encourage the child (not nag him) to imitate. The vocal organs are now ripe for utterance and should be exercised. If the child does not develop the speech organs during this nascent period he will ever be slow, halting, or deficient in the use of words. Certainly it is that new words are accumulated with amazing rapidity during this budding period. The two years old child has amassed, within a year, from three hundred to twelve hundred words, representing ideas, and may have as many more parrot-words; *i.e.*, sounds imitated without an understanding of the meanings. These latter have been gathered from rhymes, jingles, and from conversation not understood and from chance association of sounds with objects or actions. Now, even these parrot-words are important, for they gradually acquire fulness of meaning. Words are, as Dr. Harris has said, like bags; once acquired they hold all the perceptions and reflections that relate to the idea symbolized by the word.

Not only should the child be assisted in enunciation, but his environment should be such as to lead to the production of ideas. Although I do not coincide with the renowned Max Muller that there can be no thinking without words, yet it is doubtless true that the best thinking utilizes words as instruments. The child that is properly environed, who gratifies his appetite for seeing, hearing, and touching things, who is led to think about these things (for thinking does not hurt children), and who is not overstimulated, will as surely acquire words as mature people acquire tools to accomplish their mechanical work.

The instinct of curiosity, the constructive instinct, and the inborn tendency to play, all co-operate in the acquisition of language. The child must see and examine things for himself; he should not stumble upon them all by chance; designedly he should be led to where things are; he must be helped to see them right; he must have facts told about them; he must be questioned about them; and above all, he must have questions answered that he will surely ask. In this way he will pick up much language; he will have given to him many new words; he will ask terms from you, and he will even coin them for himself.

Curiosity

The child, through his instinctive curiosity, is a born investigator. Normally he pulls things to pieces to see how they are made and how they go. His unwise elders often condemn what they believe to be innate destructiveness, but he is simply trying to satisfy his craving for knowledge. To keep alive this instinct and further its normal development is high teaching art. Too often before the end of school life the instinct has completely atrophied. To get the college student to desire to know is the most difficult task before the college instructor. Not infrequently before the college is reached all knowledge is taken in prescribed doses and largely because ill consequences are feared if directions are not followed.

Curiosity is a fundamental instinct, observable far down in the scale of animal life. It is apt to be coupled with fear in the presence of strange objects. Who has not seen horses, cattle, sheep, and swine hovering around a newly discovered and strange object, oftentimes walking round and round, hovering in its vicinity, but ever with nerves tense ready to make off with the greatest speed on the discovery of apparently harmful or undesirable signs? Any one who has tried to catch a horse in a pasture by luring him with a pretence of food has received a lasting remembrance of this blending of curiosity and fear. Fowls and birds exhibit the same characteristics. Small children, and even adults, often manifest similar states. I have seen my child of one year cry with fear on seeing an umbrella, but no amount of persuasion could bring her away from its vicinity, so fascinating it seemed. Who has not gone through a dark wood, a dark room, all quaking with fear but curious to ferret out some mystery? Every one would fain take a turn at hunting for spooks in a haunted house. Sully tells us that: "A very tiny child, on first making acquaintance with some form of physical pain, as a bump on the head, will deliberately repeat the experience by knocking his head against something as if experimenting and watching the effect." This is clearly a case of curiosity overpowering fear.

Spencer says:

"Whoever has watched, with any discernment, the wide-eyed gaze of the infant at surrounding objects, knows very well that education does begin thus early, whether we intend it or not; and that these fingerings and suckings of everything it can lay hold of, these open-mouthed listenings to every sound, are the first steps in the series which ends in the discovery of unseen planets, the invention of calculating engines, the production of great paintings, or the composition of symphonies and operas. This activity of the faculties from the very first being spontaneous and inevitable, the question is whether we shall supply in due variety the materials on which they may exercise themselves; and to the question so put, none but an affirmative answer can be given." Lloyd Morgan gives expression to a coincident opinion where he says: "Herein, then, lies the utility of the restlessness, the exuberant activity, the varied playfulness, the prying curiosity, the inquisitiveness, the meddlesome mischievousness, the vigorous and healthy experimentalism of the young."

Activity and Constructiveness

A child of six months accidentally knocks two tin cans together and discovers that he has done something. He immediately strives to continue this experiment, and his beaming countenance gives ample evidence of the satisfaction gained. At eight months my child accidently dropped a teaspoon upon the floor. When the teaspoon was given to the child again, he at once began to exert himself to repeat the dropping process. After that, whenever the spoon was given to him the dropping recurred. Evidently the child's desire to repeat the action was prompted not so much by the pleasurable noise as the satisfaction of doing something. From the time children can walk I have found them anxious to do things that grown-up people do. They are anxious to dust, sweep, wash, iron, bake, make beds, carry things, read, write, and go on errands. They are called lazy a little later on, but I believe that a normal healthy child has not a lazy fibre in its make-up. Their muscles, nerves, and senses are hungry for exercise, and every effort is made by the child to satisfy these cravings. The child may be lazy in the sense that your particular kind of occupation may be repugnant to him, but if you watch the little feet trot all day you can hardly have the heart to call him lazy.

Constructiveness is a fundamental instinct of so much importance as to merit special consideration. All children exhibit early tendencies toward making things. I have noticed a child of seven months trying to place one block upon another in imitation of other children. Miss Shinn tells us that her niece as early as seven months would not listen contentedly to older persons playing the piano, but that she was satisfied only when trying it herself.

In these inborn tendencies to activity and constructiveness are the teacher's and parent's golden opportunities. The parent should encourage the little ones to help. In this way the work habit will be instilled, and by the time the child is five years of age it may save its mother many steps every day. It can pick up and put away its own playthings, and run on errands (I have known four years old to go half a mile and purchase correctly things from a store and to go daily for little grocery orders in the near neighbourhood). Most children are born carpenters; that is, the love of carpenter's tools is well-nigh universally manifested among healthy children.

They want to hammer, and saw, and make. A child can have no more useful educative appliances than a hammer, some nails, and boards into which he may have full liberty to drive the nails. I have noticed children of two years amuse themselves in this way for hours at a time. They may not develop into carpenters when grown up, but they have gained an education through the process. It is a pity that children cannot have a set of tools and that instead of having all their toys, sleds, carts, etc., made for them they are not allowed and encouraged to construct them for themselves.

James has put the matter very aptly in the following paragraph: "Constructiveness is the instinct most active; and by the incessant hammering and sawing, and dressing and undressing dolls, putting of things together and taking them apart, the child not only trains the muscles to co-ordinate action, but accumulates a store of physical conceptions which are the basis of his knowledge of the material world through life. Object teaching and manual training wisely extend the sphere of this order of acquisitions. Clay, wood, metals, and the various kinds of tools are made to contribute to the store.

A youth brought up with a sufficiently broad basis of this kind is always at home in the world. He stands within the pale. He is acquainted with Nature, and Nature in a certain sense is acquainted with him. Whereas the youth brought up alone at home, with no acquaintance with anything but the printed page, is always afflicted with a certain remoteness from the material facts of life, and a correlative insecurity of consciousness which makes of him a kind of alien on the earth in which he ought to feel himself perfectly at home...... Moreover,.... how important for life,—for the moral tone of life, quite apart from definite practical pursuits,—is this sense of readiness for emergencies which a man gains through early familiarity and acquaintance with the world of material things.

To have grown up on a farm, to have haunted a carpenter's and blacksmith's shop, to have handled horses and cows and boats and guns, and to have ideas and abilities connected with such objects are an inestimable part of youthful acquisition. After adolescence it is rare to be able to get into familiar touch with any of these primitive things. The instinctive propensions have faded, and the habits are hard to acquire. "Accordingly, one of the best fruits of the 'child-study' movement has been to reinstate all these activities to their proper place in a sound system of education. Feed the growing human being, feed him with the sort of experience for which from year to year he shows a natural craving, and he will develop in adult life a sounder sort of mental tissue, even though he may seem to be 'wasting' a great deal of his growing time, in the eyes of those for whom the only channels of learning are books and verbally communicated information."

Play

The educative value of the play instinct has been recognized by kindergartners since the time of Froebel. It has recently received much study by others, and undoubtedly is means of intellectual and moral discipline. I believe that both free play and regulated play whose ends are certain discipline, are valuable. In the first five or even six years the play should be almost entirely free play, without adult restrictions imposed upon it. In the first place, the tonic effects of play upon the nervous system are of great moment. When mental exercise has been engaged in which absorbs one part of the brain only, free play causes what Warner designates as 'augmenting, spreading movements' of nervous energy. The spontaneous play calls into action fresh brain areas and the successive discharges from one centre to other centres serve to reinforce the nerve currents as they proceed to the muscle which produces visible action. A good laugh, which usually accompanies free play, being a series of acts commencing with small muscles and ending with the large ones, may completely change the previous mode of brain action. To remove temporary fatigue there is absolutely no substitute for the good old-fashioned recess, with its laugh and shout and capering wildly about.

Play, then, during the early stage of childhood before the child has gained control over the accessory muscles should be largely spontaneous and unrestricted. I say largely, because even then something may be done to regulate and direct play which does not involve fine co-ordinations. The kindergarten games which include movements involving the larger muscles of the trunk, those controlling the head, arms, legs, etc., may be engaged in to great advantage. These should have in view the exercise of the social instincts. Many little social duties and amenities may be thoroughly inculcated in children through play which is organized and directed by the teacher. My children had a birthday party the other day.

The whole direction of the affair was given by the mother. They were helped to arrange the little table, were assigned places, given a few directions, and through imitation of others they carried out the rest of the programme. Now the little games which the kindergartner directs (though she may seem to be asking their advice) are of immense value in helping children through imitation and obedience to learn the fundamental laws of society. These plays should certainly be well adapted to the capacity of the children, never predominantly inhibitive or restraining, rather the reverse. But enough of control should be sought to lead the child to form habits of self-control. It must be done by easy gradients. It is like gradually training the colt by accustoming him early to the halter, to being led, and to being bridled, so that when his colt-hood is ready for the harness he needs no 'breaking.'

The entirely unrestrained child is like the wild horse; subsequently he may be broken but is never safe. A violent outbreak may be expected at the least unusual occurrence. It has been shown by several writers that many boy's organizations (base-ball teams, etc.) do not hang together well but go to pieces on slight provocations. Bryan concludes from this that therefore play up to about twelve years "should be unhampered, spontaneous and careless of ends." While I recognize the fact that children do not hold together in 'team work' of themselves, I should be inclined to attribute it to the very fact that childhood cannot produce leadership. In Professor Bryan's own words in the same article: "Unquestioned obedience to rational, intelligent authority should be the principle in the management of young children, and freedom from this principle will increase with the development of the child."

From a considerable observation of kindergarten games and household games of children, I am led to believe that their enjoyment is in no way curtailed by wise direction, and certainly the educative features derived are much superior to the play that is entirely 'careless of ends.' The child in his spontaneous play is not always 'careless of the end.' My little girl of five goes coasting, and of her own free will and with no instruction save imitation and experience has learned to steer the sled almost as skilfully as an adult.

Children of eight or ten often learn to skate beautifully, learn to ride bicycles in a manner that puts to blush the adult, and it is all play to them. Now provided they enter into organised games with the same zest, and I believe they may, why is it not as much play when directed? It should be no more hurtful to the child to cheerfully obey simple directions in a kindergarten game than to learn to 'pat-a-cake', to learn to button his own clothes (which my children have begged to do), to learn to hold a knife and fork properly, to maintain reasonable silence in presence of company and at the table, etc.

The social instinct is one that early exhibits itself. The babe of a few weeks old shows signs of lonesomeness when left alone, especially if it has been much tended. By the time the child is five or six months old absence of accustomed members of the family, especially children, causes no little irritability, Perhaps a caution may be thrown out against over-stimulation of the immature nerves during the early days of childhood.

If allowed too much companionship, although he enjoys it, the child may become irritable and his normal growth be seriously hindered. By the sixth month the child may safely watch other children at play for some hours daily. A little later on he will take a hand in playing with objects on his own account. The child should be the one to manifest a desire to play with things. This is first exhibited by grasping as indicated above. Too often, however, things are forced upon him by nurses who seek to keep his quiet by continually increasing the stimuli, The more the child frets the harder they toss, and pat, and pinch, and tickle, and talk, and sing. What the babe needs under such symptoms is something that will act as a sedative, *i.e.*, to be left alone and to have quiet around him.

The social instinct furnishes a starting-point for the complete training of the individual for his place in society. The laws of the society can be learned only by being in social organizations. A child isolated from the world grows up a social monster, because of the abnormal development of his selfish nature. Rousseau taught that man is by nature a pure being becoming corrupt by contact with artificial society. Therefore he isolates himself from his fellows from birth to manhood. But such an individual could not live in society because he has found no place in it. Law and order, the basis of our social fabric, are meaningless to him. Hence the child must learn the fundamentals of social organizations by subjecting himself to the restrictions imposed by society for the benefit of the whole and the individuals composing the whole.

The family is the first to impose restrictions and extend privileges. Instinctively the child learns about the family organization and also instinctively imitates their reactions toward one another. By this undesigned process the child unconsciously forms numberless habits, which will be priceless to him through all his life. He learns, or should learn, how to treat his parents, brothers and sisters, strangers, how to behave at the table, not to disturb family or neighbourhood peace, etc. But even this would leave him undisciplined in multiple essentials of the relationships imposed by society at large.

There is the school toward which the child instinctively yearns to go. I believe all children want to go to school not because it is school, but because many children are there. Now, too early formal school work is injurious, but there is the kindergarten and if properly conducted it is a blessing to all children. There the children can assemble and under pure, wholesome influences, through exercises appealing to the instincts of sociability, expression, and constructiveness, learn through play some of the most valuable lessons of their lives.

Children of the most disagreeably selfish dispositions may with little or no coercion develop the control and proper emotional attitude for most amiable actions. Through imitation of their fellows, they learn to do many things which could not be beaten into them, and they drop many habits which could never have been beaten out of them.

PSYCHO-GENESIS AND LAW

The great contribution of evolution has been in rendering a new interpretation of the origin of present modes of activity. Instead of regarding any action as causeless or as supernatural, it finds an explanation of the present in the records of the past. Dr. Stanley Hall in particular has given an entirely new meaning to education. His great admonition is to study the actual child of today if we wish to develop an ideal man of tomorrow; and if we would know the real child of today, we must not only view him as he is, but we must know him historically. The paleo-psychio records of race growth must be searched diligently to know how the child of today came to be what he is. Then only are we ready to plan for the morrow. Otherwise our blunderings may cause only arrests, retardations, and malformations.

He says:

> "Man is not a permanent type but an organism in a very active stage of evolution toward a more permanent form. Our consciousness is but a single stage and one type of mind; a late, partial, and perhaps essentially abnormal and remedial outcrop of the great underlying life of man-soul. The animal, savage, and child soul can never be studied by introspection." Dr. Hall has emphasized more strikingly than any one else how each individual comes into the world freighted with all the influences of the past. Though each rational being undergoes great modification, yet the initiation of most phenomena of the present has its origin in the remote past and can only be understood by comprehending that past. Evolutionary history is the key to the understanding of the present and no great progress in education can ever be effected without the prophecy made possible by revelation of what and how the present came to be. He further writes: "We must go to school to the folk-soul, learn of criminals and defectives, animals,

and in some sense go back to Aristotle in rebasing psychology on biology, and realize that we know the soul best when we can write its history in the world, and that there are no finalities save formulas of development. The soul is thus still in the making, and we may hope for an indefinite further development.... There are powers in the soul that slumber like the sleepers in myth, partially aroused, it may be, in great personal or social crises, but some time to be awakened to dominance. In a word, the view here represents a nascent tendency and is in striking contrast to all those systems that presume to have attained even an approximate finality." In his classical study of fears, Dr. Hall also wrote: "We must assume the capacity to fear or to anticipate pain, and to associate it with certain objects and experiences, as an inherited *Anlage*, often of a far higher antiquity than we are wont to suppose."

In this way he has sought an explanation of the multitude of activities which have hitherto been merely catalogued and regarded as static or supernaturally given. In his psychology and pedagogy everything has a natural history. Royce has contributed much in the same direction in his *Outlines of Psychology*, in which he explains initiative, docility, will, and conduct as the resultant of complex impulses which are the outgrowths of inherited and individual experiences that become organized into latent tendencies.

PAST VS. PRESENT

The beginnings of all great types of action have their roots far back in the past, that is, they are instinctive. Even conception, judgement, and reason—which we are apt to regard as the antipodes of instinct—are themselves in part instinctive.

The more efficient they are, the greater the instinctive capital with which they start. Royce has said of walking, creeping, etc., that their mastery was "very slowly reached as the result of a training whose details were nowhere predetermined by heredity, while on the other hand, every step of the process was indeed predetermined by hereditary constitution to tend, in the normal child, toward a result that would give it, under the circumstances of its individual life, the powers of locomotion suited to a human being."

In a similar manner Marshall accounts for religion, duty, and conscience upon a genetic basis. He says: "We here conceive of conscience as the protest of a persistent instinct against a less persistent, but momentarily more powerful one, and we are led to the belief that conscience has been evolved by natural evolutionary forces. We are thus led, therefore, to look upon conscience as being in general the surest guide we have to mark the way in which we should direct our lives if we would act in accord with what we call the law of development." Oliver Wendell Holmes wrote: "But mind this: the more we observe and study, the wider the range of the automatic and instinctive principles in body, mind, and morals, and the narrower the limits of the self-determining conscious movement."

Dr. Hall says: "There is one thing in nature, and one alone, fit to inspire all true men and women with more awe and reverence than Kant's starry heavens, and that is the soul and the body of the healthy young child. Heredity has freighted it with all the accumulated results of parental well and ill-doing, and filled it with reverberations from a past more vast than science can explore; and on its right development depends the entire future of civilization two or three decades hence. Simple as childhood seems, there is nothing harder to know; and responsive as it is to every influence about it, nothing is harder to guide. To develop childhood to virtue, power, and due freedom is the supreme end of education, to which everything else must be subordinated as means. Just as to command inanimate nature we must constantly study, love, and obey her, so to control child-nature we must first and perhaps still more piously study, love, obey it. The best of us teachers have far more to learn from children than we can ever hope to teach them; and what we succeed in teaching, at least beyond the merest rudiments, will always be proportionate to the knowledge we have the wit to get from and about them."

INITIAL PERIODS

The term nascent period is employed in chemistry to designate that state of a compound in which it is just beginning to form. It has already come into use in biological interpretations of education to indicate the time of the budding of instincts. The instinct begins to manifest itself when the organism is mature or ripe in development. Structure and function develop together.

Consequently whenever a new instinctive tendency appears it is indicative of the approaching maturity of the correlative structure. Baldwin has called attention to the fact that the instinct for vocal speech begins to manifest itself synchronously with the preferred use of the right hand. Up to the age of eight or nine months the child is ambidextrous. During the same period no attempt has been made to talk. Since they arise at the same time and since the centres controlling the two functions are so closely situated. Baldwin regards the two processes as functionally related and as having the same nascent period. My own experiment with children confirm Baldwins' conclusions.

A study of the prominent human instincts shows that there are nascent periods in the development of each of them. Fear is not displayed at birth, but develops after a few months. Walking is deferred from nine to twenty-four months; curiosity is scarcely worthy the name for some years; the collecting instinct is not noticed in most children for some years; the sex instinct, the parental instinct, the religious instinct, all have their special budding periods. During these periods the golden opportunity for their cultivation is presented.

Nascent Periods in Motor Development

Mosso wrote: "In man the brain develops later than in all other animals/ because his muscles also develop later. The striped muscles are more incomplete at birth in man than in any other animal. For this fact that the human brain develops so slowly, I am able to discover no other reason than this, that at birth the organs which effect movement over which the brain exercises its authority, are not yet complete."

He says further:

"If we wish to hasten the maturity of the brain, we must decide whether the formation of the myelin can better be hastened by stimulations of the senses and intellectual work, or better by muscular exercises. The latter way seems to be the more natural. We must, therefore, to begin with, consolidate the motor nerve paths which develop first, and after that seek to develop the portion of the brain concerned with intellectual work. Modern views show a tendency to confirm what the great philosophers of Greece already recognised, *viz.*, that children ought to begin to read and write only with the tenth year. The conviction is again slowly maturing that our children begin to learn too early, that it is injurious for the development of the brain to be fettered to the school-desk when only five or six years old. The conviction is slowly making its way that no more time should be devoted to intellectual work than to muscular exercise. The modern education of youth, however, resembles more an artificial hot-house culture than a natural training of the human plant."

Similarly we may regard the progress of development of all inherent capacities and powers. Even those more indefinite powers, like power of mechanical memory, ability to learn abstract arithmetic and grammar, have their periods of budding vigour when their cultivation can be best effected. The chapters on motor ability and on the development from fundamental to accessory, give ample evidence that the child of five has very little control of the accessory muscles. Manual dexterity requiring fine co-ordinations should not be attempted in childhood. Fine writing and the use of small tools should be deferred until later. The nascent period for the acquisition of manual skill is early youth. The maximum dexterity is not attained then, but the cultivation must then begin if the fullest fruitage is to ensue. Many superintendents are convinced that manufal training in its complete forms should be begun not later than the grammar grades. Authorities in colleges of engineering argue for manual training in the secondary schools because those who defer it until the college is reached fail to acquire the same degree of skill. To gain great skill in playing the piano and other musical instruments, it is well understood that it is absolutely necessary to begin in early life.

Nascent Period for Language

There is a special period in the life of the child when his capacity and interest in acquiring vocalized speech are at their best. The child gives abundant evidence of this period by his constant chatterings and his amazing acquisitions. In a few months he acquires a vocabulary which would take an adult as many years to acquire. This period is at its best from about one and a half years to ten or twelve. During this period the child should be in an environment where, through imitation, he can absorb without difficulty all the knowledge of the mother tongue that he will ever need for practical purposes. An ordinary child of a dozen years of age who has been reared in a refined home where correct language is spoken and who has had ample opportunity to talk will be able without schooling to use his mother tongue with facility, force and precision.

During the same nascent language period there is a golden opportunity for acquiring the ability to speak foreign languages. There is abundant evidence that ordinary children can, in addition to their native tongue, master two or three foreign languages as spoken languages by the time they are ten years of age. This means that they can understand readily what they hear and can use effectively the language in expressing their ideas orally. We have wholesale illustrations of the fact that childhood is the nascent period for acquiring a spoken language. Foreigners who come to this country in childhood acquire such a mastery of the language in a few months that they cannot be distinguished from the native-born. The parents of the same children, however, seldom acquire the language so as to use it with any great degree of precision or skill. It is not because they do not try but because the vocal organs and the centres controlling them have passed beyond the nascent period of economical functioning in new ways. Children who have acquired these accomplishments know as much of arithmetic, geography, and of other usual school subjects as do the children who have not acquired the additional languages. The children suffer no impairment of health because of the additional acquisitions.

And in spite of such ample evidence we persist in America in organizing our curricula in such a way as to give practically no opportunity to learn foreign languages until too late. To the objection that there is no time, it should be said that there is abundant time if we only would arrange the curriculum so as to adapt it to the stages of development of the unfolding child. We are uneconomical in forcing things at unseasonable times. The Germans and the French can teach us how to arrange our curriculum so as not to waste so much of the child's time.

"The introduction of athletics affords a striking illustration of the decline of the learning power with the progressing years. When golf first came in it was considered an excellent game for the middle-aged; and you have all watched the middle-aged man play. He was so awkward, he could not do it. Day after day the man of forty, fifty, or even older, would go to the golf field, hoping each time to acquire a sure stroke, but never really acquiring it. The young man learned better, but the good golf players are those who begin as children, twelve and fourteen years of age, and in a few months become as expert and sure as their fathers wished to become, but could not. In bicycling it was the same. Eight lessons were considered the number necessary to teach the intelligent adult to ride a wheel. Three for a child of eight. And an indefinite number of lessons, ending in failure, for a person of seventy...... As in every study of biological facts, there is in the study of senescent mental stability the principle of variation to be kept in mind. Men are not alike. The great majority of men lose the power of learning, doubtless some more and some less, we will say, at twenty-five years. Few men after twenty-five are able to learn much. They who cannot, become day-labourers, mechanics, clerks of a mechanical order. Others probably can go on somewhat longer, and obtain higher positions; and there are men who, with extreme variations in endowment, preserve the power of active and original thought far on into life. These of course are the exceptional men, the great men."

GREAT INTERESTS AND INSTINCTS

It is no less true that there are nascent periods for acquiring a knowledge of abstract grammar, abstract arithmetic, philosophy, science, and other subjects. Every great interest presupposes a corresponding innate ability. No one ever developed a great headway of interest in anything for which he did not possess some real capacity. The boy who can without training sprint a hundred yards in eleven seconds is interested in reducing his time to ten seconds; but the clumsy fellow who requires fifteen or more seconds develops no special interest in sprinting—that is, in sprinting himself. He may develop the gambler's interest in seeing others sprint. Many think they are interested in football and other sports, but most of them are merely interested in being amused, not in participating. Only those with innate abilities are so interested. Similarly with music, art, mathematics, or language. The interest which leads people to be patient workers and producers in any of these lines is coupled with inherent capacity in the given direction.

On the extreme importance of recognizing nascent periods in education, Dr. Balliet remarks: "There is a nascent period for each physical and mental power, a period of rapid growth when new aptitudes and interests are developing. It is our dense ignorance of most of these nascent periods that makes it impossible for us as yet to prepare a proper course of study. Hence our courses of study are little more than conscientious guesses. When we shall know more about these nascent periods, we shall be able to arrange a course in which the various phases of every study will be presented at the proper period when they will appeal most strongly to the child. Such a course of study must take into account three types of children...... the observer, the thinker, and the doer. The last type has but recently been recognized in education."

Many Instincts Transitory—It has only recently become understood that instincts are not functional in a fixed manner all through life. Most people, for example, think that wildness, methods of food-getting, etc, are given once for all and are in no way affected by individual experience, *i.e.*, education. But two important laws should be remembered in this connection: (*a*) Many instincts develop at a certain age and then disappear; (*b*) Many instincts, if unexercised or unaided by environment, fail entirely to develop, or remain stunted and dwarfed.

Every one knows that playfulness is a characteristic of the young rather than of the adult. That the adult does not play is not a matter of environment or circumstances, but a result of the fading of the instinctive impulse to play. Tadpoles breathe by means of gills instead of lungs; the frog naturally adopts a new mode of existence in response to new instincts and in consequence of the passing of old ones. The young calf instinctively follows, but in time the tendency fades. The young child at first instinctively gets food by sucking, but later the impulse fades and is replaced by a no less instinctive tendency to bite and chew. Allusion was earlier made to the instinctive function of swimming movements, and the transient power of infants to hang by their hands. In fact, numberless rudimentary instincts, like vestigial organs, come into function, survive a brief time, and then either partially or completely atrophy. In a sense all the organs and functions of infancy are rudimentary. They subserve a purpose for a given stage and then give way to a higher form.

Atrophy of Unexercised Instincts

Spalding, the renowned observer of animal habits, tells of a friend of his who "reared a gosling in the kitchen, away from all water. When this bird was some months old, and was taken to a pond, it not only refused to go into the water, but when thrown in scrambled out again, as a hen would have done. Here was an instinct entirely suppressed." All dogs have an instinct to bury bones, old shoes, gloves, and other articles. It was doubtless necessary for their ancestors to bury food for self-preservation. James remarks that dogs brought up for the first few weeks of life on a hard floor where there is no possibility of really burying anything, will nevertheless obey the promptings of instinct and will make an attempt to bury sundry articles. The futile attempts are, however, abandoned after a time and are not repeated all through life. The lack of exercise of the instinct was the cause of its atrophy. Spalding and James both record that calves and chicks, which always manifest the instinct to follow the mother, lose this impulse in a few days if put under different environment which develops other habits.

DEVELOPMENT CHOCKED

In case of boys and girls, the latter grasp the subject much more easily and better than the former. The minds of the adults become so habituated to thinking the elementary processes that a transition to higher processes are rendered difficult. While we should fix, in the form of habits, all activities that must be continually repeated in the same way, yet we should guard against too definite crystallization of thought processes. Every habit tends to enslave its possessor. Pupils and parents are continually making a mistake in requesting that the children be allowed to "go over subjects again so as to get them thoroughly." If it is found inadvisable because of immaturity to promote children who have made a reasonable passing grade, it would be far better to have them take new matter of an elementary nature rather than to review all the old material in exactly the same fashion. A pupil should never be kept back in all his studies because of failure in a part of them.

Arrest occurs (*a*) through the premature or excessive exercise of a function or (*b*) through lack of exercise during the nascent stage. Not only do physical and intellectual arrests occur, but also emotional, volitional, and moral arrest may as easily ensue through the same causes. Darwin tells us with great sadness in his later years of his utter inability to appreciate music and aesthetic effects in general. He attributed the lack to atrophy, due to disuse. His extreme devotion to an intellectual ideal had left no room for aesthetic culture. It is a pity that the beautiful in nature and art has not been considered of as great importance as the crassly utilitarian.

A survey of our almost parkless cities, undecorated or fussy architecture, the lack of beautiful paintings, the ugly house interiors, the bleak farms without trees, flowers, or artificial adornment, all attest that we are pursuing methods, which tend to stifle all aesthetic impulse. The lack of adornment and beautification in life, however, is certainly not because of total degeneracy in aesthetic life. The fact that even the working people will select the best music and the best art when free to them is evidence enough of aesthetic instincts which struggle for assertion.

The will may suffer arrest in a great variety of directions. The child who is always pampered and never required to exercise deliberation or put forth effort, grows up with undisciplined powers. When the power of control would make him a conqueror he finds himself the slave of appetite and passion, and the victim of chance environment. Every drunkard despises himself in his sane moments and yearns for the nobility of self-control, but the flabby will cannot withstand the tempter's voice. Habits of virtue and righteousness have never been established and all the wishes and yearnings he can muster are overpowered by the habits of vacillation or of absolute unrighteousness.

In the case of undesirable instincts it is well to know when and how to arrest development. Royce has very aptly said that "childhood is a great region of life for the sprouting and first springing of the young weeds of future mental disorder. The full-grown maladies of the asylums need older brains to live in; but child psychology is often full of elements from which future troubles may come. It therefore behooves the teacher of young children to be, if possible, psychologist enough to know, and by sight too, those symptoms of instability of brain which are so common in early years."

Hall wrote that systematic gymnastic exercises applied at the right time may produce immediate and often surprising development of lung capacity. The same attempts with boys of twelve utterly fail because the nascent period has not yet come. Donaldson demonstrated that forcing open the eyelid of a young kitten prematurely and stimulating with light arrested the development of medullation. He also wrote of arrested development in another connection, saying: "Development and the changes involved in growing old, are by no means synonymous, so that although in those animals with a fixed size there are always to be found undeveloped cells, yet it is not a correct inference that these cells are also young in the sense that they might still complete their development. It appears, rather, that the capacity for undergoing expansive change is transient, and that those cells which fail to react during the proper growing period of an animal have lost their opportunity forever."

Mistaken notions concerning the teaching of arithmetic and grammar have doubtless been responsible for a multitude of pedagogical sins. The formalist regards the course of study as a pedagogical grindstone upon which the wits of the child are to be sharpened. We remember in this connection Robert Recorde's arithmetic book called *The Whetstone of Witte*. Mathematics is said to develop the reasoning powers and many have believed that the earlier it could be introduced the greater would be the development. Little children have been forced to take it in allopathic doses in the hope of prying up their reasoning powers. Abstractions in grammar have been likewise forced upon them. Not only have the children failed to comprehend the abstractions, but their reasoning powers have been stunted and dwarfed rather than developed. The forcing process caused arrest of development.

Dr. Harris, former Commissioner of Education, was the first to call attention in a striking way to the subject of arrested development in education caused through overtraining. He remarked that the attempt of many teachers, in their very zeal for good teaching, "to secure what is called thoroughness in the branches taught in the elementary schools, is often carried too far; in fact, to such an extent as to produce arrested development (a sort of mental paralysis) in the mechanical and formal stages of growth.

The mind in that case loses its appetite for higher methods and wider generalizations. The law of apperception, we are told, proves that the temporary methods of solving problems should not be so thoroughly mastered as to be used involuntarily, or as a matter of unconscious habit, for the reason that a higher and more adequate method will then be found difficult to acquire. The more thoroughly a method is learned, the more it becomes a part of the mind, and the greater the repugnance of the mind toward a new method. For this reason parents and teachers discourage young children from the practice of counting on the fingers, believing that it will cause much trouble later to root out this vicious habit and replace it by purely mental processes. Teachers should be careful, especially with precocious children, not to continue too long in the use of a process that is becoming mechanical; for it is already growing into a second nature, and becoming a part of the unconscious apperceptive process by which the mind reacts against the environment, recognizes its presence, and explains it to itself.

The child that has been overtrained in arithmetic reacts perceptively against his environment, he counts and adds; his other apperceptive reactions being feeble he neglects qualities and casual relations." It is more important that the child should learn to curb his temper, control his fists and tongue when under provocation, bear defeat and pain heroically, move his muscles economically and gracefully, stand surprises without shock, abstain from strong drink, tobacco, and vicious habits, than to know the multiplication table or grammar. The Scriptures even go so far as to assert that 'He that ruleth his spirit is greater than he that taketh a city.' But positive control is a much higher control than negative. The child who goes into tantrums, pampers his appetites, shirks his lessons, escapes all physical labour, has his will hopelessly arrested. Habits of righteous volition must be ingrained early or the man is doomed to go through life a nerveless sentimentalist. No one ever develops athletic prowess after maturity, nor is it much more possible to develop positive moral virtues unless the foundations have been laid in childhood and youth.

Arrest of religious development may occur through precocity induced by too early memoriter learning of dogmatic forms and formulas. The acquisition of any proverb or formula not understood may bias wrongly one's whole course of life. We all know how the unfortunate knowledge of the superstitions concerning the number 13, Friday, charms, omens, and amulets torments us and even causes us to act upon them although against our best judgment. Similarly antiquated medical advice which we learned when young, and which is sometimes absolutely pernicious, is so hard to abandon that we heed it even at our peril. In the same way dogmas and formulas which really possess symbolical or metaphorical meaning are accepted literally and in their distorted misinterpretation become permanent mental possessions. Our minds become so indurated with these modes of functioning that higher and truer development becomes impossible.

The child's mind perceives things literally and in the concrete, but abstractions in science and morals, which are mumbled and misinterpreted, become a menace to higher growth. On the other hand, to fail to give the child the concrete foundations in science, conduct, or religion means that subsequent comprehension of abstractions is forever precluded. Many a man who might have become a scientist by learning early the concrete facts out of which higher concepts could be evolved, has never glimpsed scientific realms because his early experiences have contributed no background of apperceiving masses. Likewise in morals and religion, lack of concrete personal experiences out of which diviner conceptions could evolve has doomed many to dwarfed moral and religious development.

WINDING-UP

The study of instinct reveals very clearly that mankind is not a finished product but that the race is ever in the making. There is ceaseless change. There can be no standstill. The change may be either upward or downward, progressive or degenerative. The same forces which produce fuller, more abundant racial life, if perverted, may cause degradation and extinction. The effects of life experiences—education—do not cease with the individual. All posterity shares in the heritage received by the individual and modified by his life. The life experiences of one generation become the impulses of the next and all future ones.

Education is thus magnified in importance. The full realisation of its meaning should lead from selfishness to the highest altruism. It is the business of education to select and create for perpetuity those instincts which will contribute to the development of the highest ideals of life. Harmful instincts should be allowed to atrophy through disuse or to be shunted off into useful channels. For example, many tendencies toward vice, immorality, and crime should be allowed to decay by accentuating good impulses. In some cases they must even be considered as diseases and therefore combated. All organic diseases, mental defects, and moral degeneracy should be eliminated. Purposive selection should be employed to aid chance natural selection. Purposive selection should even correct natural tendencies, for heredity preserves defects as well as excellencies. In many cases the continuation of characters represents no selective process. Heredity simply continues what has been acquired in previous generations. For example, ugliness is never perpetuated through selection, but heredity nevertheless causes it to persist through generation after generation of the same family.

One great problem of education is to so understand instinct as to correlate the individual with his environment and secure the fullest and richest measure of life. Each individual should be more highly developed than his ancestors and should have fewer undesirable tendencies. Getting rid of original sin means eliminating some harmful hereditary traits, abridging others, and shunting others.

Pessimists often raise the cry that no race progress is discernible. They argue that the world is no better today than four thousand years ago, that no one possesses a higher grade of intellect than in the earliest historic times. There is no warrant for such pessimism. There were giant intellects in the palmy days of Greece and Rome, and in the time of the Pharaohs, but the world average then was vastly lower than now. It may even be seriously doubted whether the giants of old would be so conspicuous were they alive today. The high level of today might make them sink out of sight by comparison.

Today there are thousands planning and executing enterprises as gigantic as the erection of the pyramids or the generalship of the Peloponnesian War. In every civilised country there are many writers, statesmen, kings of finance, inventors, scholars, educators, who have accomplished as great things as are recorded in the annals of ancient Rome, Greece, Egypt, or Palestine. They may never be singled out because the same degree of intelligence is so common.

That new instincts, physical, intellectual, and moral, have been developed, and are being developed, there can be no doubt. That some impulses have become atrophied and are dying out there is equally little doubt. The uniform attainments in poetry, music, scholarship, statesmanship, and commerce are greater than ever before, and it is reasonable to suppose that there is a close relationship between attainments and ability. Many troublesome instincts like pugnacity, selfishness, and sensuality are becoming subdued and controlled. The higher instincts of reason, morality, conscience, altruism, and religion have become expanded and strengthened. We now have less of war, carnage, gluttony, and lust, and more of refined courage, altruism, and love, than ever before in the world's history. The deeds of men as recorded in the annals of history, sacred and profane, make a splendid record of the growth of the higher and nobler powers and the crushing to heel of the baser instincts. The very fact of the conservation of energy teaches that forces may become cumulative and tendencies or impulses to action be created. The facts of memory, habit, and heredity lead to the same inevitable conclusion. If we believe in evolution and the development of civilised man from primitive savagery, we cannot escape it; for is not the greatest difference between savagery and civilisation one of instincts?

When we remember that interests are determined largely by instincts, it is at once seen that a knowledge of instinct is of great importance in determining courses of study. In the light of a knowledge of instinct the course of study is adapted to the capacities of individuals. The school is fitted to the child rather than the child to the school. The intelligent administration of the entire elective system must be thoroughly grounded upon a knowledge of the fundamental instinctive powers of the individual. There have been altogether too many misfits in the world because of a lack of recognition of innate possibilities and needs. Education is not only to minister to thoroughly apparent needs and interests of the individual, but one of its most important functions is to discover interests and aptitudes.

A better knowledge of nascent periods of development would effect many readjustments in the position of different subjects and topics in the curriculum. Already the fruits of even our limited knowledge of the subject are becoming apparent. The kindergarten work has been remodelled, formal arithmetic work is disappearing from the primary grades, concrete work is finding its place in the elementary schools, elementary algebra and concrete geometry have been shifted from the high school to the grammar school, and the abstract arithmetic has been relegated to the high school. Formal grammar is less emphasised in elementary work, and ought to be pushed still higher up.

It is being recognised in practice that modern foreign languages can be most advantageously begun between seven and twelve. There are well-marked stages in the growth of interest and power in drawing which should serve as a guide in arranging drawing courses. Already the ultra-logical course in drawing has been replaced by a more rational psychological arrangement recognising the well-marked stages of development. The organisation of manual training departments and schools is in part a tacit recognition on the part of educators that the instincts for motor activity and of constructiveness are the most valuable allies in the training of childhood and youth, and must be utilised if education is to be normal and balanced.

The head, the hand, and the heart, metaphorically speaking, all have claims asserting themselves which must be recognised if we would avoid malformation. As a final illustration, we may cite the recent recognition of the peculiar period of adolescence. The main value of the recent study of adolescence has been in the appreciation that there is a special time of budding of the most powerful instincts of the human race. The proper adjustment of the curriculum and the better recognition of nascent periods of development would guard against arrest of development, and enable educators to co-operate with nature in developing children normally from one stage to another and into the fullest and noblest manhood and womanhood.

CHAPTER TEN

The Intellect

BIOLOGICAL AND SOCIAL FRAMEWORK

It has been pointed out that within the general biological and social framework, every individual tends to be different. To quote Tyler "variability from one individual to another individual is a universal phenomenon." The differences on the whole tend to be quantitative rather than qualitative.

Individual differences are a matter of degree but not a matter of kind. The extent to which individuals vary constitutes their distinguishing qualities. Thus, individuals differ from each other. Everybody has his own peculiarities which make him a separate individual from others. Individuals differ in many respects. They differ in height, weight, intelligence, knowledge, interest etc.

Areas of Individual Difference

It has already been said that individuals differ in many areas. Some of them are discussed below for bringing the fact here to us.

Difference in Physical Development

Individuals develop in similar fashion, they are all alike in constitution. But still we find that some children are tall some are short. Some are lean and thin.

Difference in Intelligence Level

Children differ in the amount, make up and rate of development of mental abilities. Most of the studies demonstrate that most children possess average I.Q.'s and a very few children possess high I.Q.'s.

The educational programmes of the students should be chalked out on the basis of their respective I.Q.'s. When the teacher gives stress on the average children, the gifted are neglected. If the emphasis is on the gifted, the slow learners are frustrated.

Differences in Achievement

We find that some variables or traits are positively correlated and some others are negatively correlated. There is positive high correlation in between intelligence and achievement.

Thus, differences in achievement are also found among those children who are at the same level of intelligence. This is due to various factors of intelligence and difference in previous experiences or interests.

Differences in Motor Abilities

Children also differ in their motor ability. There are differences with regard to muscular co-ordination motor co-ordination, speed of performance steadiness of control and resistance to fatigue.

Differences in Attitude

"An attitude is a predisposition to act in a certain way. It is a state of readiness that influences a person to act in a given manner." It is a general disposition towards a group of people or an institution. Different children have different attitudes towards authority institution etc. This attitude the child learns from his very childhood.

Differences Due to Sex

There are individual differences in men and women. Some qualities are unique in women. They differ from men in those qualities. Women are more delicate while men are more sturdy.

Emotional Differences

Individual reach to different kinds of stimuli. But they differ on their emotional reactions to a particular situation Emotions are present in every individual. But there are differences in degree but not in kind. For example, the emotion of anger. That is present in every individual. But some people get angry very soon and some others do not get angry so easily. One may laugh at a thing, another may take the same thing seriously and may be ready to commit murder. This shows the emotional differences among the children.

HEREDITARY FACTORS

It has been pointed out, "heredity and environment are the basic factors that brings about variability in human beings. Other factors such as sex, age, race, physique are also important in causing variability in human beings. Almost 20 years ago it was a debatable topic whether heredity or environment is more significant in causing individual differences.

There are some psychologists and biologists who give more stress in heredity. On the contrary, there are relatively few psychologists who give primary importance to the environment and a secondary position to heredity. Many studies have been undertaken, in this regard. Some studies reveal the importance of heredity and some other studies on environment.

Study by Dr. Lienship

Dr. A.E. Lienship undertook a study on some educated families. Richard Edward married a famous lady "Elizabeth." Some persons of his family could rise to the occasion. They became doctors, professors, orators and politicians.

After some years Edward married an ordinary women from whom only ordinary persons were born. This study well explained the importance of heredity in causing individual differences.

Twins and Differences

Individual differences are also found in case of identical twins, fraternal twins and siblings. Thorndike conducted a good number of studies on pairs of twins and got positive correlation between the twins. In case of identical twins r =.90 and in case of fraternal twins r =.69.

Pearson undertook another study on 200 pairs of siblings with respect to trait-vivacity, self-assertiveness, popularity etc. He got positive co-efficient of correlation of +.50. Other studies in this regard also show that there is a positive correlation.

Similar study was done by Merriman on identical and fraternal twins by the Stanford Binet, Army beta and national intelligence test. He obtained r =.90 and +.70 in case of identical twins and fraternal twin respectively.

Gallon Frances

Another remarkable personality is Gallon Frances in the study of heredity. He conducted a study on 977 nearest blood related individuals. Out of them 536 come out to be successful famous individuals. He also studied 977 common individuals out of them 4 became famous. In 1869 he came to the conclusion from his studies with 977 persons that "the superior family gave birth to the children of superior ability who were distinguished in the field of art, literature and science. Opposed to this generalization, the lower category of family gave birth to criminals, feeble minded and bad characters."

Human nature is shaped through the interaction between human organism and environment. We cannot therefore deny the importance of environment in shaping human behaviour and causing individual differences.

Research by Gordon

Gorden an English psychologist conducted a study on children living in a very poor environment. The children were in the margin of mental deficiency possessing IQ of 69.6. But with the increase in age their IQ were depressed. It was studied that the child of the age group of 4-6 had an average IQ of 90 and another of the age group 12-22 had an average I.Q. of 60.

Catel another environmentalist stressed the importance of environment in causing individual difference. He had conducted studies on 1000 individuals and at last came to the conclusion that "Individual differences are due to environmental factor"

Race, Nationality, and Culture

There are significant innate differences in mental abilities among the several racial groups and national groups. In U.S.A. a study was undertaken among 25 Negroes and white children. It was seen that 25 per cent of Negroes were more intelligent than the white people. Climberg conducted a study among individuals from France, Germany and Italy. The differences found after the study was not due to the heredity of the individual but it was due to environment.

Differences on Account of Sex

Sex is also responsible for causing individual difference. Numerous studies have been carried out in this regard. For instance, male children show superiority over the girls or females in number, concept and arithmetic ability, manual performances and mechanical abilities. Girls are generally superior to boys in linguistic ability.

ROLE OF INTELLIGENCE

Human Intelligence

It has been observed, oftentimes, knowingly or otherwise, under various circumstance we estimate, evaluate and/or comment upon the abilities and capacities of somebody or the other. The teacher faced with the problem of admitting students to pursue a course of study; the employer wishing to hire persons to particular jobs, the defence authorities wanting to recruit men for various services and the counselor desirous of suggesting suitable vocations to his clients, etc., all of them strive to assess and evaluate the capacities and abilities of people to fulfill the demands of the respective tasks. Depending upon such assessments (whether they are accurate and reliable or otherwise) we label these individuals as being 'bright' or 'dull', 'efficient' or 'inefficient' or 'intelligent' or 'dullard'.

Intelligence is Ability

Intelligence is a general ability to acquire and utilize knowledge and skills of different kinds. Some others have expressed the view that intelligence is the capacity to adopt oneself to the demands of reality and deal with it effectively. There are still others who say that intelligence includes specific mental abilities such as word, fluency, memory, ability to deal with numbers, etc.

Besides these, other factors that are taken to be indicative of intelligence are ability for making use of symbols and abstract thinking, facility for fertile imagination, capacity to learn new tasks, ability to solve problems, being efficient to act purposefully and many more. The above analysis regarding the nature of intelligence is that it includes many kinds of abilities and varieties of capacities. Since intelligence includes such diversified abilities, it necessarily has many dimensions. Important among them are power, width and speed.

Power is revealed by the ability of the individual to perform tasks of various levels of difficulty and complexity. Speed refers to the quickness with which an individual can perform a certain tasks. Width or range refers to the area or spaciousness and is indicated by the number and varieties of tasks an individual can successfully and effectively perform. All this points to the fact that the nature of intelligence is complex.

ASSESSMENT OF ABILITIES

In the beginning of the last century, when psychology was just getting started, members of the Paris School Board approached Alfred Binet and asked for his assistance. They asked him to develop an objective method for detecting children who were mentally retarded and in need of special help. In short, they asked him to devise a simple workable test of intelligence. Binet was already at work on related topics so he readily agreed. In designing their test, Binet and his colleagues Thedore Simon were guided by the belief that the items used should be ones children could answer without special training or study.

They felt that this was important because the test was designed to measure the ability to handle intellectual tasks-not specific knowledge gained in class. In order to accomplish this goal, Binet and Simon chose items of two basic types. First, the selected questions which were so new or unusual that almost none of the children tested would have any prior experience with them. And second they chose items which were so familiar that virtually all of the children would have been exposed to them in the past.

The first version of their test was published in 1905, and it contained 30 items of these two types. Much to Binet's and the school board's pleasure, the test was quite effective in attaining its major goal. With its aid, children in need of special assistance could be readily identified. Encouraged by this early success. Binet and Simon broadened the scope of their test so that it could measure variations in intelligence among normal children. This revision, published in 1908, grouped items by age. Specifically, six items were included at each level between 3 and 13 years. Individual items were placed at a particular age level if about 75 per cent of the children of that age could pass it correctly.

Sample items from the first intelligence test developed by Binet & Simon.

The child is asked to:

- Recognize the difference between square of chocolate and square of wood. Execute simple commands or imitate simple gestures.
- Name object shown in pictures.
- Repeat a sentence of 15 words.

- Tell how two common objects are different.
- Draw a design from memory.
- Make a Rhyme (what rhymes with-?")
- Complete sentences begun by the examiner.
- Use three nouns mentioned by the examiner in a sentence.
- Define abstract terms (for example, what is the difference between esteem and friendship).

When intelligence has become so important, to us discuss the term also. Different psychologists have tried to define it in different ways. It is so complex that all definitions vary from each other. So far as the dictionary meaning is concerned it is the ability or capacity to acquire and apply knowledge. But a good number of definitions have been evolved by the psychologists according to their own outlook and experience of the term intelligence.

Being digested with a number of definitions, Boring defined "Intelligence is what intelligence tests test". Thus, to define intelligence is a very difficult task. Since last fifty years, many studies have been carried out on intelligence and measurement and many complicated definitions have been developed. It is worthwhile to mention some of the definitions here.

1. Stern: Intelligence is capacity to adopt to relatively new situation.
2. Terman: Intelligence is capacity for distract thinking.
3. Ebbinghaus: Intelligence is the capability to complete the part into a whole.
4. Thorndlike: Intelligence is the power of response from the point of view of truth or fact.
5. G. Stoddard defines: "Intelligence is the ability to understand activities that are characterized by difficulty, complexity, abstractness, economy, adaptiveness to a goal, social value and the emerges of originals and to maintain such activities under conditions that demand a concentration of energy and resistance to emotional forces."

Charles Spearman

Intelligence is the analytic and synthetic ability of mind.

Buchingham

Intelligence is the ability to learn.

Huggarty

It is a practical concept connoting a group of complex mental processes traditionally defined in systematic psychologies as sensation, perception, association, memory, imagination, discrimination, judgements and reasoning.

Thus, there are a number of definitions regarding intelligence. Some are biological, some are educational and some are empirical in nature.

E.L. Thorndike has classified intelligence into three categories namely. Abstract Intelligence, Concrete Intelligence and Social Intelligence. We exhibit abstract intelligence while dealing with symbols, words, numbers, formulas, diagrams, etc.

Concrete intelligence is the ability of the individuals to comprehend concrete situations and to react to them. Social intelligence refers to the ability of an individual to react to social setting or situations. Adequate social adjustment is the index of social intelligence. The term 'intelligence' has the following characteristics:

(a) It is an inborn natural power.
(b) It helps man to face the difficult circumstances, problems, difficulties and complicated situations.
(c) It helps man in learning things.
(d) Intelligence is largely influenced by heredity.
(e) Environment has also a considerable effect upon intelligence.
(f) Intelligence is different from that of knowledge.
(g) It is different from acquired traits.
(h) It is experimented that children are of medium intelligence and ability.

These are some of the characteristics of intelligence. Various theories also have been developed on the nature of intelligence.

Measurement of Intelligence

The ultimate nature of intelligence has a theoretical faculty and cannot be measured. There probably is no Perfect test of intelligence. Mental abilities are so complex that they can not be measured adequately by any one or more tests yet constructed.

They can not be seen or felt or heard. They measure the manifestation of intellectual capacity in action or in behaviour. There was long struggle in order to devise means and methods of measuring intelligence. The most notable development in the history of intelligence testing was the work of Alfred Binet in the early years of the 20th century. Prior to Binet Sir Francis Gallon in England and J.M. Cattell in America studied individual differences in intellectual make-up but could not devise any method for studying intelligence.

The first credit goes to Binet for devising a scale of measurement of intelligence in the year 1905. It contained tests for the group 4 to 15 years. In these test items the chronological age and mental age (C.A. and M.A.) were correlated. There were six items in the test meant for each age (one test for one year). Each item indicated two months of mental-age. The basic factors which were intended to be measured were reasoning, imagination and judgement. Binet's tests were quickly adopted and revised from time to time. Terman, at Stanford University revised Binet's scale. This scale is therefore known as "Stanford Binet". He made some modifications over Binet's scale. He introduced the concept of "Intelligence Quotient" (I.Q.) here as the ratio of the mental age to the chronological age.

Meaning of I.Q.

It is the ratio between mental age (M.A.) and chronological age (C.A.)

$$I.Q. = M.A./C.A. \times 100.$$

Mental age is obtained from the performance of a student in an intelligence test.

For example a child possessing a mental age of six and a chronological age of 10 will have an I.Q. of 60.

$$M.A. = 6 \quad C.A. = 10$$
$$I.Q. = M.A./C.A. \times 100 = 6/10 \times 100 = 60$$

Thus, the I.Q. indicates the rate of mental growth. Children may have same I.Q. but have different C.A's or may have same M.A. but different I.Q's.

It has already been said that Intelligence Quotient (I.Q.) is the ratio of the mental age to the chronological age. In order to compute I.Q. we have to know what the mental age is. A child's mental age is got from his performance on an intelligence test. His success on different items of tests is calculated and it gives his mental age. Suppose there are six items in a test of intelligence meant for a age group 8. If a child answers all the items he gets through 12 months.

Thus, one item related to 2 months. The child belonging to age-group-8 gets basal age of 8 if he answers all the items meant for that age. He answers 2 items of the age-group (out of six items) he gets a credit of 4 months. If he fails to answer all the items he gets '0' credit. In case of this child mental age is 8 years 4 months (Basal age-8, credit-4 months.)

In this way mental age is calculated. However; it has to be considered in terms of chronological age (the real age). The ratio between one's M.A. and C.A. gives Intelligence Quotient or I.Q.

Computing I.Q.

When we are aware of one's mental age and chronological age, we can easily compute his I.Q. For example a child possesses M.A. of 10 and it is equivalent with his C.A. So in this I.Q. will be.

$$M.A./C.A. \times 100 = 10/10 \times 100 = 100$$

A child possessing M.A. higher than his C.A. definitely has an I.Q. of higher level. Let his M.A. be 10 and C.A. =8.

$$I.Q. = 10/8 \times 100 = 125$$

In this way we classify children into different groups according to their I.Q.

1. IQ 130 and above—Genius.
2. IQ 120—129—Superior.
3. IQ 110—119—Above average
4. IQ 90—109—Normal or average
5. IQ 80—89—Below average
6. IQ 70—79—Dull or border lines
7. IQ 50—69—Feeble minded
8. IQ 25—49—Imbecile
9. IQ 0—25—Idiot.

ROLE OF WISDOM

How a person becomes self-actualized is not a simple matter. The environment must not be restrictive, the circumstances must be right. Self-examination, self-knowledge, and productivity all seem to be involved in self-actualization. According to Maslow (1965) in the course of self-actualization man reaches the point where he fulfils his deficiency needs (his biological needs and needs of security) and can devote himself to the fulfillment of higher needs such as love and creativity. Presumably a loving person will be "good". Maslow strongly condemns the view that man's nature is evil.

Nature of Creativity

Though there might be differences of opinion with regard to the exact nature of creativity, the characteristics that are manifested by persons who are creative may be stated and described. Creative persons show a preference for finding out solutions that are less frequent and less ordinary. That is, they show a uniqueness of approach to solve problems.

The process of this thinking is more complex. Their thinking is characterized by a disposition of independence and openness. They show a high degree of aesthetic, emotional and social sensitivities. Creative thinking sequentially seems to go through the following stages:

- (*i*) Preparation,
- (*ii*) Incubation,
- (*iii*) Illumination,
- (*iv*) Evaluation, and
- (*v*) Revision.

Preparation involves formulation of the problem and the collection of materials considered necessary for the solution. More often than not the creative thinker, at this stage comes to feel that he cannot solve the problem even after working at it for a considerable length of time and hence sets the problem aside.

This is followed by the period of incubation during which time, certain of the ideas which hindered, with solution the problem slips into background. But the attempt at the solution of the problem may be continuing at an unconscious level. Illumination is taken to occur when the solution to the problem seems to occur quite suddenly and unexpectedly. It is what is referred to as insight.

The next is the stage of evaluation when the creative thinker checks whether the apparent solution is really useful and correct.

Either the solution may be correct, but may need some modification or it may have discarded and new solution worked out. In any case, revision is made into final stages of creative thinking to make the solution useful, meaningful and significant, but it is hoped that further investigation would throw light on the exact nature of the process involved.

The Correlation

There seem to be a significant positive correlation between measures of general intelligence and creativity. Since tests of intelligence measure just the available knowledge without showing how they will be put to use in the use of the solution of problems, a number of psychologists feel that though a minimal level of general intelligence is essential for creativity, a high IQ score does not really indicate creativity. In other words, a person with an IQ of 140 or above may not be creative whereas a person with an I.Q. 120 may make creative contribution.

CHAPTER ELEVEN

Perception of Thought

The layman uses the term 'thinking' quite often and without much reflection as to what it means. When a man for instance says 'I think it is 8' o'clock now' he means that he guesses. On the other hand when a mechanic 'thinks' of fabricating a gadget, it means that he tries to perform a complicated mental activity in which he plans, remembers and tries to 'connect' or 'associate' many of his past experiences with what he wants to build or make presently. In a third case when a person says I think it was a Monday when I met you last 'it refers to the process of remembering'. Having referred to the various possible connotations of the word, let us examine the characteristics of the process of thinking.

"Man is differentiated from animals because of his ability to think. As far as two thousand years ago, Aristotle referred to man as a thinking animal. The term Homo sapiens used by biologists refer to human beings, means thinking or wise man. The seat of human thought the cognitive process, the neocortex or the 'new brain' of the human being is very large. In terms of evolution, the development of neocortex is a new development. Paleocortex or the 'old brain' which is below the neocortex, controls the biological function and this the man shares in common with other lower animals.

THE CLASSIFICATION

Though the term, thinking seems to elude any precise definition from the characteristics involved in the process, we can arrive at a working definition. Thinking is a higher mental process which includes verbal symbols internal visual and auditory images, ideas, concepts and mathematical symbols. It takes into account past experiences, future possibilities and external reality as well. Thinking usually takes place when the individual is exposed to an unfamiliar situation in which habitual responses are inadequate for adjustment. Such a situation is known as problem situation. In a purposeful activity that is goal directed interference with the smooth functioning of behaviour may occur in two ways.

1. It may be in the form of physical obstruction between the individual and the goal. This could occur in the form of missing element in the conceptual sequence that would logically link an intellectual question with its undetermined answer.
2. It may be in the form of a temporary inability to perceive the similarity between the existing situation......and some familiar situation to which appropriate and adequate responses have been established already. Since the problem situation interferes with process towards a goal it provokes thinking and this thinking process continues until this interference is done away with.

In summary we can say that thinking refers to many processes including (1) formulating and testing hypotheses (2) acquiring and making use of concepts (3) manipulating symbols of language like that of words and (4) manipulating various kinds of images.

SOME CONCEPTS

As we have seen thinking involves language symbols such as words. Here we have to differentiate between three related concepts the sign, signal and symbol. Sign is a general term referring to any stimulus that stands for something else. As a matter of fact, signal and symbol are 'signs' but they point out to an intention to communicate something of significance. Signal indicates that the time and place for something to occur is ahead *e.g.* cloudy sky, enabling a forecast of rain symbol is a sign representing something else. For example, a traffic light (redlight implying an instruction to stop) is both a signal and a symbol.

Thinking and language are closely interrelated because the symbols used by human beings are often words and language. Language supplies us with innumerable symbols and the rules for using them. The use of language symbols makes human thinking sophisticated and differentiates it from animal thinking. Besides language, images are other kind of symbols involved in thinking processes.

It has been pointed out that modern "cognitive psychologists" have developed several powerful new techniques that allow them to study portions of mental life in the objective manner demanded by science. We shall start with the traditional approaches to thinking: the "associationist" and Gestalt approaches, both based upon learning and perception. The associationist approach was an extension of early behaviourism aimed and expending stimulus-response model of human thought. The Gestalt approach viewed thinking as based upon the same concepts as perception. A newer approach to thought borrows information processing techniques from computer science and engineering. We will discuss this approach, in which the information flow within human mind is considered to be the most important part of thinking.

No discussion of thinking would be complete without considering mental images. We shall see how these pictures inside the mind help us to play chess and to find our way from one place to another. Although we know from our own experience that mental images exist and can be very useful. It has taken psychologists some time to develop the technology to study imagery in the objective manner demanded by science.

To complete our coverage of cognition, we will conclude with a discussion on decision-making. Although people are seldom perfect decision-makers in a mathematical sense, there is still consistancy in their behaviour. We shall explore some relatively simple ways to make decisions. We hope that some of these techniques may help you to make some of your own decisions or atleast to help you to understand why some decisions can be difficult.

The symbols that we use in thinking are often words and language, and therefore thinking and language are closely related. A language makes available hundreds of thousands of potential symbols and gives us rules for using them. To a large degree, the availability of language symbols is what makes human thinking so much, more sophisticated than the thinking of other animals. Although language is a powerful tool in human thought, as when we "talk to ourselves" internally images are another important type of symbol used in thinking.

When we use images to think, they are not usually complete "pictures in the head". They are usually incomplete.

Perception of Thought ■ 237

RESEARCH CONSEQUENCES

McKellar (1972) draws a distinction between autistic thinking and rational thinking. Autistic thinking has no rational purpose. It is the brain's manipulation of the information available to it, from the senses or from stored material, without any particular purpose. Day-dreaming is an example of autistic thinking. Rational thinking, on the other hand, is logical and rational and directed towards a purpose. When you are solving the clues in a crossword puzzle you are engaging in rational thinking.

FREUDIAN CONCEPT

For Freud and the psychoanalysts, thinking is closely related to their view of basic human motives. For them, the basic human motive is the satisfaction of bodily needs. Where these needs are not fully satisfied, memory of them is brought into play. This memory is associated with the kind of excitation that actual food, warmth and contact evoke. For example, a hungry infant hallucinates about food, but this hallucination is not in itself satisfying. Some of the energy released is devoted to solving the problem, to changing the environment so that the food, the warmth or the contact is obtained. This is essentially autistic thinking, driven by emotional rather than by rational processes. Freud makes a distinction between primary and secondary thought processes. While secondary thought embraces rational conscious thought of which we are normally aware, primary thought processes are normally unconscious. There seem to be three separate levels of thinking:

Preconscious Thought, which comprises those thoughts and ideas which are not engaging our consciousness at the moment, to which we are currently not paying attention but which nevertheless exist for us.

Conscious Thought, to which we are currently paying attention and on which we are engaging our minds.

Unconscious Thought, which remains inaccessible to our consciousness but which nevertheless plays a part in determining our behaviour.

PIAGET'S THEORY

Piaget termed the building blocks of an individual's intelligence schemata. They are continually being modified or added to by contact with the environment so that the individual's adaptation to that environment becomes more complete. The process involved is one of equilibration. When something new manifests itself in an individual's environment his or her mind is thrown into a state of imbalance or disequilibrium. This is uncomfortable, so there is motivation to find a new balance. This new balance occurs through adaptation, which takes the form either of assimilation or else of accommodation. With assimilation, an object or an idea is understood in terms of the concepts or actions (schemata) which the child already possesses. With accommodation, concepts and actions are modified to fit the new situation.

GESTALT PERCEPTION

There is a classic account of a German psychologist Wolfgang Kohler interned on the island of Tenerife during the First World War, who set problems for a chimpanzee named Sultan. Kohler saw the principle concerned here as one of isomorphism the notion that the mind always attempts to restructure the elements of a problem so that the brain fields adopt good form, or Pragnanz, as the Gestalt psychologists described it. There is an inborn tendency within the brain to seek order out of chaos. This is in accordance with the Gestalt laws of organization.

STUDY OF BEHAVIOUR

Behaviourists found some difficulty in explaining thinking. It did not seem to accord well with their principle that all mental processes were essentially the forming of associations between stimuli. Watson (1913) viewed thinking as subvocal speech. The process of thinking inevitably (as Watson saw it) involved inner language.

This was a motor theory of thought. Some work was done with deaf mutes. It might be expected under Watson's theory that they would move their fingers more than a normal group of adults when they were thinking: they used their fingers for sign language, after all.

There did seem to be a higher correlation between motor activity in the fingers and thinking than in a hearing group of adults. Skinner later viewed thinking as private behaviour as opposed to overt behaviour, and believed that it was similarly subject to stimulus control and reinforcement. In his book *Verbal Behaviour*

(1957) he attempted to show that both overt behaviour and thinking were controlled by operant conditioning. In overt behaviour, there was an interaction with someone else, while, with thinking, individuals are their own listeners. There is in effect an interaction with themselves.

COGNITIVE METHOD

Cognitive approaches to thinking have attempted to examine the mental processes which occur during thinking. Miller et al. (1960) identified what they referred to as heuristic strategies. These were models which enabled them to stimulate the way in which the mind solved problems.

The complexities of a problem might be simplified by working out a series of rules of thumb. These could then be applied one at a time. Though this did not guarantee that a solution to the problem could be found, it reduced the problem to manageable proportions. A computer could then be programmed to deal with it. For example, in programming a computer to play chess, a set of instructions had to be devised such as 'check that the king is safe' or 'make sure that the queen cannot be taken'.

Newell and Simon (1972) attempted to mirror human problem solving and behaviour in a heuristic way. To validate the models set up, they relied on individuals' verbal reports of what was going on in their heads while they attempted to solve problems. In this way, computer models constructed of how problems were solved. Within these models the programme was analogous to the set of rules or instructions within which a person operated: the computer memory was analogous to the memory of the individual, and the input and output from the computer represented the problem proposed and the solution found.

However, because human brains are not computers and cannot be so rigidly controlled there were difficulties, including the following:

It is not very useful to think of human beings as machines. Any analogy is bound to be partial only, as we do not fully understand the principles on which the human brain operates.

Computers, while they are very accurate and efficient calculators and solvers of logical problems are not capable of creative thinking results.

CHAPTER TWELVE

Grades of Learning

Simply knowing that wide variations in level of mental development exist at every grade level is not enough. We need specific information about these variations, and specific reference points, in order to judge what each child can be expected to accomplish. Here are some questions that will guide us in our study of the variations in learning ability:

1. What measurable traits are the best indicators of general learning ability?
2. What variations in these traits do children of the same chronological age show? How much overlap is there is learning ability among different chronological age groups? For example, what proportion of 10 years old children equal or exceed the average ability of 11 or 12 years old children?
3. How is age related to variations in learning ability? Is there a greater difference between bright and dull 12 years old children than between bright and dull six years old children? If so, how much difference?
4. Do bright and dull children of the same mental age show differences other than differences in learning ability that require classroom adjustments?
5. What can children with various I.Q.'s be expected to accomplish? What final educational and vocational levels can they achieve?
6. How can we use the results of intelligence tests to predict learning ability? How much faith can we have in various types of intelligence tests?
7. What special abilities and aptitudes should we consider as we work with children? To what extent are special abilities, such as artistic and mechanical ability, independent of general mental development?

8. What general educational plans are used to adjust instructional goals and materials to differences in learning ability? What elements in these plans can we use in the classroom?

In order to answer these questions, we need to assemble specific information from many different sources. For example, even though M.A. is not a perfect indicator of learning ability, nor is I.Q. a perfect indicator of rate of growth in learning ability, still they are the best indicators that we have. And the process of developing and standardising intelligence tests, especially the two best-known individual intelligence tests, has given us a great deal of information concerning just what specific I.Q.'s and M.A.'s mean. In addition, these same data tell us a great deal about the differences in vocabulary, memory span, and other determinants of ability to learn that occur among groups of children of the same chronological age. Still other important data have been assembled by using intelligence tests to study selected groups of children and adults. To supplement our data concerning the level of mental development and achievement that dull average, and bright children can be expected to reach, we can draw on expert opinion. Our reason for studying these data and opinions is to establish reference points that will help us to understand the children we teach and to establish goals to guide us in selecting materials and methods and in appraising the results of our instruction.

GRADES OF LEARNING ABILITY

For 50 years or more, makers of intelligence tests have been trying to identify measurable traits that will serve as accurate predictors of learning ability. They have discovered that certain traits are excellent indicators and that others are worthless. They know that size and strength, facial expression and height of the forehead, reaction time and sensory discrimination, and artistic and mechanical talents are useless as indicators of learning ability. But they have found that memory, number sense, actual school achievement, ability to solve problems and to follow directions, ability to handle abstract concepts and to recognise similarities and differences, ability to solve certain types of puzzle and to learn mazes, and general ability to reason are extremely valuable indicators of learning ability. So the modern intelligence test is made up of problems that measure the degree to which an individual possesses these traits.

Although you may never actually administer an intelligence test yourself, you must know how to interpret the results of such tests, and you will certainly want to know how to read the signs that indicate whether or not a child can learn quickly.

In general, intelligence tests use one or both of two methods of determining learning ability: (1) They make a direct test of a child's memory, reasoning ability, and ability to handle abstractions by presenting him with problems and materials that are new to him. (2) They make indirect estimates of his ability to learn by determining what he has already learned both in and out of school. The direct approach measures the child's memory for a group of numbers, a sentence, or a simple design. The indirect approach uses problems that are designed to find out how much the child has learned from the experiences that are a part of the environment of nearly all children. For example, the child may be asked to tie his shoe laces, to identify common coins, or to draw a picture of a man.

In your own day-to-day appraisal of a child's ability to learn, you will use both approaches too. You will estimate ability by observing how well the child follows directions, how quickly he learns a short poem, and how far he has progressed in reading and other school subjects.

ROLE OF AGE IN LEARNING ABILITY

How wide are the variations in learning ability within a large group of children of the same chronological age? How much do various chronological age groups overlap in learning ability?

To gain specific information on these questions, let's examine some measurable aspects of ability to learn—memory, for example. The Stanford-Binet Tests of Intelligence test children on their memory for numbers that are pronounced at the rate of about one digit per second. The procedure is as follows:

The examiner says, "I am going to say some numbers and when I am through I want you to say them just the way I do. Listen carefully, and get them just right." The child is given three opportunities to succeed. Three different sets of digits are used, with the same number of digits in each set. The child is given credit for success if he makes one correct response out of the three attempts.

The following table shows the percentages of children of various ages who, under these conditions, have a memory span of from two to nine digits. Since the ability to accomplish the kind of task used to measure intelligence ceases to improve after ages 16 or 18, the achievement of age groups older than 16 is not shown in the table.

Percentage of Persons of Various Chronological Ages Able to Memorise Number Series of Various Lengths

Number of Digits	Chronological Age														
	2	3	4	5	6	7	8	9	10	11	12	13	14	15	16
Two	38	86	98	99											
Three	15	76	91	98											
Four	1	18	47	77	85	97									
Five		8	25	41	70	81	87	96	96	95	96				
Six			9	19	35	48	67	63	76	80	87	88	92		
Eight					3	9	12	13	19	22					
Nine						2	3	4	4	6					

According to the table, 4.2 per cent of four years old children fail to memorise a two-digit number, but 8 per cent of them succeed in memorising a five-digit number. We see that 9 per cent of six years old children succeed in a learning task (memorising a six-digit number) that 8 per cent of 16 years old children fail.

Obviously, memory for numbers is only one indicator of a child's ability to profit from instruction. Most intelligence tests derive their final estimate from measuring several more or less independent indicators. But the ability to memorise numbers does give us some indication of a child's ability to focus his attention on a problem, and these test findings give us some idea of the range of a child's ability. Some six years old greatly exceed other six years old. Some four years old exceed some 13 years old. Let's look at some other indicators of learning ability that have been included in the Stanford-Binet Scale. Table lists eight of the problems used. Here again, we see the wide variations in ability among children of the same age and the overlapping of abilities among chronological age groups. For example, 22 per cent of seven years old can draw a simple design from memory but 8 per cent of 14 years old fail to do so.

244 ■ Educational Psychology

All these tasks are similar to those that the child meets in the classroom. And we can see the vast differences in ability to handle them that exist among children of the same age when they are doing the best they can. We must recognise that we cannot drive any one child to perform at a higher level than he is capable of; all we can do is to adjust the level of his activity so that he is able to meet with some success.

Percentage of Persons of Various Chronological Ages Able to Accomplish Certain Tasks on the Revised Stanford Binet Scale

Task	Chronological Age														
	2	3	4	5	6	7	8	9	10	11	12	13	14	15	16
Copy a circle	12	62	94	98											
Naming opposites		3	48	78	93	99									
Memory for a 10-word sentence			2	27	64	83	94								
Gives examiner various numbers of blocks			3	43	71	94	96	99							
Sees absurdities in picture			0	5	39	59	78	85	96	98					
Memory for designs					2	22	31	50	60	72	76	91	92		
Name 28 words in one minute					9	28	40	55	66	70	83	86	88	94	
Interprets proverbs									5	11	22	28	45	51	

AGE AND VARIOUS ABILITIES

The above tables also give us information about how the range of learning ability within a given chronological age group increases with increasing age. For example, in the first table we see that only 1 per cent of two years old children have a memory span for four digits but that five years later (age seven) 97 per cent can perform this task. But as we get into older age groups (memory span for six digits, for example) we find a much wider spread of abilities—9 per cent of six years old handle a problem that 8 per cent will fail ten years later (age 16). And although only 12 per cent of two years old children and 98 per cent of five years old children can copy a circle sufficiently well to pass this test, on a more difficult test (memory for designs) we find 22 per cent of seven years old children passing a test that can be passed by only 92 per cent of 14 years old.

Vocabulary development is an especially accurate indicator of level of mental development. The child's performance on the vocabulary section of the Stanford-Binet Tests of Intelligence (45 words ranging from very easy to very difficult) gives a better indication of the total score that he will make on the test than does any other section of the test. Thus, if we were to use only one trait to predict learning ability, we would choose vocabulary development. Wechsler, the author of the other best-known individual intelligence test (which uses a list of 42 words), has this to say about the importance of vocabulary as a measure of intelligence:

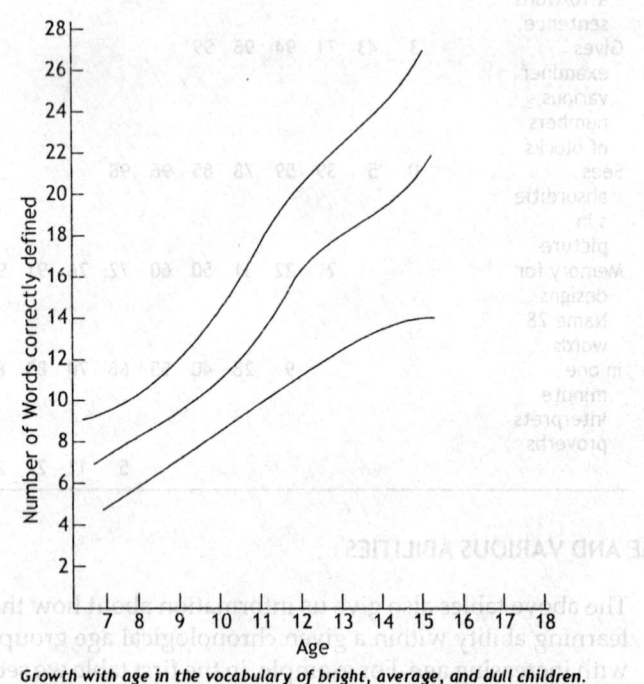

Growth with age in the vocabulary of bright, average, and dull children. (I.Q.'s of about 115, 100, and 85 respectively.)

Source: [Adapted from Quinn McNemar, *The Revision of the Stanford-Binet Scale*. Boston: Houghton Mifflin Company, 1942].

Contrary to lay opinion, the size of a man's vocabulary is not only an index of his schooling, but also an excellent measure of his general intelligence. Its excellence as a test of intelligence is seemingly derived from the fact that the number of words a man knows is at once a measure of his learning ability, his fund of verbal information and of the general range of his ideas. The one serious stricture that can be made against the Vocabulary Test as a measure of a man's intelligence is that the number of words a man acquires must necessarily be influenced by his educational and cultural opportunities. It is seemingly unfair to illiterates and persons with a foreign language handicap.

Figure shows the Stanford-Binet vocabulary test scores of moderately superior, average, and moderately dull children at different ages. The vocabulary development of moderately superior children (I.Q. 115) is shown by the upper line of the graph. These children are not the brightest you are likely to find in any one class, since more than 15 per cent of all children have I.Q.'s higher than 115. The lowest line of the graph shows the vocabulary development of moderately dull children (I.Q. 85). Here again, more than 15 per cent of all children have I.Q.'s lower than 85.

When we look at the moderately superior child's rate of vocabulary development, we find that by age 14 he has reached the level that the average child does not reach until he is 18, and that by age 11½ the moderately superior child has already surpassed the ultimate (adult) level of growth of the moderately dull child. The increasingly wide variations in learning ability that develop as children become older are shown by the tendency of the three lines on the graph to become wider apart at the upper age levels.

Perhaps a more vivid proof of the wide range of learning ability among groups of older children is provided by the distribution of M.A.'s among large groups of children of the same chronological age. Figures showed us that although 50 per cent of the children in any chronological age group have I.Q.'s between 90 and 110, 10 per cent have an I.Q. of 80 or below, and 10 per cent have an I.Q. of 120 or above. Similarly, about 3 per cent are below 70, and 3 per cent are above 130. We know that there is a strong tendency for children to maintain about the same rate of mental growth from year to year and that approximately the same percentage (10) of six and 12 years old children have I.Q.'s of 80 or below. But as a group of children of the same age grow older, the dull child falls further and further behind the bright child in ability to learn (M.A.). Thus a knowledge of how intelligence quotients are distributed in the general population helps us to see why there is such a large increase in the individual differences in ability to learn and why there is so much overlap in learning ability between a group of children of chronological age six and a group of chronological age ten, for example.

Since we know that M.A. is our best indicator of ability to learn, let's examine the mental age distributions that we find among five chronological age groups (four, six, eight, ten, and 12 years old). It is easy to understand why the bright and the dull children (the upper and lower ends of the five distributions) grow further apart in mental age as they grow older. At age 6, a child of 125 I.Q. has a mental age of 7½; at age 12, he has a mental age of 15. Thus, at age 6 he was but 1½ years above average in mental age, but at age 12 he is 3 years above average. The child of 70 I.Q., on the other hand, is 1.8 years below average in mental age at age 6, but 3.6 years below average by the time he is 12 years old. As we can see from Fig., the difference in mental age between any two 4 years old children doubles by age 8 and triples by age 12. Although the spread of mental ages within the middle 80 per cent of the group (I.Q. 80 to 120) is only slightly more than 1½ years at age 4, it is over 3 years at age 8 and nearly 5 years by age 12. We can see, then, that although many of the children with the lowest I.Q.'s drop out of school after about the eighth grade, the gross differences in mental age are greater in the high school than in the elementary school.

Actually, when we work with groups of older children, the problem of finding materials and tasks of appropriate difficulty is even greater than these differences in ability to learn suggest. The child who is learning new materials rapidly at 14 was also learning rapidly at age seven, and in the intervening years he has acquired a much greater background of knowledge and experience than the slow-learning child has. Since most school tasks require background as well as ability to learn new material, the classroom needs of these two pupils become disproportionately different as they grow older.

TYPES OF CHILDREN

Although a 15 years old child of I.Q. 80 and a 10 years old child of I.Q. 120 have the same mental age (12), they show many differences other than those caused by their different chronological ages. For one thing, the bright child has found success in school; the dull child has found only failure. Their attitudes toward the whole learning situation will vary accordingly.

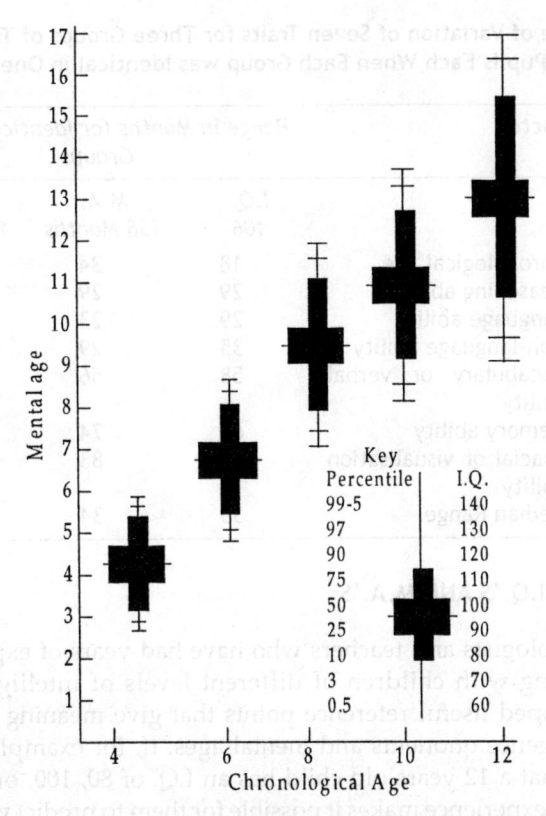

The range of mental ages among each of five chronological age groups.

Moreover, their interests depend on their different degrees of physical development and on the interests of their respective peer groups. Thus, when we are adjusting the educational activities of the school to the individual child's needs, we must consider many factors other than his mental age alone.

Examples of other types of variations that can be expected among children of the same mental age are shown in the following table. Three different groups of 25 children each, who were identical on measures of one trait, were compared on measures of other traits.

The children whose scores are reported in column 2 were all of the same mental age (11½). But even on traits that we think of as being closely related to mental age (vocabulary, reasoning ability, and memory) there was a variation within the group of from 2½ to 5 years.

Grades of Learning ■ 249

Range of Variation of Seven Traits for Three Groups of Twenty-five Pupils Each When Each Group was Identical in One Trait

Factor	Range in Months for Identical Ability Groups		
	I.Q. 106	M.A. 138 Months	C.A. 129 Months
1. Chronological age	18	34	—
2. Reasoning ability	29	29	58
3. Language ability	29	23	42
4. Non-language ability	35	29	79
5. Vocabulary or verbal ability	58	56	59
6. Memory ability	60	74	59
7. Spacial or visualisation ability	79	83	114
Median Range	35	34	59

DEFINING I.Q.'S AND M.A.'S

Psychologists and teachers who have had years of experience in working with children of different levels of intelligence have developed useful reference points that give meaning to specific intelligence quotients and mental ages. If, for example, they are told that a 12 years old child has an I.Q. of 80, 100, or 120, their broad experience makes it possible for them to predict what can be expected of such a child in the classroom.

Although nothing can really take the place of experience in working with children, you can make a start at developing your own reference points by studying reports on the average I.Q.'s of children from different environments and by reviewing the opinions of experienced psychologists on what can be expected of children with different I.Q.'s. Let's examine some of this information.

Although children with I.Q.'s under 70 are commonly referred to as feeble-minded, most of those with an I.Q. of 50 or above (and some with an I.Q. of less than 50) attend the regular public school instead of being sent to special homes for the feeble-minded.

Whether or not a child with an I.Q. below 70 is able to care for himself in a community depends more on the demands of his environment than upon the exact level of his intelligence.

Thus, the degree of feeble-mindedness that necessitates institutional care is determined by social pressures as well as by psychological measures.

However, psychologists rather generally recognise three levels of feeble-mindedness:

1. Idiots (I.Q.'s from 0 to 25) even as adults are unable to guard themselves against common physical dangers. They would soon die if others did not protect and care for them. Even the brightest of this group never advance mentally beyond the level reached by the average two years old baby. The highest-level idiots may learn to dress themselves or become able to say a few words but at the lowest level they are unable to sit up and may remain in bed all their lives.
2. Imbeciles (I.Q.'s from 26 to 50) can learn to care for their own physical needs but they require close supervision either in an institution or by their families. They can learn to do simple routine work such as making beds, mopping floors, or digging ditches but cannot develop any clear understanding of money or of their legal or moral responsibilities. The highest-level imbecile may as an adult attain a mental age of about seven.
3. Morons (I.Q.'s 51 to 70) can learn to read and write and as adults can perform many routine jobs satisfactorily. In general, their adult level of mental development will be equal to that of the average child seven to 11 years of age.

One investigator has summarised numerous studies of the intelligence of various groups of children and adults, including the predictions of psychologists on the levels of educational and vocational development that can be attained by persons of different levels of intelligence. His conclusions appear in the following table.

Reference Points for Establishing the Meaning of an I.Q.

120	Needed to do acceptable work in a first-class college with normal effort.
114	Mean I.Q. of children in Midwest city, from white-collar, skilled-labour families.
107	Mean I.Q. of high-school seniors.
104	Minimum I.Q. for satisfactory (*i.e.*, average) work in high school, in academic curriculum.

93	Median I.Q. of children in eight one-teacher rural schools in Texas.
91	Mean I.Q. of children in Midwest city, from low-income, socially depressed homes.
90	Adult of I.Q. 90 can assemble some parts requiring some judgment, can operate sewing machines where threading and adjusting the machine is required. Child of I.Q. 90 can progress through eight grades with some retardation. With persistence may complete high school with difficulty.
70	Adult of I.Q. 70 can set and sort type, do farm work. Child of I.Q. 70 will be able to attain fifth grade and may do average work there.
60	Adult of I.Q. 60 can repair furniture, paint toys, harvest vegetables.
50	Adult can do rough painting, simple carpentry, domestic work.
50	Child above I.Q. 50 can profit from special classes in regular schools, need not be segregated.
40	Adult can mow lawn, handle freight, simple laundry work.

We found that a relationship exists between the socio-economic level of the family and the intelligence of the child. The following table gives us the results of one study of how the intelligence of children is related to the occupation of the father.

This type of information is helpful to us in two ways. Since the I.Q.'s of parents and their children are closely related, we gain a clue to the level of intelligence required for average success in various occupations.

Mean I.Q's According to Age and Father's Occupation

	Father's Occupational Classification	2-5 ½	6-9	10-14	15-18
I.	Professional	116. 2	114. 9	117. 5	116. 4
II.	Semi-professional and managerial	112. 4	107. 3	112. 2	116. 7
III.	Clerical, skilled trades and retail business	108. 0	104. 9	107. 4	109. 6
IV.	Rural owners	99. 1	94. 6	92. 4	94. 3
V.	Semi-skilled, minor clerical and minor business	104. 3	104. 6	103. 4	106. 7
VI.	Slightly-skilled	95. 1	100. 0	100. 6	96. 2
VII.	Day labourers, urban and rural	93. 6	96. 0	97. 2	97. 6

```
                Urban (N-1962 Cases)
          ········  Rural (N-940 Cases)
```

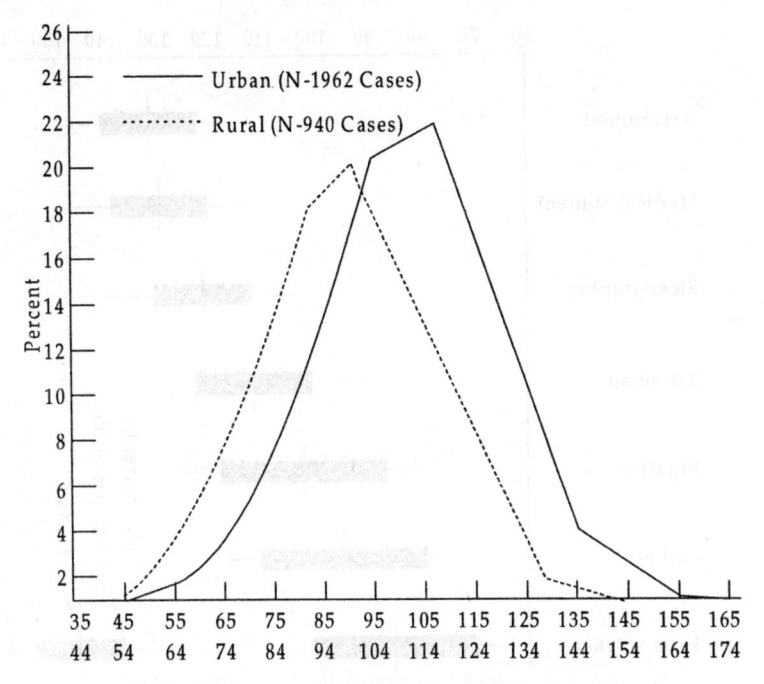

Distributions of I.Q.'s for rural and urban groups.

And we can see here the apparent effect of meager or of rich home environment on the child's vocabulary, memory, and general ability to learn.

Differences in intelligence between rural and urban groups of children have also been reported. For example, during the process of standardising an individual intelligence test, the children tested were divided into two groups, those living in areas with a population density of more than 1000 per square mile (urban) and those living in areas with less than 1000 per square mile (rural).

The I.Q. distributions of these two groups are shown in the above figure.

Information on the relationship between occupation and intelligence is provided by studies of the scores made by enlisted men taking the Army General Classification Test, a group intelligence test, known as the A.G.C.T. The following figure shows seven selected occupations from the more than 200 occupations that have been studied. As you look at this figure, remember that it is based on A.G.C.T. scores, not on I.Q.'s.

Grades of Learning ■ 253

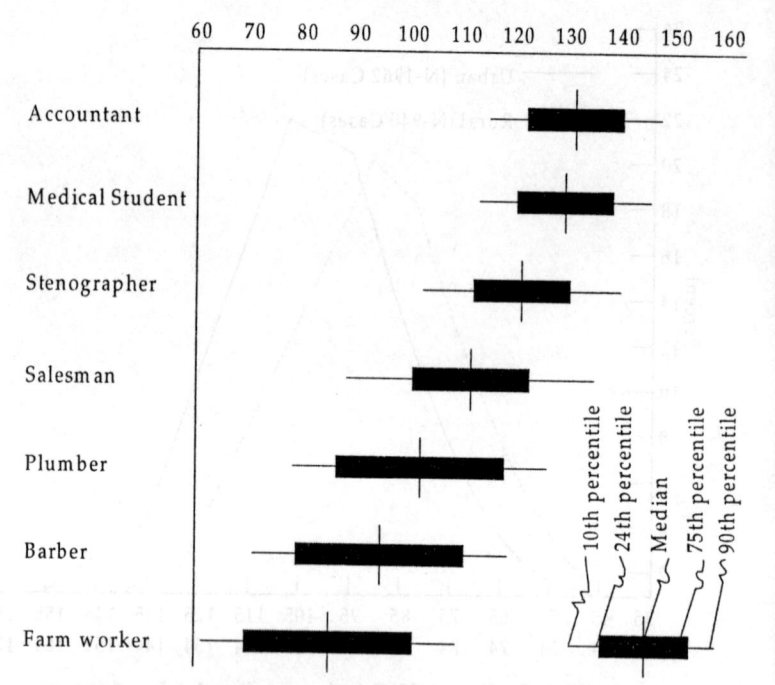

Army General Classification Test scores for certain occupational groups (enlisted men). From Naomi Stewart, "A.G.C.T. Scores of Army Personnel Grouped by Occupations".

The above figure is important for two reasons: (1) It makes clear the wide differences that exist between the medians for the seven occupational groups. (2) It also points up the tremendous overlap in abilities between the groups. In the lowest-ranking occupations, there are always some individuals with sufficient ability to be at least equal to the average person in the highest occupational groups. A certain minimum amount of intelligence is necessary for success in the higher-level occupations (note the short range), but no level of intelligence guarantees that an individual will choose a high-level occupation. The data in above figure are of special importance to us as teachers because they indicate how often our schools fail to guide children with high levels of intelligence to make the best use of their abilities.

Many children with high potentialities end up as unskilled or semi-skilled labourers.

Distribution of I.Q.'s for All High-School Students in St. Louis, Missouri, 1936-37

I.Q.+	Percentage
140 plus	1
130-139	4
120-129	12
110-119	24
100-109	31
90-99	20
80-89	7
Below 80	1

+ The I.Q. was obtained from a group intelligence test—the Henmon-Nelson Tests of Mental Ability.

A look at two final studies of the intelligence of special groups will give us additional points of reference to use in the classroom. One study of the distribution of intelligence among high-school students in St. Louis, Missouri, is reported in the above table.

The other study shows the differences in median I.Q. found in American colleges. All freshmen in 323 colleges took the American Council (group) intelligence test. The following table gives the average scores converted into I.Q.'s that are roughly comparable to Binet I.Q.'s.

Median I.Q.'s of Freshmen in American Colleges

	Median I.Q. of Freshman Class
Highest-ranking college from a group of 323 colleges	123
Median I.Q. of all freshmen in the 323 colleges	109
Median of four-year colleges	109
Median of junior colleges	105
Median of teachers colleges	105
Lowest-ranking college from a group of 323 colleges	94

ROLE OF INTELLIGENCE TESTS

Although a knowledge of the intelligence quotient and mental age of each child should lead to better teaching, many school administrators refuse to make the results of intelligence tests available to classroom teachers. One reason is that the teacher who has only a general understanding of the I.Q. and does not recognise the limitations of intelligence tests can make serious errors in interpreting test results. For example, he may classify children with low scores as hopeless and fail to provide them with the same stimulation that he would have provided had he not known their I.Q.'s. Or he may classify children with high scores as successful rather than as potentially successful, accept their work without challenge, and fail to hold them to the standard of work that they are capable of.

Another danger is that the teacher may forget that every intelligence test score is merely an estimate of the child's intelligence, and that intelligence is only a portion of the child's total abilities. If this estimate is secured by a skilled examiner using an individual intelligence test, it will be fairly reliable. It is a much better estimate than can be obtained in an hour, or perhaps even in weeks, by any other means. However, it is still an estimate. As teachers we must never close our minds to other sources of information about the capabilities of the child. Although the individual intelligence test give an excellent estimate of the general ability of the child, success in certain vocations and even in certain types of school work is not highly related to intelligence test scores.

The administrator sees another important reason why he cannot make test results available until he is sure that the teachers fully understand their implications. Most parents have at least a vague understanding of the meaning of I.Q. They suspect that the intelligence of children is related to the intelligence of the parents. If a child is classed as a moron, the implication is clear to the parent. If a child is classed as brilliant, the parent is likely to take a lively interest in I.Q.'s—particularly in those of his neighbour's children. The inexperienced teacher might erroneously conclude that there is no danger in telling the parent of a brilliant child just how brilliant his child is. But parents have a natural tendency to discuss their children's strong points with other parents; if one parent reports that his child has a high I.Q., other parents begin to wonder where their children stand. They make inquiries, and the administrator begins to encounter problems! Actually, these may be just the sort of problems that the administrator and the teacher should wish to encounter. Ideally, parents and teachers should work as a team in sharing information for the welfare of the child. But parents as well as teachers must thoroughly understand the meaning of intelligence test scores before they can use them to the child's advantage.

And there is another reason why we must be cautious even in the case of the parent whose child has a high I.Q. Both he and the child may begin to take a high I.Q. as an indication that the child has already achieved success. Such an attitude may result in an undue inflation of the ego and a barrier to the development of good work habits.

All these dangers threaten to reduce the potential value of intelligence tests. How are we to avoid them? Obviously, the first step is to acquire a clear understanding of the implications of intelligence test scores and a professional attitude toward the proper use of all information that concerns the child and the school.

The Individual Intelligence Test

The individual test is worth while only if the examiner is well-trained and skillful in encouraging the child to make his best effort. He must know how to interpret the child's responses to a series of carefully determined questions and tasks. He knows how the average child of every age will perform each task and respond to each question, because he is familiar with the responses that hundreds of other children of all levels of ability have made previously.

The tasks and questions included in intelligence tests are designed to sample how the child will react to real-life situations in which he must meet new problems, handle abstractions, use language, and learn new materials. Although the individual intelligence test has been developed only in the past 60 years, it has already become an extremely important educational tool both for predicting the present performance and rate of mental growth of individual children and for studying the environmental factors that are related to mental growth.

In addition to the actual test scores, the examiner learns a great deal about children from his experiences in giving intelligence tests. He develops a rich understanding of the methods of attack and the abilities of the typical child at each age level. If every teacher could become skilled in using the individual test, his understanding of children would be greatly advanced. But the attainment of this skill requires many hours of study and instruction. And even after this basic training has been completed, testing experts say that the examiner must test 50 to 100 children before he can acquire sufficient skill to make his findings reliable. For this reason, training in administering the individual intelligence test is seldom included in the basic programme of teacher preparation. Many teachers, however, seek this training when they work toward advanced degrees.

The Group Intelligence Test

To test each child with the individual test requires the services of a skilled examiner for nearly an hour's time. But the group intelligence test can be used by a careful person after only a short period of training. Of course, we must be more cautious in interpreting the results of the group test, but, if we use it wisely, it can give us valuable information about the children in our classroom.

Ordinarily, the scores made on group tests are in fairly close agreement with the scores made on individual tests. However, the accuracy of the scores depend largely on how carefully the examiner follows the instructions furnished with the test. In addition, he must provide the children with working conditions that are as nearly perfect as possible. The room must be well lighted, there must be ample seating space and a good writing surface, and any needed materials, such as pencils and scratch paper, must be made available. Since time is an important element in most group tests, a stop watch is needed. The examiner must be careful to make clear all the directions and illustrations that are called for, and no more. He should reduce distractions to a minimum; he should not walk around the room, look at papers, or make unnecessary comments. He should read the "Directions to Examiner" beforehand and should follow them carefully. The examiner must be scored exactly as specified by the instructions.

Many group tests are accompanied by tables for translating the scores into mental ages and intelligence quotients that have about the same meaning as those obtained from individual tests. However, some group tests make use of percentile norms, with separate norms provided for each age group. If we find that a 12 years old child makes a score equal to the 75th percentile, we know that only 25 per cent of the 12 years old group that was used to standardise the test made better scores than that child. In addition, if the group of 12 years old children that was used to standardise the test was a representative sample of all 12 years old children, the 75th percentile is equivalent to an I.Q. of about 110, because about 25 per cent of all children at any age level have I.Q.'s above 110.

If the group test is so convenient and economical to use, then, why is the individual test better for diagnosing children with educational problems? To answer this question let's compare the two types of tests.

The individual intelligence test uses both direct and indirect methods for estimating the child's learning ability. The group testing situation, unfortunately, makes it difficult to test directly the child's memory, ability to follow directions, and the like. So the group test must rely on the indirect method and sample what the child has learned from his environment. Fortunately, this ordinarily leads to a reasonably accurate prediction of learning ability. For example, achievement in reading and arithmetic, vocabulary development, and even knowledge of current events are closely related to the ability to learn.

Unfortunately, however, some children, because of emotional problems, absences from school, and other reasons, have not learned as much as they were capable of learning. For this reason, the group test greatly underestimates the ability of individual children with educational problems.

Estimates of mental ability provided by group intelligence tests, then, have all the weaknesses and dangers of estimates provided by individual tests, plus the weaknesses of underestimating certain children. Children who have a special disability in reading, for example, tend to make extremely low scores on group tests. The danger lies in the possibility that a teacher will accept the low score as positive proof that the child is dull. This is particularly serious because the bright child with a reading handicap could benefit tremendously from remedial instruction. But once he has become labelled as "dull" he is unlikely to receive such special help.

The alert teacher guards against this danger by examining every possible indication of learning ability. If a child does better work in arithmetic than in reading, if he follows directions and has a good memory, and if he understands information that is presented orally, it is likely that he has a special reading problem rather than low intelligence. Thus, although the group test is useful in identifying children who can profit from an enriched programme, it must not lead us into depriving the other children of the maximum opportunity to learn.

PECULIAR TRAITS

We know that general intelligence is an excellent indicator of the child's ability to learn subject matter, to reason, to understand, and to adjust to social situations. However, there are many other determinants of success in these and other areas of human achievement. We are already familiar with the importance of motivation and physical health, for example. In addition, there are several special abilities that bear little relation to one another or to general intelligence, such as musical, artistic, and mechanical aptitudes.

Individual differences in special abilities arise in part from psychological differences (sense organs, reaction time, coordination, and the like) and in part from differences in opportunity. Each child succeeds in one type of experience and fails in another. If he meets with success in working with tools, in drawing, or in music, and finds it difficult to succeed in his other school courses, he tends to spend more and more time on the activities that provide him with security. Consequently, he develops increased excellence in those activities. Even within areas that are highly related to general intelligence—mathematics, for example—we sometimes find that a child has developed special excellence through extra application even though he has fallen below his general level of intellectual development in other areas.

DIFFERENT ABILITIES

There is probably no school in the country that fails to make some provision for individual differences. Every school and every teacher makes some adjustment in the levels of performance expected of the child with an I.Q. of 70 and the child with an I.Q. of 130. And during the last decade or two, the tendency has been toward making more and more provision for individual differences in the classroom. With our increasing emphasis on the professional training of both teachers and administrators, and with continuous improvements in instructional materials and laboratory facilities, we can expect this trend to persist.

Certain educational plans for adjusting instruction to the abilities of the individual child are so well known that they have been given special names. It is worth while to examine these plans for ideas that you may want to use in your own teaching, even though you do not teach in a school system that has adopted a special plan.

The *Dalton Plan* attempts to make instruction completely individualised and tailored to pupil needs. The classroom becomes a laboratory, with no formal recitations. The plan is best known for its "contracts", in which each student plans a unit of work with his teacher and finishes one contract before he starts another. Individual progress graphs encourage self-improvement rather than competition with other members of the class. Some educators have criticised the Dalton plan's emphasis on the individual contract, since social cooperation is an important product of learning and since social stimulation is an important motivator of learning. Even though social forces cannot be entirely eliminated by any formal plan, it is possible that their impact may be reduced by the use of individual contracts.

The *Winnetka Plan* individualises instruction, but not to the same extent as the Dalton plan does. It starts by identifying those core curricular elements that all children are expected to master. The core is broken into units, and each pupil works on a unit until he has achieved perfect or nearly perfect mastery. The core is so designed that a child of about 95 I.Q. or better should be able to make a year's progress in a year's time. Each child devotes about half his time to the core, and the other half to activities for which no standards are set, such as social studies, fine arts, dramatics, and sports. An attempt is made to place pupils in groups based on social maturity.

A third plan, known as "ability grouping", came into use soon after intelligence tests began to be accepted as educational instrument (1916-18). At first, groups were formed on the basis of mental maturity. However, numerous problems arose, since a group of children may be homogeneous on any one trait but may vary widely on others. For example, when the children were grouped on the basis of mental age, it was found that they showed wide variations in chronological age, social and emotional maturity, and special abilities.

In more recent applications of ability grouping, only temporary groups are set up. Each group is composed of children whose interests are similar enough for them to cooperate successfully on a given project. Even in a widely heterogeneous group, a skillful teacher can provide individualised assignments and instruction.

Other plans call for the setting up of special classes, particularly in the larger schools, to provide for the needs of one or both of the intellectual extremes. A special class for slow-learning pupils, for example, makes it possible for the teacher to provide them with additional help. But it has another advantage. Where the slow-learning child is in the regular classroom the teacher can give him extra help only at the expense of the average or superior student. Special classes for the most able children have been tried with some success, but they are by no means as common as are special classes for the slow learners. Perhaps the success of any plan designed to accommodate individual differences depends more on the skill of the teacher and on the cooperation among teachers than it does on the specific details of the plan. Most of the plans contain elements that can be used by the alert teacher even though the plan has not been adopted by the school as a whole.

Summary

Our reason for examining data and opinions on individual differences in learning ability has been to form concrete reference points that we can use in planning our procedures, selecting our materials, setting our instructional goals, and evaluating our efforts as teachers.

The modern school is a child-centered school whose goal is to help every child achieve maximum growth. Since each child has many present and future needs, including, but going far beyond, cultural knowledge, we must know a great deal about him as an individual if we are to give him maximum help in his preparation for later life. We must know how he resembles and how he differs from other children in his group.

As a teacher you must be a realist. You must work with the child where he is in the process of development. You must work with what the child has in abilities. And working with the child where he is and with what he has, you must help him achieve maximum growth.

ROLE OF PSYCHOLOGY

Educators are getting more and more to recognise that the dedication of the American democracy to the philosophy of equal educational opportunity does not mean the same education for all. On the other hand, trying to be all things to all children in the face of the marked differences that exist among them has complicated the task of the school to the point that it has not been particularly effective in dealing with a sizeable portion of its population. Some administrators have become reconciled to the view that, no matter how hard one tries, only so much can be done and that inevitably someone will suffer; others, spurred by pressures and criticisms from the public as well as complaints from classroom teachers, have tried various innovations with varying degrees of success. Common among the latter are the special programmes for exceptional children: what needs to be recognised is that everyone is, in a sense, exceptional and in need of a special programme for, as many classroom teachers will testify, there is no typical child for whom a standard programme can be fitted without alterations.

SCOPE OF PERSONAL DIFFERENCES

The fact that individuals differ from one another is fully accepted even by the layman. The extent to which people differ is, however, seldom appreciated. Differences in height, weight, complexion, and other physical characteristics are obvious to all, but not quite so fully realised are the differences among people with respect to such psychological traits as intelligence, social and emotional adjustment, interests, special aptitudes, and general readiness for a given activity. This discussion will be oriented toward differences as they apply to the learning of academic material but, in this, it will be doing violence to the psychological concept of the total personality. It should be remembered that the child is unique and that two children even with the same IQ are not intellectual equals for the child is more than the summation of his characteristics. Thus, when for the sake of analysis and discussion, reference is made to gifted children no implication is made beyond their relative similarity with respect to intellectual ability, for even within such a group tremendous differences exist.

To appreciate the range of individual differences to be found in the classroom, one might first consider the implications of the range of IQ. If we, for instance, consider children of CA = 12 and for the sake of simplicity of discussion ignore the top 2 per cent and the bottom 2 per cent of the distribution, we will find the MA of the remainder, as determined by the Revised Stanford Binet, to range from an MA = 8 to an MA = 16. Thus, there are children in the average grade six class who are capable of working at the tenth grade level while others are fully challenged by the work of grade two. This range of ability would be found in any subject area, whether it involves vocabulary, reading ability, arithmetic, or social studies. And this is not to mention the 2 per cent at the top of the distribution or at the bottom.

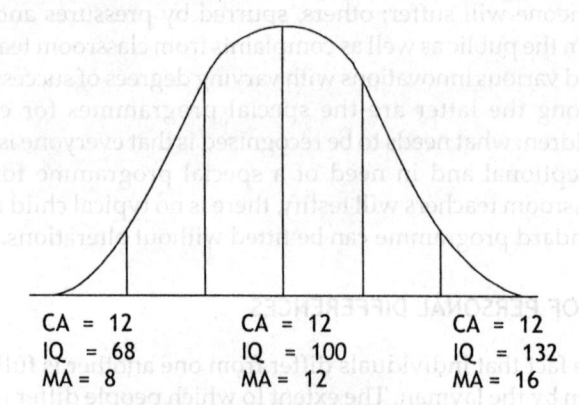

```
     CA = 12           CA = 12           CA = 12
     IQ = 68           IQ = 100          IQ = 132
     MA = 8            MA = 12           MA = 16
```

Range of individual differences

There is a great deal of overlapping from grade to grade:

(a) As shown in the accompanying figure, IQ data suggest that one-sixth of the sixth graders are above the median for grade eight in ability and, conversely, one-sixth of the eighth graders are below the median for grade six.
(There is a one-third overlapping between consecutive grade);

Degree of overlapping in ability between grades 6 and 8

(b) The upper 10 per cent of high school seniors are more competent than the median college senior and, conversely, the lower 10 per cent of college seniors would fall below the median of high school seniors—and this would be true of any subject area—although with different comparisons different students would be included in that 10 per cent, *i.e.*, a given high school senior, for example, might surpass the college median in reading but not in mathematics.

In the Learned and Wood study, it was found that if graduation from college had been on the basis of accumulated knowledge rather than on the basis of accumulated credits, the graduation class would have consisted of 28 per cent of the seniors, 21 per cent of the juniors, 19 per cent of the sophomores, and 15 per cent of the freshmen. The average score of the class that would have graduated, had graduation been based on the comprehensive tests given, would have fallen at the 84th percentile of the class that did graduate and the average chronological age would have been two years lower.

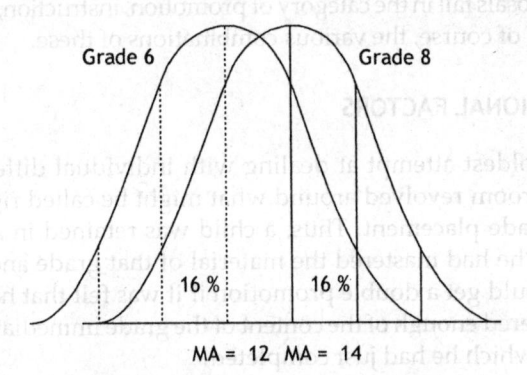

```
        Grade 6        Grade 8

           16 %    16 %
        MA = 12  MA = 14
```

Many other examples could be given, including the fact that there are high schools and colleges in the United States where the dullest pupil is a mental giant by comparison with the brightest student of some other high school or college. Suffice it to say that individual differences are real and they are large. The more important question is what to do about it.

Our schools are not too well organised to deal with such differences; children start grade one at the same age, move one grade per year, use the same textbook, follow the same curriculum, do the same assignments, and face the same standards—all much after the pattern of an industrial assembly line. Despite all that is known about individual differences, many teachers still operate on the assumption that grade levels mean definite stages of educational achievement and that all children have the required readiness and that they can do the work "if they'll only apply themselves" or they use the other version that, with the large classes they have, there is nothing that the teacher can do about children who 'can't' or 'won't' learn! Both views are equally bad: frustration, maladjustment, misbehaviour, and drop-out are among the usual outcomes of such pedagogical malpractice.

PERSONAL DIFFERENCES

A number of schemes have been advanced to deal with the situation and, although none has been a complete solution to the problems of the classroom teacher faced with thirty or more children combining all the permutations and combinations of differences possible, it is profitable to consider at least the major plans. Generally, these proposals fall in the category of promotion, instruction, and grouping with, of course, the various combinations of these.

MOTIVATIONAL FACTORS

The oldest attempt at dealing with individual differences in the classroom revolved around what might be called rigid standards of grade placement. Thus, a child was retained in a given grade until he had mastered the material of that grade and, conversely, he could get a double promotion if it was felt that he had already mastered enough of the content of the grade immediately following that which he had just completed.

Acceleration was particularly prevalent in the old ungraded school where a gifted child could go through the first eight grades in perhaps four or five years. In fact, repeated double promotions could result in college graduation perhaps as early as age fifteen. It has been frowned upon in recent years on the argument that it overemphasises the intellectual at the expense of the other phases of the child's all-round development as stressed by modern educators and that the accelerated child may become a misfit from the standpoint of physical, social, and emotional adjustment.

At the other end of the continuum are those whose work is below par and who, according to the older view on the subject, needed to be retained lest they get hopelessly bogged down with the more advanced work to come and slow down the progress of students in the next grade.

Before we proceed to a discussion of the validity of this position, let us consider the question: "Why fail students?" Whereas the specific answer to that question varies from case to case, the general policy of failure "where warranted" is considered by the advocates of rigid standards to serve three important functions:

(a) To motivate students who apparently will put in an effort only when the threat of failure is kept constantly before them. This, as we have seen, is not true—and fortunately so, for it would be a sad commentary on the appropriateness of our curriculum and our methods if it were! Failure is a last ditch attempt at motivation and it ought to be possible for the few teachers who still rely heavily on fear of failure as a motivational device to use more positive measures.

(b) To maintain standards. Some people feel, for instance, that the high school is losing its academic reputation by graduating students who have been carried along for years and parent and community groups have, in some cases, demanded a return to the "good old standards" where one did not graduate without a certain amount of knowledge. They overlook the fact that the solution in those days consisted of simply forcing the student to drop out, sometimes long before he got to high school.

(c) To reduce the variability within the classroom. It is argued that the child who fails to master the work of the grade ought to be retained since, by the next year, his increased mental development and the general overview of the work of the grade which he has had will make it possible for him to do well as he repeats the grade. This has not been realised in practice. As early as 1911, Keyes showed that repeaters do worse, rather than better, than they did the first time. Cook and Klene and Branson likewise showed that potential repeaters profited more from being promoted to the next grade than from being retained. Thus, Cook compared schools having rigid standards as represented by an average retardation of nearly two years in grade seven, with a matched sample of schools having liberal promotion policies with a corresponding average retardation of only 17 of a year and found a significant difference in achievement favouring the schools with lenient promotional policy. He found no difference in the range of individual difference in the two sets of schools. Likewise, Coalfield and Blommers found that children who reached grade seven in eight years (due to failing) knew no more than did children who had reached grade seven in seven years. Evidently, the standards of a school cannot be raised by accumulating the dullards any more than the standards of a ball team can be raised by keeping the unfit. Of course, in school, emphasis must be on the individual child but, if our concern has to be for the standards of the school, let us, at least, be logical and eliminate, not retard.

Also to be considered, especially in view of the modern emphasis on the total child, are the effects of the child's retention on his personality. Although the evidence is not entirely conclusive, the consensus relative to such effects would be in agreement with the statement by Goodlad that "throughout the body of evidence runs a consistent pattern: Undesirable growth characteristics and unsatisfactory school progress are more closely associated with nonpromoted children than with promoted slow-learning children."

In view of his need to maintain a consistent self-image, the child who is retained is likely to conceive of himself as dumb, tough, or unconcerned as many teachers who have repeaters in their classes can attest. These children, having been separated from the group in which they belong and often being out of step physically, socially, and emotionally with the new group, generally find it difficult to get accepted and often react to the whole situation by becoming discouraged, mischievous, and hostile.

Evidence points to the fact that retention is not effective in reducing the range of individual differences and that it tends to have negative effects on the academic achievement and personality of the child. It does not follow, however, that retention should be completely eliminated from our schools: no doubt, there are times when a child who is retarded physically, socially, and emotionally as well as mentally, can profit from being put into a somewhat younger age group; each case should be evaluated on its own merits.

The decision to promote or to retain should be made only after consideration of all the factors—not just the academic—and generally the teacher should show cause why the child should be retained in terms of how he can be helped more by retention than by promotion.

The important thing is not to promote or to retain but rather what the teacher does after having made this decision, for the element of failure is not eliminated simply by having universal promotion. Unless the teacher is prepared to take the child at his level—as he has to do with all the other children in the class—and make whatever adjustment and adaptation of the instructional methods and materials (*e.g.*, individualised instruction, subgrouping, and remedial work) necessary to bring the material down to his level, the child had better be retained, for otherwise classwork will become progressively more baffling to him.

If he has to be frustrated, it is hard to tell whether it is more devastating to be frustrated once a year or continually throughout each day of the year.

Retention should not be thought of as a form of punishment but rather as a matter of optimal grade placement for maximum growth. At all times, the instructional needs of the child should take precedence over the convenience of the teacher and if, by special help and remedial procedures, he can be kept in with his group without taking too much of the teacher's time and energy away from the other children, he should be promoted. When the decision is reached that he should be retained, he should be prepared for the decision. It is most important, for instance, that he be convinced that those who made the decision had his welfare at heart. It is also most important that the parents be in on the decision, for their reaction, if unfavourable, might well make an otherwise wise decision to retain, unwise.

To avoid the objections to complete failure, various compromises have been worked out including partial failures, (failure for one semester, or in one or two subjects only), conditional failures where the child is given the option of attending summer school, as well as such programmes as the Winnetka, the Dalton, and the Morrison plans. Another proposal which seems to have some merit is that of having fewer promotion periods: the Milwaukee public schools, for instance, have a primary block, consisting of six semesters which can be shortened or extended up to eight semesters before the child moves into grade four. There is no passing or failing: the child simply covers the material of the first three grades at his own speed. The effectiveness of these solutions varies from case to case but none can be considered a cure-all.

GUIDING PROCESSES

Teachers in the classroom are in a difficult strategical position in that they have to get children of widely different ability and background up to satisfactory standards by the end of the year. In other words, they have to extract similar performances out of children who are far from being similar. And they manage to do just that through, the simple expedient of limiting their objectives.

Thus, in spelling, the teacher announces that all the words the children need to know for the examination are the words in certain lists. In history, the material to be mastered in order to pass the course is found in Chapters 1 through—of the prescribed text, and so on. Thus, whether it is the one hundred additional facts or the work of grade nine algebra, it makes no difference if the bright child knows it all at the beginning of the year; he can sit and be bored while the teacher prods and pushes the dull past the finish line before the end of the year. For the same reason, teachers sometimes emphasise facts and other aspects of the course that can be memorised, since this is an area in which the dull, if they try hard enough, can achieve relatively well—at least, relatively better than they can in the area of reasoning, of dealing with applications and implications, and of the other higher mental processes. And so, at the end of the year, the class tends to put on a seemingly homogeneous performance.

Putting a ceiling on what students in a given course have to cover, besides stifling originality and initiative, takes all the joy out of class work. It may also account for the fact that the correlation between intelligence and achievement is as low as it is and the fact that children may lose up to a half of their so-called education in the brief months of summer vacation. Apparently, somebody is forgetting that "equal educational opportunity" implies that the only ceiling which should be imposed on education should be imposed by limitations in ability.

However, as for reducing individual differences—when the goals are unlimited and related to the higher mental processes, instruction will increase, not reduce, individual differences; it is only when the goals are restricted that instruction will reduce the variability. If education is to be a matter of opportunity to profit from instruction in accordance with one's ability, status after training must diverge in the same way as the IQ lines for various ability levels shown in the accompanying chart diverge; and the greater the quantity and the effectiveness of instruction, the further apart in achievement students of different ability will be.

And this is precisely what happens when the goals of education are measured in terms of vocabulary, of getting meaning out of a paragraph, of solving a problem in mathematics, of organising ideas, of using effective English, and other phases of education that really matter, for this is the type of material found in intelligence tests. Unfortunately, these are the things which teachers often neglect.

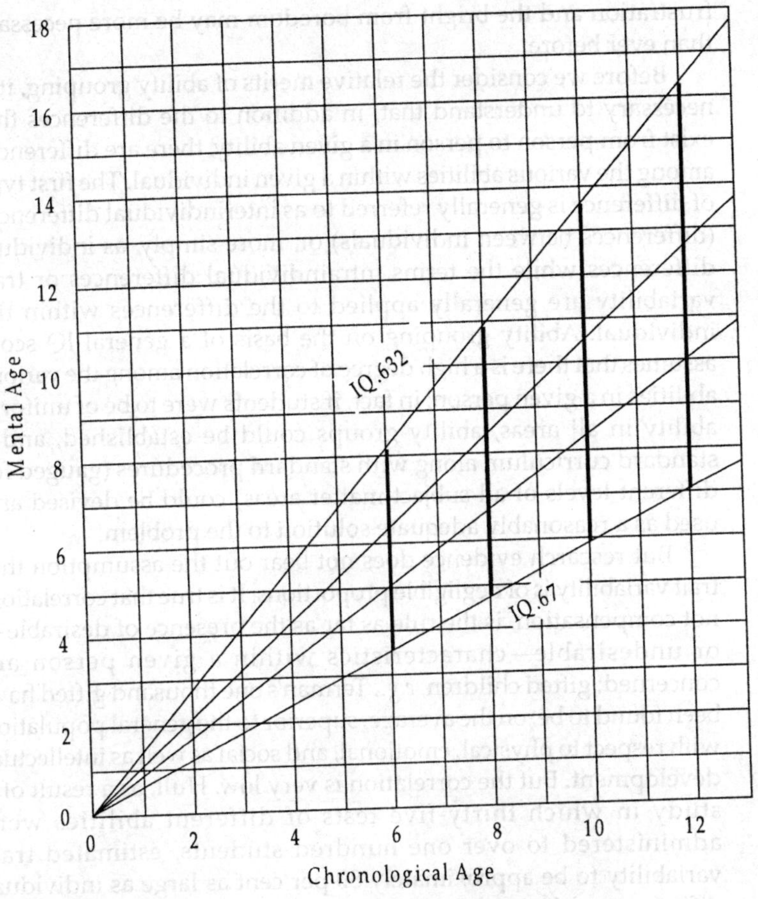
Mental Age
Chronological Age
18
16
14
12
10
8
6
4
2
0
0
2
4
6
8
10
12
IQ.632
IQ.67

INCREASE IN INTELLECTUAL DIFFERENCES WITH AGE

Different Abilities

A solution to the heterogeneity of ability in the classroom that keeps coming back and which finds many supporters is that of ability grouping (or homogeneous grouping, as it is sometimes called). This method is not new: it is essentially what schools did years ago when they passed only the competent student—they simply forced those of lesser ability to drop out of school which saved them the inconvenience of providing seperate classes. Actually, because of the wider range of ability enrolled in school today, ability grouping as a means of saving the dull from frustration and the bright from boredom may be more necessary than ever before.

Before we consider the relative merits of ability grouping, it is necessary to understand that, in addition to the differences that exist from person to person in a given ability, there are differences among the various abilities within a given individual. The first type of difference is generally referred to as interindividual differences (differences between individuals) or, more simply, as individual differences while the terms intraindividual differences or trait variability are generally applied to the differences within the individual. Ability grouping on the basis of a general IQ score assumes that there is a high degree of correlation among the various abilities in a given person; in fact, if students were to be of uniform ability in all areas, ability groups could be established, and a standard curriculum along with standard procedures (gauged for different levels of all subject-matter areas) could be devised and used as a reasonably adequate solution to the problem.

But research evidence does not bear out the assumption that trait variability is of negligible proportions. It is true that correlation, not compensation, is the rule as far as the presence of desirable—or undesirable—characteristics within a given person are concerned: gifted children, *e.g.*, Terman's one thousand gifted have been found to be, on the average, superior to the general population with respect to physical, emotional, and social as well as intellectual development. But the correlation is very low. Hull, as a result of a study in which thirty-five tests of different abilities were administered to over one hundred students, estimated trait variability to be approximately 80 per cent as large as individual differences and it is generally agreed that grouping, say, high school students into a high and low ability group on the basis of general ability, will reduce by some 20 per cent only the overlapping is normally found between the two groups in specific subject areas when students are assigned to groups at random.

Thus, general ability grouping is only partially successful as a means of reducing the range of individual differences in the classroom. Actually, it is somewhat more effective in grade school than in high school and college, for there is evidence to show that trait variability increases with age. Thus, a youngster with considerable ability in all subjects is more likely to be found in lower-grade school than in the upper grades: besides the relative lack of specificity in his abilities, the curriculum at that level is more homogeneous. Some people show somewhat less variability in their traits than others but, as we have seen such person who is tops in every ability being exception rather than the rule and, whereas some students get A's in all subjects, it does not mean that they put in the same time and effort on each. Therefore, if ability grouping is to be successful in high school and college, the grouping has to be on the basis of, not over-all IQ, but rather on the basis of whatever special aptitudes are involved in the various courses. Thus, a high-school student whose verbal aptitude is high might be placed in a superior class in English and history but perhaps in an average class in algebra if his numerical aptitude should turn out to be less impressive.

Ability grouping on the basis of general IQ in the grade school and on the basis of relevant abilities in high school can effect some reduction in the range of individual differences to be found within a given classroom and some school systems are successfully grouping their students. On the other hand, many arguments against such a plan have been advanced, the following being among the more common:

(a) Grouping on the basis of mental ability overemphasises the intellectual and ignores equally important aspects of the child's all-round growth. It is argued that it tends to disregard, for example, the role played in learning by such factors as motivation, and that it may cause the child to encounter difficulties in the area of social and emotional development as a result of insufficient contact with children of lesser or greater ability. The term undemocratic is sometimes thrown in to befog the issue with an emotional overtone. In order to meet this criticism, some schools are using a partial segregation plan in which the gifted are grouped homogeneously for half a day and returned to their regular classroom for the other half-day.

(b) Grouping on the basis of mental ability is likely to give some students a feeling of superiority and others a feeling of inferiority. This argument tends to overlook the fact that the gifted child could also feel superior as a result of his being the cock of the roost in an ungrouped class, and that we have already accepted ability grouping for the retarded child.

(c) Grouping does not result in sufficient homogeneity in ability to do classwork to warrant the effort and difficulties involved, especially since, in a small school, there may not be enough students from whom to choose so as to effect any degree of homogeneity in the subgroups. And, even when children are grouped according to ability, teachers still have to take care of individual differences in the classroom. This last point is well taken and probably constitutes the strongest argument against ability grouping. The ideal is to place each child in the educational setting that will give him the best opportunity to achieve an optimal well-rounded growth; but one must not assume that ability grouping is the only way of dealing with children at their level. A competent teacher can make provision for differences among individual pupils whether or not his class is grouped according to ability; it is not uncommon to have students in the primary grades, for instance, sectioned into three ability levels for a particular activity and reshuffled among the groups for a different activity. Such subgrouping can be particularly effective in that it takes maximum advantage of the benefits of individual participation and of social reinforcement while maintaining the whole-group feeling. Of course, subgrouping entails certain difficulties but none is insurmountable. Anyone who has had experience in ungraded rural schools would feel little sympathy for the teacher who is incapable of providing each child in his classes with five days of learning experiences per week simply because his students do not happen to be of a single-ability level in all subject-matter areas. The teacher who complains that he does not have time to provide special help and to individualise the work of the classroom needs to realise that he must find the time to do it. Unless he does, some children will get progressively more lost and soon will become problems whereas a little attention in time will save trouble later. After all, the number of deviates who require special attention is generally sufficiently small and it should pose no impossible task to a teacher willing to use a little ingenuity.

Thus, ability grouping is not an end in itself: it is a means which some schools consider advisable for facilitating the teacher's task of dealing with children of widely different ability. When ability grouping is used in a school, the word ability should be interpreted in a broad sense and made to include such factors as IQ, special aptitudes, past scholarship, motivation, perseverance, social competence, and general maturity. Hence, the admission of students to the various classes should involve an evaluation of each case on its own merits. It should also be emphasised that ability grouping implies a differentiated curriculum fitted to the abilities and needs of the group and of the individual students in the group: to try to present the same material at a slower or faster pace just will not work.

SPECIAL CHILD

The advent of Sputnik once again focused attention on the gifted child who alternately becomes our most valued natural resource and the forgotten student. Because he is able to take care of himself academically, he gets less attention from the teacher and because he can get by without effort, he is not encouraged to make use of his talents to the extent the duller child does. Hollingworth estimates that children with IQ's of 140 and better waste half their time in the usual classroom and those of 170 and better waste practically all their time. This is in general agreement with the opinion expressed by Terman and Oden that more than half of the children of IQ's of 135 or above have already mastered the school curriculum to a point with two full grades beyond the one in which they are enrolled and some of them as much as three or four grades beyond. Some educators and laymen are convinced that, whereas we have accepted the idea of special provisions for the dull, we still discriminate against the bright, boring them, and causing them to seek outside of school (and often in antisocial ways) the feeling of achievement and self-esteem we deny them in school. Many display signs of apathy, boredom, unhappiness, and even maladjustment. In fact, many do not even go to college.

Generally speaking, the teacher in the average classroom cannot take care of the gifted along with the average and the dull children. As a result, the gifted are simply neglected. Often their intelligence is not even recognised, partly because many conceal their true ability so as not to appear different. Therefore, instead of being encouraged to develop their potentialities and to make a contribution in keeping with their superior ability, they are often forced into habits of indifference, carelessness, and indolence by being made to adjust their pace to that of the class.

When the question of doing something for the gifted child is raised, the solutions mentioned are generally along one of three lines: acceleration, adaptation or enrichment, and grouping. All three have their merits and their limitations and the most desirable procedure to use would depend on the particular situation involved. It must be emphasised that intellectual superiority is a matter of degree and that it is, therefore, impossible to devise a standard programme that will take care of the needs of the gifted for, just as their more average counterparts, gifted children display individual differences in all areas, including the intellectual. The only saving feature from the standpoint of the teacher is that they possess a great deal of ingenuity and initiative (when it has not been beaten out of them) so that, in contrast to the duller children who often hang onto the teacher's neck like millstones, the bright can make their own adaptations of the curriculum when allowed a certain amount of freedom.

Acceleration has definite possibilities for the gifted. Allowing them to go through the second and third grades in a single year, or allowing them to enter grade one a little earlier may be desirable in many cases, especially since some of these children are superior in other aspects of growth as well as the mental and would, therefore, fit in well with a group older than themselves. This will permit them to reach college one or two years earlier and the head start may be to their advantage in view of the fact that getting established in a profession, such as medicine, is a slow process. This procedure is recommended by no less an authority than Terman and rather well supported by research showing that, generally, students who skip a grade are apparently none the worse for it. Nevertheless, where acceleration is used, it would seem better to have accelerated classes which may, for instance, complete the work of junior high school in two years instead of three, rather than permit students to skip a grade.

Ability grouping has already been discussed. It has definite possibilities as a means of dealing with gifted children and many school systems have successfully implemented a programme of this sort. Not only does experimental evidence tend to favour ability grouping from the standpoint of academic progress but such grouping is also endorsed by the gifted themselves.

The general consensus is that, while experimental data are not entirely conclusive, the evidence in favour of special classes, in the words of Norris and Noonan, "indicates certain advantages and minimises the claimed disadvantages." Of course, grouping is not in itself sufficient; its effectiveness depends on what adaptations of standards, materials, and methods are made to provide the gifted child with experiences at his level and the extent to which this is done may be a factor involved in the conflicting evidence as to the relative superiority of grouping over nongrouping. Partial grouping may be a satisfactory compromise in view of the arguments for and against complete separation of the gifted.

Enrichment or adaptation of the material to the ability level of the child is a must whether or not the child is accelerated, for the gifted child could not be accelerated enough without doing him harm from an emotional and social standpoint. Enrichment can take place in special classes or in the regular classroom where the child is given freedom and encouragement to pursue the subject beyond the requirements for the other children in the class. Unfortunately, while ideal in theory, enrichment as the sole means of dealing with the gifted is seldom adequate in practice. Too much time is wasted by the gifted child doing the work other children are doing—in fact, often doing more of the same whereas he should be doing less—and the teacher is often too busy working with the rest of the class to give the needed help and encouragement. Some schools allow gifted children to use the study hall or library period to work on projects of their own, but they are entitled to more positive direction from the teacher if they are to make the most of their abilities. Excusing them from routine work and allowing them to take an extra subject during the study hall period is generally to be recommended wherever it is feasible, but probably the best approach involves a combination of acceleration, enrichment, and segregation. Most school systems of any size ought to be able to work out some arrangement along these lines.

DISABLED CHILD

The slow learner also has special needs but his needs are generally much more obvious to the teacher than those of the gifted child so that, whereas the gifted is often neglected, the dull is constantly being prodded which, while it may lead him to greater use of his limited talents, also may lead him to frustration and maladjustment. The special provisions that need to be made for such a child depend, of course, on the situation. It is generally agreed that for the children of IQ below 70 or so, special classes are preferable to attempts to deal with them in the regular classroom. What such a child needs is special help and understanding and especially freedom from pressure and emotional distress resulting from emphasis on unrealistic demands.

Likewise, his curriculum, rather than involving coverage of the same material as the regular class but at a slower rate of speed, needs to be oriented toward the concrete and the specific with a strong vocational bend. It is also necessary that he be given practice in effective living under conditions that are pleasurable. For children somewhat less retarded, ability grouping through guidance into special areas where the relative lack of intelligence will be less of a handicap is, of course, advisable but it must not be assumed that the child will be good in shop or that he will have a lot of drive in motor mechanics simply because he lacks what it takes from the standpoint of the academic curriculum.

As pointed out in a previous chapter, Davis and Eells make a rather strong case for the slow learner from the lower socio-economic classes. They point out that such a child makes slow progress in school, not so much because of lack of mental ability but rather because of the unsuitability of the middle-class oriented curricular diet served in our schools.

Regardless of the validity of their contention—and Shaw found correlations ranging from 27 to 41 between measures of socio-economic status and academic achievement in various subjects—the fact that taking care of individual differences also implies orienting the curriculum toward the needs and purposes of the child must not be overlooked.

HOW TO DEAL PERSONAL DIFFERENCES?

None of the proposals we have discussed is capable in itself of taking care of the large range of individual differences found among students in the classroom. Some of the proposals occasionally made to deal with the problem are relatively useless; others, such as ability grouping, can be only partially effective. Any administrative plan can facilitate the work of the classroom teacher but cannot solve the problem for, in any grade—whether with liberal or strict promotion, whether with or without ability grouping—there will always be differences and, even if pupils were to be equated today, by tomorrow some would already have separated themselves from the rest. In the final analysis, it is the teacher who is the key to any plan in dealing with individual differences, for it is he who has contact with the "customer."

Thus, we need teachers who are not only familiar with the principles of individual differences and their implications in terms of educational practice but who also are sensitive to individual needs and are sufficiently dedicated to their work to want to adjust curriculum and standards to the level of the child. They also have to be possessed of ingenuity in vitalising the curriculum and competence in the use of pupil-centered techniques which tend to have greater flexibility and which can be more easily adapted to differences in ability and background than the chapter approach: a project in transportation or in sanitation, for instance, contains aspects that would challenge both the first grader and the college graduate. It must also be remembered that if given a part in the selection of the goals for which they are to strive and provided with a classroom atmosphere of understanding and encouragement children can be depended upon to find their own level. The teacher needs to accept individual differences as both a challenge to his professional competence and a blessing: what if everyone were equally adept at mathematics and no one had any ability in the area of motor mechanics? He needs to know the resources of the class and to capitalise on these in connection with group projects as a means of building up group feeling and of giving the individual member a sense of worth and belonging through his contribution to the attainment of group goals.

Getting acquainted with each and every child is obviously a prerequisite to dealing effectively with the problem of individual differences. This involves the teacher having at his disposal various test scores, family data, developmental history data, and any other information that will help him understand the child as a unique individual. Implied is the need for a thorough testing programme and for mutual sharing of information with the home for the welfare of the child. An up-to-date, concise, and convenient cumulative folder where this information is readily available is essential and a lightened teacher-load would certainly help. It may also be advisable—although objections to such a plan can be raised—to have a rotation system that would permit the same teacher to remain with a given group for more than one year. Such a plan may help high-school teachers become acquainted with some of their students to a greater extent than they do now. The core programme in which a teacher in high school has the same students for two periods a day is a move in the same direction. Lastly, there is need for a wide variety of course offerings and co-curricular activities together with an effective guidance programme that will orient students into areas which are suitable in terms of their abilities, interests, and backgrounds.

THE INFERENCES

It is a fundamental idea in American education that every child should be provided with an education in keeping with his abilities in order that he may attain maximum self-realisation. If teachers are to be successful in making this possible, they need to become familiar with some of the basic concepts of individual differences as they pertain to the work of the classroom. The following are among the major points on the subject which have been discussed in this chapter:

(a) People seldom appreciate the wide range of individual differences. As an example of such differences, as they relate to the classroom, the top third of the students in a grade six class, for instance, have the mental development that would permit them to do above-average work in grade seven while the lowest third would probably do below average work in grade five.

(b) Our schools are not too well organised for dealing with individual differences. Uniformity in age of entrance, in curriculum, in textbooks, and in promotion is, unfortunately, rather rigidly accepted as standard practice.

(c) A number of schemes have been advocated for dealing with individual differences. Of these, ability grouping appears to be among the most effective. When used in high school and college, ability grouping has to be based on a consideration of special aptitude as well as past scholarship, general maturity, motivation, social competence, and other factors peculiar to the individual case.

(d) It is difficult to deal effectively with the gifted child within the framework of the regular classroom and special provisions in terms of acceleration, enrichment, and special grouping are generally necessary. Enrichment is essential regardless of what else is done.

(e) The needs of the duller child in terms of special classes, special curriculum and special methods have been more fully appreciated.

(f) None of the schemes discussed is, in itself, an adequate solution to the problem. At best, these plans can only facilitate the work of the teacher in dealing with the wide range of individual differences in the classroom but it is the teacher who, in the final analysis, must make the adaptations of the classroom experiences to fit the ability level of the individual child.

CHAPTER THIRTEEN

Making Disciples Read

A child can satisfy his psychological needs through reading and listening only to the extent that he understands what he reads and hears. He can gain new experiences, security, self-esteem, and the esteem of others from written or spoken language only as he is able to attribute meaning to language. The child who cannot understand what he reads has no good reason for reading. When we find a school in which the general level of reading ability is low compared with the general level of pupil intelligence, we can be sure that there has been poor instruction, poor curriculum, or both.

The child who cannot read well cannot succeed in mastering geography, history, science, or any other school subject that requires reading. He will suffer threats to his security and self-esteem whenever he sits in a class where reading is demanded.

Inadequate reading ability causes much of the discouragement and frustration that we observe among children in the classroom. Many children create disciplinary problems or leave school altogether simply because they do not have sufficient reading ability to be able to satisfy their needs within the school situation. The poor reader is always a potential source of trouble in the classroom. Since he cannot satisfy his needs in the typical school situation, he must seek attention and security either by changing the situation or by escaping from it. We cannot expect a child to keep up his interest when his efforts go unrewarded.

Reading, then, is a fundamental concern of the school and of every teacher within the school. Even though the quality of reading instruction in the lower grades of the elementary school is excellent compared with what it was as little as 25 years ago, it remains an important educational problem.

The reading ability of the average ten years old child of today is far above that of the average ten years old child of a generation ago. The following changes in the teaching of reading in the primary grades are the major reasons for this improvement: making words and phrases, rather than the ABC's, the unit of instruction; emphasising silent rather than oral reading; selecting materials of a difficulty appropriate to the developmental level of the child rather than forcing all the children to use the same books; choosing materials because they are interesting rather than because they are literary masterpieces; making reading instruction interesting, informal, and rewarding to the child instead of driving him through formalised recitations; and providing materials of progressive difficulty so that even the first-grade child can read many books rather than just one or two.

However, today's curriculum and the society for which it prepares the child demand greater reading ability than was required a generation ago. Unfortunately, during the later grades of the elementary school and throughout the secondary school we do little to encourage the continued development of reading skill and we do an inadequate job of choosing appropriate reading materials.

The problem of adjusting the difficulty of reading materials to the developmental level of the child is particularly difficult at the high-school level. Where 50 years ago few children with I.Q.'s under 100 or 110 attended high school, today many high-school students have I.Q.'s below 100 and even below 90. The machine age has eliminated the need for boys and girls under 18 or 21 to work full-time. Under the guidance of skilled teachers working toward sound goals, a child or adolescent with an I.Q. of 90, 80, or even 70 can progress further toward good citizenship and a happy and productive life than he could while working as an unskilled labourer or loafing on the streets.

As we discuss reading, we shall keep two distinct problems in mind:

1. Many children do not read (or listen) as well as they should. What can we do to improve their skill?
2. Many children do not have the ability to learn to read (or listen) as well as our present curriculum demands. What can we do to adjust our curriculum to their levels of attainment?

MEANING OF READING

What do we mean by reading? There are many possible definitions. We might say that it is the ability to pronounce the words on a printed page; but we know that it is possible to learn to pronounce the printed words of a foreign language and yet have no understanding of their meaning. For this reason, any usable definition of reading must include a stipulation that meaning is attained. We might say that reading consists of obtaining meaning from the printed page, but even this definition leaves much to be desired. Reading must be more than merely obtaining meaning. Reading is a type of thinking. Actually, no meaning exists on the printed page itself. Meaning exists only within the reader. And what is true of reading is also true of listening, since the critical phase of each act is what happens within the reader or listener and not whether the stimulus is a printed or a spoken word. The printed page or the spoken word must arouse meaning within the individual who reads or listens, and that meaning must be integrated with other related meanings. If integration does not occur, the reader derives little benefit from his activity. Reading must parallel and include reasoning. The reader must challenge what he reads on the basis of what he already knows and he must re-examine his present ideas in the light of what he reads.

Certainly the mere skipping of the eye across the printed page is not reading, and the mere understanding of the printed word, without challenge or integration, is at best a low level of reading. For at its highest level then, reading requires both thinking and learning. The reader takes what is on the printed page and uses his store of ideas to accept or reject—and he himself is changed in the process.

Words may suggest thoughts to us, but they cannot transmit ideas or meaning directly from the mind of another to our own mind. For words have different meanings and shades of meaning and these meanings may vary with how the words are arranged in the sentence and what sentences precede and follow. The past experiences and purposes of the writer determine what meaning he intends to transmit; the past experiences and present needs of the reader govern what meaning he receives.

The child has learned to challenge and integrate what he hears and sees and to interpret words in light of the situation long before he learns to read. He discovers that the word "No" has a different meaning when it comes from one person than when it comes from another. An assurance that food is "good" cannot always be accepted without evidence; spanking may be in fun or in anger; and heat may be pleasant or unpleasant.

An excellent measure of the value to us of any material that we read is the extent to which it causes us to think. We learn little by taking the hand of the author and following him passively through a situation. As we know, we learn only as we meet problems and are forced to search for solutions. The learning that we do as we read may add to our stock of ideas or it may strengthen or weaken what we previously have believed.

METHOD OF READING

Although the simplest element of the printed page is the letter, we read neither by letters nor by combinations of letters. We read by words and phrases. The total pattern of the word—its length and the picture given by the combination of letters—is the smallest unit of reading. Just as in a painting we see meaning in the completed pattern of the picture rather than in the strokes of the brush, so we are unaware of the individual letters that make up the word.

To have a sympathetic understanding of the difficulties a child meets as he learns to read, we must remember that neither the printed word or letter, nor the spoken word, has any meaning except as a symbol to which we have learned to attribute meaning. The only meaning such symbols can possibly have is the meaning we ascribe to them by mutual agreement. The combination d-o-g is no more closely related to the animal of that name than is the combination x-y-z, except that we have agreed to use "dog" instead of "xyz" as a symbol for this special animal. With but few exceptions, the words that make up our oral and written language are arbitrary substitutes for objects or situations. Meaning is conveyed from the speaker to the listener or from the writer to the reader only to the degree that both ascribe the same meanings to the symbols used. The first step in the development of reading ability, then, is the development of an adequate vocabulary. Normally, the child first acquires a listening vocabulary and then a reading vocabulary.

The primary purposes of reading are to add to information already possessed, to challenge ideas and concepts presently held, and to obtain vicarious experiences. Thus, the person who has little experience or knowledge of his own will gain little from reading. He must have a background of ideas and experience if he is to profit from reading. The richer his background, the more he will gain from reading. In many cases, the reading that we do and that we expect children to do is so far removed from experience that little is gained from it.

The problem of obtaining meaning from reading is rather cruel in its implications. The child or adult who carries most to the printed page gains most, and the one who carries least gains least. Thus the bright and the dull emerge from the reading of an assignment further apart than they were before.

AIMS OF READING

Our Primary purpose for studying the reading process is to learn how to help the child to read effectively. What are the goals of reading development? Obviously, first we must teach the child to understand what he reads. And second we teach him to integrate what he reads with what he already knows. We recognise speed as a goal of reading development only when we are ready to consider the efficiency with which the child reads.

Although the skillful reader can read rapidly, his most important characteristic is his marvellous ability to adjust his pace to the difficulty of the material and to his purpose in reading it. His comprehension remains high for all materials, but his rate fluctuates from as low as 50 or 100 words per minute to as high as 600 to 800 words. He reads slowly when he encounters difficult materials, when he finds it necessary to consider implications, or when he wants to remember a number of facts. By contrast, an unskilled reader with the same level of mental ability plods through both easy and difficult material at about the same rate of speed. His comprehension suffers when he encounters difficult material and, since he maintains the same pace on easy materials, he finds them unchallenging and his attention wanders.

This difference and flexibility between good and poor readers is analogous to a farmer ploughing a field. Since the tractor has a limited amount of power, as the farmer runs into heavy soil he must make a choice between adjusting the depth of ploughing or reducing the speed of his tractor. The unskilled reader pulls his plough to a shallow depth but maintains about the same speed; the skilled reader shifts to a more powerful gear and thus drops to a slower speed.

If he is to read most effectively the many different types of material that he encounters, the child must become a flexible reader. For effectiveness as well as efficiency, different types of materials are read at different rates. The high potential speed of the skilled reader helps him in two ways: it holds his attention to easy materials and greatly increases the amount he can read per minute. Flexibility is more than a simple adjustment of the over-all reading rate to the difficulty of materials, however it is a much more subtle process. In almost everything he reads the skilled reader varies his rate from moment to moment. Certain sentences or paragraphs he disposes of rapidly, other portions he reads more slowly. He may even intersperse recitation with reading.

READING PERFORMANCE: FACTORS

There are five factors that determine how efficiently and how effectively a child reads a given selection:

1. The knowledge and experience that he takes to the printed page.
2. His mental set or intention, including his emotional state.
3. His general reading habits and skills.
4. His general level of mental development (M.A.).
5. The quality of his sensory equipment.

Knowledge and Experience

If the child is to broaden his experience through reading, he must have some background with which to begin. What he gains from reading about a topic is determined by the experiences he has already had with the objects, ideas, and concepts discussed. That is one reason why the programme in beginning reading starts in the kindergarten and first grade with the development of common experiences and vocabulary. If, for example, children are to begin their work in reading with material based on farm life, you will first want to spend considerable time discussing farms with them and showing them pictures of farms, farm animals, farm chores, and farm recreation. You may be able to complete this preparation with a visit to a farm to make sure that the children have common experiences upon which to build. Such experiences must precede formal instruction in reading, since all the members of a large group of first-grade pupils seldom possess the necessary background to begin reading. For this reason, pre-primers consist almost entirely of pictures, and many publishers provide additional pictures to supplement those in the books. These pictures serve as conversation pieces to broaden the children's experiences and vocabulary.

There is a close relationship between a child's reading ability and the excellence of his vocabulary. On the average, children from culturally favoured homes are better readers than are children from homes lacking in cultural opportunity. Education of the parents, occupation of the parents, exposure to music and art, and the number of books in the home are related to children's reading ability. This relationship is not surprising when we remember that reading is a process of converting symbols into words and ideas. For the symbols to stimulate ideas, the reader must have a background of experience, including a knowledge of the meaning of the words.

At all age levels, both comprehension and speed depend in part on the reader's background. Much that a pupil reads is new and difficult. Lacking the required points of reference or the background concepts, he may find it impossible to see the relationships and implications that the author intends him to see. A fourth-grade textbook in geography may contain hundreds of new concepts, such as Mississippi Valley, atmosphere, Great Lakes, and tides. Even such fairly common phrases as deep harbour, tall buildings, and many people may have little meaning for a child from a small town in a farming region. On the other hand, boys and girls from a large city find it difficult to understand such concepts as diversified farming, erosion, harvest, and irrigation. And neither group of children gains much meaning from a discussion of India's strange animals, Africa's primitive people or China's exotic culture until each can tie these terms to reference points within his own background of experience.

Mental and Emotional Set

Mental set is an important determinant of both reading rate and comprehension. If a pupil is simply told to read a certain selection, he will read at a much more rapid rate than if he is aware that he will be questioned on the material later on, or if he knows that he is to make some other specific use of the material. Nearly all readers are able to make some adjustment in their reading rate to suit the purpose of their reading.

Emotional state is also an important determinant of reading (or listening) comprehension. If a child's personal problems usurp his attention, he cannot be expected to concentrate on less immediate goals.

General Reading Habits and Skills

Even persons with equal mental ability show wide differences in the skill with which they adjust to different reading situations. In addition, some persons have well-developed habits of attention; others are easily distracted. Some make full use of charts, glossary, index, maps, and other aids provided by the author; others ignore them.

A study of the eye-movements of 174 university freshmen shows us how important these differences are. Fifty freshmen who were low in general reading ability were compared with other freshmen with average or above-average ability. A special camera recorded the eye-movements of each student, while he read materials varying from easy to extremely difficult. The eye-movements of both the good and the poor readers were affected by the difficulty of the materials read. But when the rate of reading and the amount of material read in one fixation were measured, the good readers were found to be much more adaptable than the poor readers. As the material became more difficult, the good readers allotted more time to each fixation unit and reduced their general reading rate more sharply than the poor readers did. These differences in flexibility between good and poor readers have been observed by a number of experimenters.

Other studies have been made of the differences between good and poor readers in eye-voice span during oral reading. Eye-voice span means the distance between the point on the printed page where the eye is focused and the point at which the voice is pronouncing a word. The eye must run ahead of the voice in order to give the reader time to recognise the word that he is to speak next. It has been found that good readers maintain a much greater average distance between the eye and the voice than do poor readers. In addition, they show greater variability in the length of this span. The good reader can allow his eye-lead to drop almost to zero when he encounters difficult words or phrases, and still maintain a smooth flow of speech. But the poor reader, who has little or no eye-lead to reduce, shows the effect of the difficult word in an immediate vocal hesitation.

General Level of Mental Development

Our main reason for studying the determinants of reading performance is to discover which ones can most easily be influenced in the classroom. But we also want to know which factors require adjustments in our assignments of reading materials, Even with the best instruction, some children will continue to be poor readers. We must try to accommodate these individual differences just as we do any other individual difference.

Reading ability and level of mental development are closely related. The correlation between scores made on a reading test and scores made on an intelligence test is almost as high as it is between scores made on two different reading tests taken by the same group of children. Authorities agree that a child can profit little from reading instruction until he has reached a stage of mental development comparable to that of the average child of about six and a half years of age.

Although few persons learn to read with the maximum efficiency that their level of mental development permits, intelligence remains a major determinant of reading performance.

Difference in Sensory Equipment

To be able to read, the child must be able to see differences in printed symbols; to develop an adequate vocabulary, he must be able to hear differences in oral symbols. Minor deficiencies in sight or hearing, although a source of inconvenience to the child, should not greatly interfere with his ability to build up a vocabulary or to perceive differences in written symbols. However, many children enter school with such marked deficiencies in sight or hearing that they are almost incapable of benefiting from the experiences that the school offers. A child with poor sight, for example, may not be able to see the relatively slight differences between words.

A child's inability to hear instructions often accounts for his inability to follow them. Each child's sight and hearing should, of course, be checked by a physician when he enters school. But you have a responsibility in the classroom to be alert to any sign of sensory defects.

PERSONAL DISSIMILARITIES

The obvious differences between good and poor readers are that good readers possess high speed, good comprehension, and great skill in adjusting to the nature of the materials they read poor readers are likely to be low in all these traits. The fastest reader in any one class usually can read at least three times as fast as the slowest reader. The reader with the best comprehension may gain as much from one reading as the reader with the poorest comprehension will gain from three or more readings of the same material.

Sixth-grade children have little in common—except that they are all in the sixth grade. Among the children in any school grade, there is a range of educational achievement and mental development of children from five to eight years. Thus, in a typical sixth grade we find some children who are able to read no better than the average child in the third grade and other children who are able to read as well as the average child in the ninth or even the twelfth grade.

Reading ability, after all, is related to intelligence, and we know that among the six years old children who start to school mental ages range from about four (I.Q. 70) to nine (I.Q. 150). Even the middle 50 per cent of six years old children have a mental-age range of from less than 6½ to more than 6/2 years. We know that these variations in mental age increase as children become older and that educational attainment is highly related to mental age. The most advanced child in any class may be from three to nine years ahead of the least advanced child.

Some of the variations in reading achievement may be due mainly to causes that can be removed by a remedial programme, but the greater number are due to factors outside the control of the school. The child who has more ability is able to make more rapid progress than the child who has less ability.

The variations in reading achievement that we can expect to find in the elementary school are shown in the following table. We see that the range of individual differences increases from grade to grade. Even in grade two, of 36 pupils we can expect three to have reached only the stage of readiness to learn to read, six to be reading at low first-grade level, and six to have achieved a level of reading ability well above the average for children in grade three. In grade six, we expect to find three or more who are below fourth-grade ability and the same number who read better than the average child in the eighth grade.

Probable Distribution of Reading Abilities in the Second, Fourth, and Sixth Grades of an Elementary School

I.Q.	Approximate Number of Pupils in a Class of 36 Who Have This I.Q.	Beginning of-the-Year Grade 2	Reading Grade Levels Grade 4	Grade 6
120 and up	3	3.4 and up	5.8 and up	8.2 and up
110-119	6	2.7 to 3.3	4.9 to 5.7	7.1 to 8.1
100-109	9	2.0 to 2.6	4.0 to 4.8	6.0 to 7.0
90-99	9	1.4 to 1.9	3.1 to 3.9	4.9 to 5.9
80-89	6	1.0 to 1.3	2.2 to 3.0	3.8 to 4.8
Below 80	3	Readiness	Below 2.2	Below 3.8

Source: Albert J. Harris, *How to Increase Reading Ability*, New York.

The importance of vocabulary and other background items has been shown by studies of how the ability to comprehend from reading a selection is related to the ability to comprehend from listening to someone else read the same material. With few exceptions, children who comprehend most when they read also gain most when they listen, and those who reach poorly gain least from listening. In the classroom, then remember that the poorest readers are also the children who gain least from your oral explanations and discussions.

The following figure presents in graphic form the differences in listening ability found among members of a group composed of university juniors and seniors. A recording of a highly factual article on the location, climate, and history of an Italian city was presented at a lecture. Following the lecture, each student took a 70-item completion test. The recording was presented two more times, and each time it was followed by the same test. On the basis of the results on the first test, two groups were chosen: the 10 per cent making the best score and the 10 per cent making the poorest score. The average test score of the lowest 10 per cent of the listeners after hearing the material three times was little better than the average score of the highest 10 per cent after hearing the materials but once. When the scores of the highest one-fifth of the class and the lowest one-fifth were compared, the differences were nearly as great as between the highest and lowest tenths.

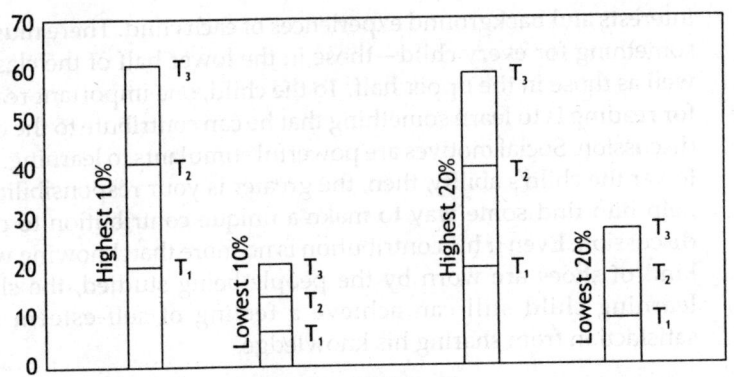

The effects of practice on individual differences.

Thus even in a group of university upper classmen (and few if any university juniors have I.Q.'s below 110), we find that a student in the lowest one-fifth gets little more from three opportunities to listen than a student in the highest one-fifth gets from one opportunity. Other studies have shown the same results with experiments in reading.

Among members of the same school grade, individual differences in ability to achieve are closely related to differences in vocabulary, knowledge, and experience, to differences in habits of reading and listening, as well as differences in level of mental development. It is not surprising that the child who goes into a learning situation with the most, gains the most; and that the child who goes in with the least, gains the least. As a result, differences in level of educational development and in capacity for further development become increasingly greater as we progress from grade to grade.

A textbook that all the members of a class can read and understand fails to challenge the better students. However, a textbook that is geared to the average level of the class is far too difficult for the students in the lower one fifth and is still unchallenging to the upper one-fifth. Whatever procedure we follow in choosing reading materials, we must be sure to provide the children of higher ability with supplementary materials that offer them a chance to enrich their store of facts and ideas.

Providing suitable supplementary materials will be one of your biggest problems as a professional teacher. In any one class, you must provide for a range in reading ability of six years or more, and within this range you must offer a variety of choices to fit the interests and background experiences of each child. There must be something for every child—those in the lower half of the class as well as those in the upper half. To the child, one important reason for reading is to learn something that he can contribute to the class discussion. Social motives are powerful stimulants to learning. The lower the child's ability, then, the greater is your responsibility to help him find some way to make a unique contribution to class discussion. Even if his contribution is no more than knowing what kind of shoes are worn by the people being studied, the slow-learning child still can achieve a feeling of self-esteem and satisfaction from sharing his knowledge.

STEP-BY-STEP PROGRESS

Many studies have been made of reading ability from the elementary school through the college years. There appears to be a rapid growth in reading ability during the first four years of school, much less during the next two or three years, and little or no growth thereafter. Most children show little improvement in basic reading skills after the sixth or seventh grade. From this time on, the rate of reading and the general level of comprehension show little improvement.

Movements of the eye, including the amount seen during any one fixation, and general maturity of eye-movements, including smoothness and lack of backward movements to re-read, show little change The child who remains in school, of course, increases in the amount of background information he takes to the printed page and shows continued improvement in his technical vocabulary.

Does this apparent maturation of reading performance in the later years of the elementary grades mean that no further increase in ability is possible? We might think so, if it were not that, in special cases, when particular attention was given to the teaching of reading in high schools and colleges, considerable improvement has resulted. The reason for the lack of improvement after the seventh grade is not that the child has exhausted his ability to improve. Rather, it is the failure of the school at the upper grade levels to nurture a need for improvement in reading.

This failure to continue to improve reading skills may be attributed in large part to the departmentalisation of the school after the sixth, seventh, or eighth grades. Typically, reading as a subject for individual emphasis is eliminated from the curriculum at the end of the sixth or seventh grade. After this time, it is left to incidental learning, which, as we know, is a good guarantee that it will be ignored entirely. In a departmentalised school, the teachers are likely to be subject-matter specialists interested primarily in science, mathematics, English, or social studies, rather than in stimulating children to learn. High-school teachers too frequently assume that the curriculum above the seventh or eighth grades is a subject-matter curriculum rather than a curriculum that must provide further development in skills.

Another reason for the school's failure to nurture reading improvement is that too frequently the examinations, particularly those prepared by state or other central certifying agencies, are designed to test competence in subject-matter knowledge—often factual attainment only—and do not seek to measure the general development of the child. This emphasis tends to force both teacher and pupil to overvalue facts and to strive only for facts.

TYPES OF READING

Leisure-time reading, which is done primarily for pleasure, and work-type reading, which is done to gain understandings in such subjects as geography, history, and science, differ in many important ways. A recognition of these differences will help you to contribute greatly to the development of general reading skills and perhaps to the development of a taste for good literature. Many teachers of literature use a work-type approach that destroys any incipient interest the child may have in literature as material for leisure-time reading. If in his reading he is forced to concentrate on footnotes, comments, analysis, and minute details of content, he will most certainly fail to gain an appreciation for what good literature can offer. And if he fails to find enjoyment in good literature, he will turn in his leisure time to comics and pulp stories or to non-reading pursuits.

On the other hand, teachers of geography, history, and science, through a somewhat mistaken faith in the value of extensive reading, often employ a leisure-time approach and fail to develop skill in work-type reading. Leisure-time reading and work-type reading are widely different processes. But we cannot expect the child to make the distinction unaided. The correct methods for each type of reading must be taught.

The child should learn to read literature as nearly any adult reader of good taste reads it. A good story or poem, like a good painting or a good song, can be enjoyed as a whole even by the relatively immature. Considerable maturity, wide experience in reading for enjoyment, and, perhaps, a special interest are necessary for the enjoyment of a detailed analysis of the various parts.

Few high-school or even college students are ready for the analytical reading of stories and poems. Reading good stories and poems as wholes and for fun contributes far more to the development of readiness for higher-level appreciations than does reading them with undue emphasis on their component parts.

On the other hand, children must read work-type materials with an intent to master them, and the material chosen must be at a level of difficulty that permits mastery. Some of the material presented in a geography, history, or science class requires a work type approach, and some of it allows for a leisure-time approach. The child must learn to recognise what approach is needed for different types of material and he must be given supervised practice in each approach. To the child, and even to many adults, reading is reading. He can discover the correct approach to different types of material only if you give him the proper guidance.

HOW TO DEVELOP WORK-TYPE READING?

Every teacher is a teacher of reading, and every teacher must have an opportunity to learn how to teach reading effectively. The high-school teacher needs to learn how reading is taught in the elementary school; the elementary-school teacher needs to know the reading tasks a child will face in high school. And both must recognise that effective reading involves skills that can be taught.

Every teacher whether he teaches history, geography, or science, must insure that the pupils develop the appropriate vocabulary and the special skills demanded by his subject. At all grade levels, part of the supervised study time should be devoted to these tasks. Not that subject matter should be shoved out of the curriculum. After all, vocabulary is basic to any specially, and the study of vocabulary is the study of subject matter. To help the child develop skill in work-type reading, some class time should be spent on exercises in which each student is asked to read a paragraph silently, look up when through, and prepare to answer questions on the material. The teacher should be careful to select a student to answer the question or to summarise the paragraph after each pupil has had time to attempt to formulate his reply. This type of exercise encourages recall and allows the teacher to show the child the specific goals of the type of reading to be done in the course. The teacher, through the type of questions that he asks, can show the child the specific goals of his assignments. Through appropriate questions, the teacher can encourage the child to draw implications or to search for cause-and-effect relationships. The questions attached to study exercises also are important because they will do much to determine whether the child searches for facts and stops, content with his facts, or goes on to see the relation between what he reads and what he already knows.

Probably the larger portion of the teaching of work-type reading skills will occur during the beginning of the year than after the year is well along, but at no time can the teacher assume that his students are skillful in the type of reading required for an understanding of the subject he teaches. In addition to these exercises in the use of recall, the child must be taught to integrate the new material with what he already knows. Older children need to learn how to take notes so that they can preserve materials for future review. The teacher must see that the child understands that a work-type study procedure is much more efficient than is the passive reading of work-type materials. We cannot expect the pupil to make the transfer from the class exercises in how to read to his own unsupervised reading of the same kind of materials unless we show him that the techniques make his study most economical and effective. Even a first-grade child soon learns to use a recall type of approach when taught to look at the whole word on a chart or picture dictionary and then to write it, rather than to copy it letter by letter.

Many skills closely related to reading are sometimes omitted from the school curriculum, even though they are necessary if the child is to become an effective reader. Among them is the ability to locate sources of information and to interpret charts and graphs. Even university graduate students are often weak in these skills.

Children need special practice in learning the parts of a book and their functions. Each pupil should learn to examine the title page, to find out who wrote the book or the article, and to judge whether or not the author is an authority on his subject. The date when the book was written is often important. The table of contents and the index have important functions that many students do not fully appreciate. Children need frequent practice in the use of the dictionary, with emphasis on the history of the language, biographical data, and the pronunciations and meanings of words. They should also become familiar with other common sources of information, such as the encyclopedia, atlas, and almanac. Practice periods in the use of these materials provide excellent opportunities for instruction in the proper care of books. Ideally, instruction in the locating, appraising, organising, and note-taking skills accompanies the assignments in which they are used, but you cannot assume that the child has already mastered these skills or that they need not be reviewed.

KINDS OF READING

The relatively recent emphasis on silent reading is an extremely important development. In the past, the school devoted a major portion of its reading time to oral reading, and even serious study was sometimes done aloud! Many schools still place far too much emphasis on oral reading.

Even when they are reading silently, most persons make considerable use of their lip and throat muscles in pronouncing individual words ("sub-vocalisation"). Their rate of reading is obviously limited by the speed with which they can speak the words. If sub-vocalisation can be eliminated, the rate of silent reading, particularly of materials that do not require a great deal of thinking time, can be increased greatly. The current emphasis on silent reading is so general in our schools that in this chapter, when reading is mentioned, it is assumed that we are referring to silent reading.

Oral reading does, however, have three important functions. First, it gives us a chance to check on a child's ability to read silently—his understanding of words, his pronunciation, and his use of punctuation to give meaning to what he reads. Oral reading is frequently used for this purpose in the first two or three grades and for an occasional check thereafter. But even in the earlier grades, we give most of our instructional time to silent reading. When we wish to check comprehension, we ask the pupil to read a sentence or a paragraph silently and then tell what the sentence or paragraph says. Second, oral reading is appropriate to certain kinds of literature. Most poetry, for example, is best appreciated when it is read aloud. Third, oral reading gives the child a chance to share his experience with others. With a book for support, a child may be able to read aloud to a group even though he could not present an extemporaneous report.

PROBLEMS OF READING

Various procedures have been developed for obtaining a mathematical index of the difficulty of reading materials. Sentence length, sentence structure, and the nature of the vocabulary are the determinants most commonly used. Although the specific procedures for obtaining an index of readability are beyond the scope of this book, references to appropriate sources are listed at the end of this chapter.

However, what is perhaps the most important determinant of readability cannot be evaluated through use of a formula. Whether or not the reader is familiar with the subject and with its special vocabulary is of primary importance, particularly for the adult. Two readers, equal in general reading skill, may differ widely in the ease with which they can read discussions off chemistry, botany, philosophy, or psychology. And even with nontechnical materials, one reader may find an article on travel, finance, photography, or politics easy to read, and another may find it difficult.

Even though the teaching of reading found throughout our elementary schools is generally of high quality, many children get out of step with the instruction. They simply have not attained a level of reading skill, and of other skills, in keeping with their stage of mental development.

There are many reasons why a particular child's reading ability may not keep pace with his mental development. Emotional blocks or unsolved problems of one kind or another are perhaps the most frequent basic causes. In general, the child's desire for new experiences, for self-esteem, for esteem in the eyes of others, and for security makes him ready and eager to learn to read. He comes to regard reading as unpleasant and to avoid rather than seek it only if the learning situation in some way threatens these basic motives.

Attempts by the parents to teach reading frequently pose a threat to the child. Parents often fail to build a need for reading and frequently do not use good teaching methods, patience, or tact. The child may be berated for stupidity and forced to attend beyond his normal span. Instruction periods that come after a day of school work are likely to exhaust the child. As a result, both reading and reading materials become charged with unpleasant associations for the child.

Parents sometimes succeed in teaching the child to read before he even enters school. When this happens, the child is out of step with his group when he joins the first grade and is denied the pleasure of discovering reading in a social situation. He finds the school unstimulating and he may develop habits of inattention.

Parents who read a great number of stories to the child may unwittingly contribute to the child's lack of desire to read. His desire for new experiences leads him to books, but he knows that he can win satisfaction more easily when someone else reads to him than if he himself is forced to read. On the other hand, a moderate amount of reading may help the child to develop his vocabulary and may whet his desire for learning to read.

You will remember the threats to emotional adjustment that were discussed earlier. Any experience that leaves the child emotionally immature is likely to interfere with his educational development. And such an experience can be particularly serious if it occurs during his first year or two in school. A home marked by bickering and strife produces a child so insecure that he can give little thought to less pressing problems.

A child who has not achieved a sufficiently high level of mental development to learn to read when we first attempt to teach him can never recapture the interest in school that he loses during this first year of failure. Age mates or even an unsympathetic teacher can so threaten security and self-esteem that the child cannot give full attention to the work of the classroom. Prolonged illness may result in so much lost instruction in important reading skills that further class work results in failure.

PROBLEMS AND THEIR IMPACT

It might appear that the intelligent child who finds himself behind his classmates in any academic area would catch up with them just as soon as the emotional or physical block was removed. But he may not be able to. His need to satisfy his motives may have swung his interests into entirely different directions.

He may have found that hobbies or other activities not closely related to the schoolroom satisfy at least a part of his need for security and new experiences. And once he gets out of step with the day-to-day instruction being received by the class, he finds it increasingly difficult to understand and use what is being offered; if he does not receive special help he will drop further and further behind in successive activities that involve the areas he has missed.

A child may develop a special disability in arithmetic, spelling, or writing, as well as in reading. Ordinarily, however, deficiencies in these areas are not so noticeable or so important as are weaknesses in reading, which may prevent success in many other areas of study.

SOLUTIONS TO PROBLEMS

From the first grade through college, some students need special help in reading. However, the remedial techniques vary with the grade or age at which the deficiency is discovered. In all cases, the first and most important step is to recognise that a certain child can profit from special help in reading. As a classroom teacher, you must accept a major portion of this responsibility.

How can we determine what child will profit from special help and what child already is reading as well as his general level of mental development allows him to read? First, of course, we must find out how well he does read. We use a general survey reading test for this purpose. Then an intelligence test, preferably an individual Binet-type test given by a qualified examiner, is used to determine his level of mental development. By comparing these two levels, we can judge the extent of his special reading disability.

The chronological age of the child is not an important factor in determining his need for remedial assistance. A 14 years old child with a reading age of ten does not have a special reading disability and does not need remedial instruction in reading if his mental age also is ten. On the other hand, a ten years old child with a reading age of ten can profit from remedial work if his mental age is 12 or 13.

After you have determined the extent to which a child's reading ability lags behind his mental ability, your next step is to diagnose his specific difficulties. Here we are looking for possible causes as well as for specific weaknesses in reading ability. A physical examination must be made of his eyesight and hearing. A special type of reading test, called a diagnostic test, is used for locating his strengths and weaknesses in reading. From such a test, you can plan the specific types of instruction that are most needed. For example, the child may be able to recognise an adequate number of common words by sight but lack the knowledge of phonics or of prefixes and suffixes that he needs for recognising the less common words.

In the remedial reading programme, you will help the child to remedy his specific defects and to advance his general level of reading achievement. If the child's difficulty is an inadequate sight vocabulary, you help him to build it up; if he needs phonic skills, you help him to develop them. In some cases, you will need to use first or second-grade reading methods and materials even though the pupil is a high-school student. You will find it profitable to study some of the better books on remedial reading.

Some schools set up special help rooms where the children may go for part of the day to receive instruction individually or in small groups. The teacher entrusted with a help room should possess great skill in diagnosing as well as in remedying reading difficulties. Only children who have special disabilities, rather than those who are slow in mental development, should be permitted to attend. Attendance in the remedial reading programme should be regarded as a real opportunity and not as an implication that the child is stupid.

In other schools, the responsibility for remedial work lies with the teacher; if the school is departmentalised, it must be a cooperative project. In nearly every classroom, you will need to devote some time to individual instruction. You may want to enlist the cooperation of the parent so that the child can come to school early or stay late. In small classes, you may be able to carry on your remedial instruction as part of the regular classroom schedule by devoting short sessions to individual assignments.

When you are attempting to remedy reading deficiencies, you must be particularly careful to find materials that the child can read and enjoy. Remember that you are not interested in whether or not the materials are appropriate to the child's grade and chronological age. You can safely ignore his chronological age, except for the cues it may give you of his interests. Once the child begins to enjoy reading, you can be sure that your remedial programme is beginning to show results.

On the high-school and college levels, special instruction is often offered in reading and in general study skills. Groups of about 15 students meet for one to three hours a week throughout a semester. They practice reading different types of assignments, set up and discuss a schedule for their outside study time, discuss and practice effective techniques for review and for preparing for and taking examinations, examine and criticise various methods for taking lecture and study notes, learn how to 'skim', and how to get the main points of a paragraph. They may take reading tests of different types and keep a chart showing their improvement in both reading rate and comprehension.

Various mechanical devices to improve reading have received considerable publicity in recent years. They include metronoscopes, films, reading-rate controllers, and tachistoscopes. It has been demonstrated that an intelligent person can greatly improve his reading speed through practice with these devices. Although flexibility rather than speed is the primary goal of the skillful reader, flexibility does require that the reader be able to attain high speed when the occasion warrants. As we know, the child cannot attain high speed so long as he pronounces to himself each word that he reads. And not only is slow reading uneconomical but, on the easier materials, the intelligent individual who must read slowly daydreams, and consequently he may fail to understand what he reads.

So far, we do not know what place, if any, mechanical devices should have in the schoolroom. We do know that the school is not doing an adequate job of helping children attain independence from habits of pronouncing each word during their silent reading. Experimental work is being done with different types of mechanical equipment at different age levels. The advantages and disadvantages of such equipment should soon be well established.

ROLE OF LANGUAGE

Language is the instrument with which we think. Mature thinking is impossible without language. We use language to make our plans, to solve our problems, and to recall our experiences. The richer our language, the greater are our opportunities to use it creatively and meaningfully. The language of a civilised people must include a vocabulary for expressing feelings, appreciations, and abstractions, as well as a vocabulary for identifying scientific, legal, and philosophical concepts. Language is basic to our cultural heritage. The modern scientist's understanding of physics could never have been arrived at and could never have been transmitted without a highly specialised vocabulary of materials, forces, time, and distance. As a teacher, you must regard the vocabulary of your special field as an important part of your subject matter.

We spend so much time in our schools trying to devise methods of instruction and to choose materials that will hold the interest of the child of low and average ability that we may fail to provide adequate stimulation for the child of high ability. Why do so few adults make significant contributions to political and social thinking? One reason is that we fail to provide reading problems that challenge adequately the child of higher ability. Few adults are able to recognise political and social problems, or to locate materials that would help them to solve a problem, or to read, appraise, and organise relevant materials. And the few who do manage to recognise the important problems and to locate and organise the relevant materials are likely to find that they lack experience in thinking problems through and in arriving at valid conclusions.

If we do an adequate job of developing those highest-level reading skills where critical thinking becomes a part of the reading process, we should find a tendency, on most issues at least, for the best-educated observers to agree on the best solutions. But what we actually find is that on almost all social and political issues nearly equal numbers of honest, intelligent, 'educated' men and women are arrayed on both sides.

The Communication of Ideas

Ideally, the words that you use and the ideas that you express should have the same meaning for you and for the child, the parent, or a fellow teacher. This seldom if ever happens because the meaning of language, whether written or oral, depends upon the background of experiences of both the giver and the receiver and no two persons have exactly the same background of experiences. When we attempt to convey our thoughts to another, certain of our words will have a connotation to the receiver different from what the giver intended. The differences in meaning are of course less when we communicate with someone who has shared many experiences with us, as in the case of children of the same family or a husband and wife. But the differences are particularly great when family, community, and national differences exist.

We see an illustration of this problem when members of different national groups gather around a conference table. Their differences in experiences make understanding tremendously difficult even when both groups understand the language used or when an interpreter explains it for them. And we have still other problems as we attempt to communicate with our pupils. In addition to the differences in backgrounds between ourselves and each child, different meanings occur because each of us tends to hear what he wishes to hear. It is easier to confirm the beliefs that we now hold than it is to modify them. The result is that though our listeners nod enthusiastically their actual understanding may be far distant from the idea that we think we are conveying.

Some Goals of Effective Speaking

Despite the difficulty of conveying exactly what we wish to convey, there are certain rules for the effective use of language that we can profitably follow whether we are speaking to a class or discussing a problem with a parent or a fellow teacher

The effective speaker tries to know the present knowledge (and opinion) of his listeners. Starting there, he seeks to take them as far as possible in the direction that he thinks they should travel. He starts at a point where his listeners are able to say, "Here is someone who thinks as I think and who values the things that I value." He realises that the attention of his audience should focus on what he says rather than on how he says it. He knows that such things as an audible pause 'aah', unusual facial contortions, awkward or unusual postures and movements, and the overemphasis of articles, prepositions, and conjunctions call attention to him and thus lessen his effectiveness as a speaker. He gains emphasis by varying loudness, duration, pitch, and phrasing.

The effective speaker influences the behaviour of his audience through offering them satisfactions for their motives. He knows that no one in his audience is interested in helping the speaker (or salesman) achieve what he wants; each listens only for the purpose of satisfying his own personal needs.

Some Goals of Instruction in Handwriting

The two primary goals of classroom instruction in handwriting are readability and speed. Neither should be sacrificed for the lesser goals of beauty, style, and originality. In writing rapid notes intended for the use of the writer alone, lower standards of legibility are acceptable than when the materials are to be read by someone else. Still lower standards are legitimate when the writer is to make immediate use of his own notes.

Occasionally, a parent may ask you what will happen if a child who shows a preference to write with his left hand is encouraged to use his right hand. Many persons have either a slight or a well established preference for the left hand. Yet our style of writing from left to right makes it necessary for the left-handed person to take an uncomfortable position if he is to avoid dragging his fingers across the written words. So it is more desirable for children to learn to use the right hand whenever possible. Actually, many have succeeded in overcoming their preference for the left hand and have become proficient right-handed writers.

For a number of years, because of certain facts about the location of the brain area that controls speech and other motor functions, it was believed dangerous to encourage the left-handed child to use his right hand. Studies have been made to determine whether or not such a change was associated with the development of speech defects, such as stuttering. The results of these studies indicate that if the change is made early in the child's life—probably not later than the first grade—and if no undue pressure is exercised by the teacher or the parent, the likelihood that the child will stutter is in no way increased. Stuttering seems to be associated not with changing hands but with emotional stress. If the child has such a pronounced preference for writing with his left hand that he must be frightened or embarrassed into changing, the experience may lead to stuttering. But, since this is a right-handed world in which left-handed writers are at some disadvantage, children who have only a moderate preference for using the left hand will probably profit from learning to use the right. However, the advantages certainly are not great enough to justify placing the child under any emotional strain.

The teacher at each grade level must help each child attain the tools he needs for the current learning activity. You must be able to identify and assist the child of normal, superior, and below-average ability and background. You must be able to recognise and make adjustments for the child with physical handicaps and special emotional problems.

The school's success in contributing to the child's education depends on the teamwork of his teachers and their supervisors. Each teacher must give first consideration to the long-range cooperative goals of the school, such as skill in reading, listening, thinking, and communicating; sound social and emotional adjustment; good physical health and health habits; high standards of morality and character; and high standards of citizenship.

Never allow your enthusiasm for special subjects or tools to prevent you from helping every child acquire all the tools that he will need for success in school and in later life. If you are to be most effective in carrying out the long-range goals of the school as well as in achieving the specific goals of your subject-matter area, you must learn each child's present abilities, skills, and attainments.

Bibliography

Anne, A.: *Psychological Testing,* Collier MacMillan Publishers, London, 1982.

Barrie, H.: *The Theory and Practice of Vocational Guidance,* Pergamon Press, London, 1968.

Brewer, J.M.: *Educational Psychology,* MacMillan Co., New York, 1962.

Bruce, Stone: *Fundamentals of Education,* Houghton Mifflin Co., Boston, 1976.

Carlton, Beck: *Philosophical Foundations of Guidance,* Prentice Hall, New Jersey, 1964.

Carrol, L.: *Occupational Information,* Prentice Hall, New York, 1961.

Cattell, B.B.: *Abilities: their Structure, Growth and Action,* Houghton Mifflin Co., Boston, 1971.

Chauhan, S.S.: *Principles and Techniques of Guidance,* Vikas Publishing House, New Delhi, 1982.

Clifford, E.: *A Basic Text for Guidance Workers,* Prentice Hall, Englewood Cliffs, 1955.

Cottle, W.C.: *Interest and Personality Inventories,* Houghton Mifflin Co., New York, 1968.

Cramer, S.H.: *Vocational Guidance and Career Development in the Schools: Towards a Systems Approach,* Houghton Mifflin, Boston, 1972.

Crites, J.C.: *Vocational Psychology,* McGraw Hill, New York, 1969.

Cronbach, L.I.: *Essentials of Psychological Testing,* Harper, New York, 1970.

Diana, V.: *Educational Theory, Research and Practice,* Rand McNally College Publishing Company, Chicago, 1978.

Donald, H.: *Developmental Counselling,* The Ronald Press, New York, 1966.

Downie, N.M.: *Preparation for Counselling,* Prentice Hall, New Jersey, 1970.

Dugld, S.: *Counselling: Philosophy, Theory and Practice,* Allyn and Bacon, Boston, 1965.

Eckerson, L.O.: *Guidance Services in Elementary Schools,* Government Printing Press, Washington, 1966.

Frank, S.: *Theory and Practice of Psychological Testing,* Oxford and IBH Publishing Company, New Delhi, 1965.

Frank, W.: *Education: Principles and Services,* Charles E. Merrill Books, Ohio, 1961.

Fullmer, D.W.: *Principles of Guidance: A Basic Text,* Allied Publishers, New Delhi, 1990.

Fuster, J.M.: *Psychological Counselling in India,* MacMillan, Bombay, 1964.

Garret, A.: *Interviewing: Its Principles and Methods.* Family Service Association of America, New York, 1942.

Ghiselli, E.: *Personnel and Industrial Psychology,* McGraw Hill Book Co., New York, 1955.

Guilford, J.P.: *Fundamental Statistics in Psychology and Education,* McGraw Hill, New York, 1965.

Hagen E.: *Measurement and Evaluation in Psychology and Education.* Wiley Eastern, New Delhi, 1969.

Hanson, J.C.: *Educational Guidance and Career Development,* MacMillan, New York, 1968.

Harold, L.: *Foundations of Developmental Guidance,* Allyan and Bacon, Boston, 1971.

Humphrey, J. Anthony and Traxler, Arthur E.: *Education Services,* Science Research Associates, Chicago, 1954.

James, A.R.: *Vocation, Education and Guidance: A System for the Seventies,* Charles E. Marril Publishing Co., Ohio, 1970.

James, C.: *Process and Procedures,* MacMillan, New York, 1978.

Jones, A.J.: *Principles of Guidance and Pupil Personnel Work.* McGraw Hill, New York, 1963.

Knight R.: *Intelligence and Intelligence Tests.* Methuen and Co., London, 1943.

Kroth, J.A.: *Educational Psychology and Guidance,* Charles C. Thomas, Illinois, 1973.

Krug, R.E.: *Ability Testing in Developing Countries: A Handbook of Principles and Techniques,* Praeger, New York, 1972.

Lester, D. and Crow, A.: *An Introduction to Guidance Principles and Practices,* Eurasia Publishing House, New Delhi, 1962.

Maclean, M.S.: *Educational Psychology,* McGraw Hill, New York, 1955.

Mahler, C.A.: *Group Counselling in the Schools*, Houghton Mifflin, Boston, 1969.

Matarazzo, J.D.: *Wechsler's Measurement and Appraisal of Adult Intelligence*, Williams and Wilkins, Baltimore, 1972.

Mehta, P.M.: *First Mental Measurement Handbook for India*, NCERT, New Delhi, 1967.

Miller, H.: *Foundations of Guidance*, Harper and Brothers, New York, 1961.

Mitra, C.R.: *Challenge and Response: Towards a New Education Policy and Beyond*, Methuen and Co., London, 1986.

Narayan, Rao: *Counselling Psychology*, McGraw Hill Publishing Company Limited, New Delhi, 1981.

North, R.D. *Techniques of Guidance*, Harper and Row, New York, 1957.

Oscar, Krisen: *The Sixth Mental Measurement Year Book*, 1965.

Pasricha, Prem: *Guidance and Counselling in Indian Education*, NCERT, New Delhi, 1976.

Patterson, C.H.: *Theories of Counselling and Psychotherapy*, Harper and Row, New York, 1973.

Ramend, N.: *Administration of Guidance Services*, Prentice Hall, New Jersey, 1958.

Robert, H.: *Education Policy and Practice*, Harper and Row, New York, 1962.

Robert, H.: *Practical Guidance Methods for Counsellors, Teachers and Administrators*. McGraw Hill Book Co., New York, 1953.

Robinson, F.P.: *Principles and Procedures in Student Counselling*, Harper and Row, New York, 1950.

Roe, Anne: *Psychology of Occupations*, John Wiley and Sons, New York, 1956.

Saraswat, R.K.: *Occupational Literature: An Annotated Biblography*, NCERT, New Delhi, 1978.

Singh, Amarjit: *Is Intelligence Inherited? — A Critical Synthesis and Review of Research Findings*, NCERT, New Delhi, 1978.

Smith, G.E.: *Education in the Secondary Schools*. MacMillan, New York, 1955.

Smith, M.R.: *Guidance-Personnel Work-Future Tense*, Columbia University, New York, 1966.

Spearman, C.E.: *The Nature of Intelligence and Principles of Cognition*, MacMillan, London, 1923.

Stewart, N.R.: *Systematic Counselling*, Prentice Hall, New Jersey, 1978.

Strange, Ruth: *Education Techniques in College and Secondary School,* Harper and Brothers, New York, 1937.
Super, Donald E.: *Psychology of Careers,* Harper Row, New York, 1957.
Thomas, F. Station: *Dynamics of Adjustment,* MacMillan Co., New York, 1953.
Thoreasen, C.E.: *Counselling Methods,* Holt Rinehart and Winston, New York, 1976.
Tolber, E.L.: *Counselling for Career Development,* Houghton Mifflin, Boston, 1974.
Vaughan, T.D.: *Educational and Vocational Guidance Today,* Routledge and Kegan Paul, London, 1968.
Vernon, P.E.: *Intelligence and Cultural Environment,* Methuen, London, 1969.
William: *Organising for Effective Guidance,* Science Research Associates, Chicago, 1965.
William N.: *Counselling and Guidance in the 20th Century,* Houghton Mifflin Co., Boston, 1979.
William, C.: *Challenges of Personal Adjustment,* Rinehart Press, San Francisco, 1972.
Zeran, Franklin R.: *Educational Psychology,* Rand McNally and Co., Chicago, 1962.

Index

Ability Grouping 261, 271, 276
Abstract Intelligence 230
Academic Curriculum 278
Acquisition of Knowledge 117
Administrative Regulations 178
Adrenal Glands 153
Aesthetic Development 34
Affection 66, 69
Aggressiveness 45
Aims of Reading 286
Allport, Garden 128, 133
Allports Theory 129
All-Round Development of the Child 49, 50
American Association of School Administrators 171
American Behaviouristic Psychologists 63
Analysis of Evidence 20
Anatomical Development 59
Anglo-American Children 39, 40
Animals Instincts 193
Anxieties 69, 71
Approach Theory 129
Areas of Individual Difference 223
Aristotle 18
Army General Classification Test 253
Arrest of Religious Development 218
Arthur Coladarci 22
Assessment of Abilities 228
Associative Areas 6
Associative Play 45
Atrophy of Unexercised Instincts 215
Attachment Behaviour 43

Attitude Inventory 181
Autistic Thinking 238
Autonomic System 149
Avoidance Learning 144

Behaviourism 132
Binet Scale 231
Binet, Sir Francis Gallon 79, 228, 231
Biological Clocks 112
Blood and Breath 55
Bodily Development 50
Bodily Growth, Definition of 51
Bookish Instruction 91
Brain Formation 150
Brains to Live 216
Brooks, F.D. 86

Campbell-Stewart 35
Capacity for Learning 28
Cardinal Traits 130
Carelessness 78
Catharsis 76
Cattell, J.M. 231
Cause-and-Effect Relationships 297
Central Traits 130
Cerebellum, Role of 156
Cerebral Ventricles 155
Cerebrospinal Fluid 155
Cerebrum 5
Ceylon 192
Change in
    Body and Behaviour 106
    Internal Organs 51
    Physical Structure 51

Child and Teacher 47
Child Discriminates 114
Childhood and Intellect 87
Childhood and Reasoning 88, 89
Childs Stability 71
Chronological Age 231
Classroom and Hygiene 161
Clinical Psychology 18
Coarse Experiments 157
Co-Curricular Experiences 60
Cognitive
    Learning 29
    -Learning Interpretations 144
    Method 240
    Psychologists 237
    Psychology 25
    Styles 13
Combining Information 15
Communication of Ideas 304
Competitive Aggressive Sports 112
Concept Formation 81
Concepts of Progress 108
Concrete Intelligence 230
Conditioning 69
Conflicts 177
Constancy of Brightness 12
Constructive Planning 182, 183
Constructive Potentialities 32
Constructiveness 201, 202
Contemporary 60
Continuity of Development 111
Co-Operative Play 45
Crime Psychology 18
Cross-Cultural Studies 41
Crying 65, 70
Curiosity 200

Dalton Plan 261
Darwin, W. 192, 193
Day-to-Day Instruction 300
Democratic Setup in the Classroom 77
Dependence 52
Development of
    Body 54
    Feelings 61
    Language 82, 91

Neocortex 235
Problem-Solving Ability 83
Development Vs Growth 106
Developmental
    Changes 117
    Process 116
    Psychology 24, 25, 31
Difference in
    Achievement 224
    Attitude 224
    Motor Abilities 224
    Physical Development 223
    Sensory Equipment 290
Difference of Intelligence Level 223
Dimension of Field Dependence 13
Direct Interview 135
Directive Principles of Programme-
    Planning 117
Disabled Child 277
Discrimination 81
Discrimination of Visual Form 85
Discussion 47
Displacement 132
Distraction 66
Donaldson 216
Dull Children 113

Early Childhood 44
Education
    Aims of 161, 162
    Goals of 23
Educational Measurement 25
Educational Psychology 18
    Boundaries of 31
Educational Science 24
Ego-Centric and Selfish 52
Embarrassment 72
Embedded-Figure Tests 13
Emotion During Childhood 64
Emotional
    Adjustment 266
    Development 33
    Differences 224
    Disturbances 78
    Education Through Sports 77

Growth 70
Immunity 76
Emotionality 67
Emotions, Properties of 63
Enrichment 276, 277, 280
Environmental Influences 119
Erikson 113
Ethical Behaviour Standards 34
Evolution of Personality 133
Excursion 47
Experimental Work 303
Expression 199
Extinction Theory 141
Eysenks Hierarchical Theory 129

Facial Expression 242
Factors of Growth 39
Fear 65, 69
Fearfulness 69
First World 239
Forebrain 150
Formulation of Hypothesis 20
Free Interview 135
Free Recall Learning 147
Freedom of Response 136
Freud 79, 113, 146, 238
    Psychoanalytic Theory 131
Friendliness 48
Friendship Gang 48
Frustrations 71
Functions of Brain 152
Fundamental Instinctive Powers, Knowledge of the 221

Gallon Frances 225
Garrison 70
General Level of Mental Development 289
General Reading Habits and Skills 289
Genesis of Instincts 190
Genetic Endorsement 122
Genetics and Atmosphere 122
Gestalt 237
Gestalt Psychologists 3
Grades of Learning Ability 241, 242

Great Interests and Instincts 212, 213
Greece 128
Group Intelligence Test 258
Group Participation 33
Growth and Development 107
Growth
    Aspects of 110
    Body in Childhood 54
    Child 44
    Definition of 104
    Intellect 80, 90
    Language 86
    Motor 55
Guidance and Mental Hygiene 168, 169
Guiding Processes 269
Guilford, J.P 134

Habits of Righteous Volition 218
Hartman, G.W. 134
Heredity 110
Heterogeneity of Ability 271
Hindbrain 151
Hippocratism 129
Homogeneous Grouping 271
Hongik, C.H. 124
Humanistic Concept 132
Hypocrites 128

Identical Twins 120
Idiots 250, 251
Imbeciles 251
Impact of Education on Growth 125
Implicit Personality Theory 15
Importance of
    Identity 137
    Spinal Cord 150
Impression Formation 14
Impulsive Child 116
Individual Education 187
Individual Intelligence Test 257, 259
Industrial Psychology 18
Infancy 84, 85
Insight Learning 144
Instincts and Habits 186

Instincts of Man 195
Instructional Methods, Adaptation of 268
Intellectual Development 79, 80
    of Child 85
Intellectual Growth 90
Intellectual Proficiency 33
Intellectualization 132
Intellectually Handicapped Children 90
Intelligence 79
Intelligence Quotient 231
Intelligence Test 228
    Role of 227, 255
    Types of 241
Interpersonal Attraction 17
Interview 135
Irrational Worries 61
Irritability 67

Jones, Earnest 118
Jungs Analytical Psychology 131
Justice Rules 17

Kelleys Attribution Theory 16
Kimble Young 134
Kinaesthetic Sense 2
Kindergarten Training 59
Kindergartner 204
Knowledge and Understanding 34
Kolesnik, Walter B. 22

Language
    Development 86
    Nascent Period for 211
    Role of 303
Latent Learning 144
Latin, John 28
Law of
    Apperception 217
    Development 208, 209
    Good Figure 4
    Organization 239
    Proximity 3

Learning
    Concept of 132
    Experience 29
    Names of 29
    of Motor 142
    Process 28
    Role of 125
    Situation 29
    Views of 34
Leisure-Time Reading 295
Linguistic Environment 88
Listening Vocabulary 285
Literature on Child Development 125
Locomotion 197

Mahabharata 61
Make-Believe and Fantasy 52
Maladjustment 170, 277
Malnutrition 55, 124
Manipulating Symbols 236
Maslow 232
Maturation 124
Maturation of Reading Performance 294
Matured Child 115
Maturity of Eye-Movements 294
Max Muller 199
Mayo Clinic 170
Meaning of Reading 283
Measurement of Intelligence 230, 246
Memory Growth 82, 86
Mental
    Ability 273
    Age 231
    and Emotional Set 287, 288
    Development 80, 287
    Fitness 158
    Growth 108
    Health Factors in the Classroom 165
    Hygiene 161, 162, 167, 184
    Illness 158
Methods of
    Evaluation 134
    Reading 284, 285

Index ■ 315

Solving 217
Microscopic Studies 120
Midbrain 151
Minnesota Teacher 181
Modification of Instincts 192
Morgan, Lloyd 188, 201
Morons 251
Morrison Plans 269
Motivational
    Cycle 146
    Factors 266
Motor
    Control Areas 5
    Cortex 157
    Development 210
    Theory 239
Muller-Lyer 8
Muscle Tissue 55
Muscle-Co-ordination 55
Muscular Development 53

Nascent Periods 221
National Association for Mental Health 159
Nature of Creativity 233
Negative
    Effects on the Academic Achievement 268
    Reinforcement 142
Negatively Accelerated Learning Curve 143
Negativism 44, 45, 70
Nervous System 84, 125, 148, 187
    Role of 149
Neurophysiology, Role of 148
Note-Taking Skills 298

Object Perception 11
Observational Learning 132
Occupational Psychology 18
Old Brain 235
Oliver Wendell 209
Onstant Criticisms 68
Optimism 123
Oval Knowledge 145

Over Affection 70
Over Stimulation 198
Overemphasis of Articles 305

Pain Sensitivity 5
Paired Associate Learning 148
Paleocortex 235
Parathyroid Gland 153
Paris School Board 228
Pattern of Growth 113
Paulsen 186, 187
Pavlov, I.P. 140
Pavlovian Conditioning 140
Peloponnesian War 220
People Perceptions 13
Perception 80
    of Objects 1
Perceptual
    Learning 12
    Motor Learning 142
    Nervous System 149
Personal
    Disparities 223
    Dissimilarities 290
Personality
    Inventory 181
    Theory 25
    Definition of 128
Philosophers of Greece 210
Phobias 66
Physical Development 60
Physical Growth, Characteristics of 58
Pituitary Gland 152
Plateau 143
Play Age 46
Positive Reinforcement 141
Positively Accelerated Learning Curve 143
Power of Imagination 89
Predictions of Psychologists 251
Prevention of Fear 66
Primary Behavioural Science 24
Primary Reinforcement 142
Primeval Forces 61
Problem of Grouping and Classification 90

Problem Situation 236
Problems and Their Impact 300
Process of Mental Growth 84
Professional Commitments 78
Progress of Mind 84
Progress, Definition of 105
Projective Techniques 136
Pseudo-Maturity 119
Psychoanalytic Theory 131
Psycho-Genesis 207
Psychological
    Principles 32
    Theory 26, 146
Psychologists of Gestalt School 134
Psychology, Principles of 182
Pupil-Centered Techniques 279
Pure Psychology 18

Quantitative
    Measurement 107
    Relationships 34
Quarrelsome 70

Rational Thinking 238
Rationalization 132
Reaction Formation by Conflicts 132
Reading
    Ability 282, 290
    Kinds of 298
    Performance 287
    Rate Controllers 303
    Vocabulary 285
Red Cross 47
Reflex Action 188
Regression 132
Relationships 177
Religious-Group Membership 46
Remedial Reading Programme 301, 302
Repression 132
Respiration and Circulation 53
Respondent Conditioning 140
Retention 269
Richard Edward 225
Role Identification 138

Role of
    Age in Learning Ability 243
    Endocrine System 152
    Heredity 124
    Intellect 79
Rorschach Inkblot Test 13, 14, 136
Ross, James 119
Rudolf Goeckel 19

Schemes of Development Stages 118
Scope of
    Educational Psychology 31
    Personal Differences 262, 263
Scouting 47
Screaming 70
Secondary Traits 130
Self-Actualization 232
Self-Assertion 52
Self-Awareness 62
Self-Confidence 70, 78
Self-Examination 232
Self-Knowledge 232
Self-Prestige 69
Self-Realisation 280
Sensation 80
Sense Organs 2
Sensitivity Elements 2
Sensory
    Discrimination 242
    Equipment 287
    Motor 125
Sentence Completion Method 137
Serial Learning 148
Set of Expectancy 9
Sex
    Appropriate Patterns 138
    Glands 153
    Role Identity 39
Sexual Development 53
Single Trait Research 130
Size Constancy 11
Skills and Competence 34
Skills for Effective Communication 33
Skinner, Charles E. 22
Slow Learner 277

Index ■ 317

Smith, Jane 179
Sociability of Upper Class 41
Social
    Adjustment 230
    Development 42, 47
    Intelligence 230
    Matrix 35
    Perception 14
    Psychologists 24
    Relations 34
Socialisation 41
Socialization of the Child 44
Societal Growth 39
Socio-Cultural Problems 20
Solutions to Problems 301
Spearman, Charles 229
Special Child 275
Specialised Sensory Areas 5
S-Shaped Learning Curve 143
Stability of Perception 11
Stage of
    Human Development 113
    Maturation 115
    Mental Development 298, 299
    Development 114, 221
    Growth 51
Staging of Drama 47
Stamping 70
Stanford University 22, 231
Stimulus
    Generalization Theory 141
    Response Model 237
Stratification of Scammon 57
Structured Interview 135
Sublimation 132
Submerged Wishes 72
Symmetrical Good Figures 4
Sympathetic Treatment 78
Sympathy 47

Teacher in Emotional Matters, Role of 73
Teacher, Role of 33
Teacher-Principal 177
Teacher-Training Institutions 181

Teaching-Learning Process 27, 31
Technical Vocabulary 294
Temper Tantrum 68
Temporary Holding of Breath 65
Testing Hypotheses 236
Thematic Apperception Test 137
Thorndike, Edward 25, 225
Thyroid Gland 153
Tiredness 71
Traditional Conditioning 140
Trait Variability 272
Typology of Kretschmer 58

U.S.A. 226
Unborn Foetus 121
Unfamiliar Situation 236
Unfavourable Mental Hygiene Factors 172, 173
Unquestioned Obedience 205
Unusual Facial Contortions 305
Unusual Postures 305

Variability of Instincts 189
Visual Deprivation 12
Vocabulary
    Development 246, 247
    Importance of 292
Vocational Development 251
Voluntary 189

Watson, John 79, 239
Watsons Theory 239
Whimpering 65
White House Conference on Child Health and Protection 159
Whole-Group Feeling 274
William James 25
William Meaninger 161
Winnetka Plan 261
Wolfgang Kohler 239
Word Association Test 136
Work-Type Reading 295
Worry 71

Zygote 120